CAMBRIDGE

Official Cambridge Exam Preparation

CB126771

PREPARE

STUDENT'S BOOK WITH EBOOK

C1

LEVEL 8

Anthony Cosgrove
Claire Wijayatilake

Second Edition

Cambridge University Press
www.cambridge.org/elt

Cambridge Assessment English
www.cambridgeenglish.org

Information on this title: www.cambridge.org/9781108913331

First published 2022
20 19 18 17 16 15 14 13 12 11 10 9 8 7 6 5 4 3 2 1

Printed in Dubai by Oriental Press

A catalogue record for this publication is available from the British Library

ISBN 978-1-108-91333-1 Student's Book with eBook
ISBN 978-1-108-91334-8 Workbook with Digital Pack
ISBN 978-1-108-91335-5 Teacher's Book with Digital Pack

CONTENTS

MAP OF THE BOOK

Key to symbols:
✔ *C1 Advanced* exam task ▶ Video

LISTENING	SPEAKING	WRITING	VIDEO
Three short conversations about personalities and friends	Personal interview		Know yourself
		Informal emails of advice	The eternal city
A talk about careers in healthcare	Speculating and describing pictures		Body of knowledge
		An essay	In two minds
An interview with two scientists about a seed bank	A discussion		The mother of invention
		A review	Once upon a time …
Five short extracts about sporting achievements and ambitions	Reacting to what people say		How to succeed
		A formal letter or email	Money, money, money

Key to symbols:

✔ *C1 Advanced* exam task ▶ Video

LISTENING	SPEAKING	WRITING	VIDEO
Three short conversations about schools	Talking about yourself		Schools of thought
		An essay	Trouble with the law
A vlog about food photography	Giving opinions tactfully		What's cooking?
		A letter	Getting away from it all
A podcast about communication and technology	A discussion		Speaking up for languages
		A report	The age of influence
Five short extracts about animals	Comparing and describing		Why on Earth?
		A proposal	Hero worship

1 WHAT ARE YOU LIKE?

? ABOUT YOU

▶ 01 **Watch the video and then answer the questions.**
How do you think your friends would describe you?
What are your best and worst personality traits?
Are there any personality traits you would like to have?

VOCABULARY AND READING
PERSONALITY

EP **1 Read the personality test questions. Which word or phrase from the box has a similar meaning to the verbs in the test?**

depend on disagree with not be included
seem understand

PERSONALITY TEST

Say ' Yes' or 'No' to each statement.

1. You don't like being alone – you have lots of friends and hate to feel left out.
2. You accept different ideas and are willing to change your views.
3. You sometimes clash with people you don't agree with.
4. You don't like being the centre of attention and prefer not to be noticed.
5. You come across as shy and enjoy being alone.
6. People can rely on you to look after their valuables.
7. You never forget your homework and always do it carefully.
8. You can relate to other people and their problems.

2 Answer the questions in the personality test and then turn to page 128 to discover what personality characteristics you have. Compare your answers with a partner.

EP **3 Complete the sentences with a word from the box in the correct form.**

clash with come across as conscientiously
extroverted feel left out introverted
open-minded relate to rely on
self-conscious trustworthy

1. Due to difficulties in finding work, many people .... their parents for financial support until well into their thirties.
2. Iago works .... in class, paying great attention to detail.
3. My sisters are twins and much older than me, so I sometimes ....
4. My mother is .... – always chatting to everyone she meets, whereas my father is more .... He mostly likes to listen.
5. People in my country have become more .... in recent years. They are more willing to accept people with different beliefs.
6. The person I .... best in my family is my grandmother – we share the same sense of humour.
7. I used to .... my brother when we were growing up, but now we get on brilliantly.
8. Sofia .... a bit unfriendly, but she's lovely once you get to know her.
9. Freddy is so .... – he hates giving presentations in class.
10. It is important to find someone .... to look after your pets when you go on holiday.

4 Discuss the questions with a partner.

1. What do you think personality tests are used for?
2. Have you ever done one?
3. How accurate do you think they are?

5 Read the article on the opposite page quickly. Which statement best summarises the writer's view?

A Personality tests are a complete waste of time.
B Some personality tests may be useful.
C Personality tests are only useful in work contexts.

6 Read the article again and match the views 1–4 to the experts.

Aurelio Da Silva Margarita Fonseka
Michael Robson Wendy Barnett

1. Companies are not very concerned about dishonesty in personality tests.
2. The Big Five Personality Traits test is better than other tests.
3. Only tests which acknowledge individual differences should be used.
4. Tests should not ask abstract questions.

How reliable are PERSONALITY TESTS?

01

We've all done it. Answered a few questions in an online quiz to 'reveal the secrets' of our personality. It's just a bit of fun, right? Or is there more to it? After all, some employers rely on these tests to hire staff, which means people's futures can be at stake. Here we explore the accuracy of personality tests with those who have used them and those who best understand them.

19-year-old students Jenny and Beth from London were looking for summer jobs last year. Jenny had never believed in personality tests, so was quite concerned when she had to take one before being offered an interview. 'I knew Beth was going to give false answers,' explains Jenny. 'She was very shy and self-conscious and didn't think she'd do well at interview, so the personality test was all-important. Beth thought that if she came across as too introverted, she wouldn't get selected.' Having given the answers that she thought the company wanted, she was rejected. Jenny, who had been completely honest in her responses was rejected too. 'I'm extroverted, which must have come through in my answers, so I've no idea what they were looking for,' she complains.

According to psychologist **Wendy Barnett**, it is not that hard to detect either random answering or fake responses. People used to believe that tests which rely on people defining their own personalities would be easy to cheat on, but due to sophisticated algorithms, that is no longer the case. Although people see questions in isolation, they are, in a good test, part of a set, and it is the analysis of all of a person's answers that gives insight into their true character.

Strangely enough, detecting that someone has given false answers doesn't automatically eliminate them from some selection processes. Barnett claims that employers accept that exaggerating or 'stretching the truth' can sometimes be an advantage in a business situation. The ability to 'play' the personality tests can actually demonstrate that the applicant is self-aware and conscious of the situation they are in. It is not necessarily a sign that they are not trustworthy in their day to day life.

The company that rejected Jenny and Beth will never know if they made the right decision, but what do the experts say about the reliability of such tests? Well, there is a huge difference between a professionally produced test and a quiz in a magazine. Personality researcher **Margarita Fonseka** of the Trent Institute favours the Big FIVE Personality Traits, scientifically developed over many decades. The test claims to reveal how conscientious, open-minded, calm and agreeable people are, as well as how extroverted or introverted they are.

22-year-old Anil took this test last year because he had read about it and was curious. 'All my friends had been talking about it for ages and I was feeling left out,' he says. Anil, initially doubtful about personality tests, was stunned by the accuracy of the Big FIVE. In particular, he was impressed that it provided insight into how he related to others. 'I would frequently clash with friends,' he admitted. 'I had never realised before that I had a tendency to insist I was right and didn't listen to the other person's point of view.' Anil believes that taking the test has made him more self-aware and improved his relationships.

Since doing the test, Anil has been trying to change his behaviour. But is he missing the point? According to experts, analysing your personality may be useful in deciding who you will get on well with, but this is not how friendships work in practice. Some people may be incompatible on paper but the chemistry between them just works. Personality is not everything. Shared interests and experiences count for just as much.

Aurelio Da Silva is a lecturer in psychology who doubts the accuracy of many personality tests, particularly those that ask strange questions like 'Do you identify with snakes?' 'It is nearly impossible to work out what someone's answers to such questions might mean,' Da Silva argues. However, most psychologists agree that some personality tests may be valid. **Michael Robson**, who advises companies on hiring staff, is of the view that in order to be valuable, tests must account for diversity and avoid 'putting people in boxes'. Overall, though, it seems more likely that the way a person has performed in their work or studies in the past will be a more reliable indicator than a score on a personality test.

7 Read the article again and answer the questions.

1 Why do you think the writer includes the story of what happened to Jenny and Beth?
2 Why might a candidate who 'faked' his or her answers on a personality test still be hired?
3 What surprised Anil about the results of his personality test?
4 What is the writer's view on the role of personality in relationships?
5 Does the writer agree that personality tests should be the main basis of hiring decisions?

TALKING POINTS

Would you be happy if a personality test was used as part of a selection process for a job or university course?
Do you think the results of a personality test could help in improving relationships between friends or family members?

GRAMMAR
PAST TENSE REVIEW

1 Read extracts from the article 1–8 and match them to uses a–h.

1 She was very shy and **didn't think** she'd do well.
2 Jenny and Beth from London **were looking** for summer jobs last year.
3 We**'ve** all **done** it.
4 Jenny **had** never **believed** in personality tests.
5 Anil **has been trying** to change his behaviour.
6 All my friends **had been talking** about it for ages.
7 I **would** frequently **clash** with friends.
8 People **used to believe** that tests would be easy to cheat on.

a a state which existed up to a particular point in the past
b an action in progress up to a point in the past
c an action that took place at an unspecified time in the past
d an action that started in the past and continues up to the present time
e a habitual action in the past
f an action in progress at a particular time in the past
g a completed action in the past
h a state in the past

2 Match each example in Exercise 1 to a tense or structure below.

present perfect simple
present perfect continuous
past simple
past continuous
past perfect simple past
perfect continuous
would + infinitive
used to + infinitive

» GRAMMAR REFERENCE AND PRACTICE PAGE 144

3 Choose the correct verb form.

1 Jan changed classes because she *hadn't* / *hasn't* been getting on very well with the other students.
2 I *used to* / *would* be quite shy but I'm much more outgoing now.
3 When my Dad got home yesterday, my brother and I *argued* / *were arguing* over what to have for dinner.
4 I've always *believed* / *been believing* you should put your family first.
5 What have you *been doing* / *done*? You're covered in mud!
6 We *were inviting* / *invited* Jaime to the party, but he didn't come.
7 When I was at primary school, I *will* / *would* always get in trouble for talking too much.
8 I wanted to help put up the decorations, but Mum *had already done* / *was already doing* it.

4 Complete Emma's message to her friend Jessica with the correct past tense form of the verbs in brackets.

Hi Jess

I still can't believe what [1] ______ (happen)!

Marc and I [2] ______ (have) a nice evening, talking about stuff, when he suddenly [3] ______ (drop) a bombshell. He [4] ______ (say) he [5] ______ (have) something to tell me. He [6] ______ (think) about going abroad for a long time, and recently he [7] ______ (decide) to do it. I [8] ______ (think) it was all talk and he would never go through with it, but now he's off to Greece!

I [9] ______ (sit) here for hours, thinking about what life will be like without him. He [10] ______ (be) my best friend for as long as I can remember.

5 Read the rest of Emma's message and decide if statements 1–4 are true or false. Correct the false statements.

Do you remember how Marc and I used to sit for hours in the park chatting? Marc used to be obsessed with sport and he'd sit and plan his trip to the World Cup Final. It didn't use to bother me too much, though, as we'd always get ice cream from the kiosk.

I'm going to miss him so much!

1 *used to* + infinitive can describe past habits but not past states.
2 *would* + infinitive can describe past habits but not past states.
3 The negative form of *used to* is *didn't used to*.
4 *would* can be shortened to *'d*.

6 Read the sentences and decide if the correct past form is used. Tick the correct sentences and correct the incorrect sentences.

1 In the 1980s, psychologists realised that many tests that were developed were not valid.
2 My grandparents would live on a farm and they would only go into town about once a month.
3 The twins were attending the local school, and doing well.
4 Ali jumped out of his seat and had shouted 'Goal!'
5 When I was born, my parents were married for 10 years.
6 The boy was totally exhausted. He's been running all morning.
7 The children didn't tell me they were going out. I was worried!

7 » WORK IN PAIRS. TURN TO PAGE 128.

VOCABULARY
ADJECTIVE AND ADVERB SUFFIXES

02 **1 You will hear two friends, Lewis and Olivia, discussing personality tests. Was Lewis's test**

a mainly accurate?
b mainly inaccurate?
c partly accurate and partly inaccurate?

EP 02 **2 Listen again and write the personality adjectives you hear. The first letters have been given to help you.**

0 kn*owledgeable* ______
1 sen______
2 opt______
3 sup______
4 car______
5 sel______
6 nar______
7 res______
8 cha______
9 jud______

3 Which nouns are the adjectives in Exercise 2 formed from?

0 *knowledge*
1 ______
2 ______
3 ______
4 ______
5 ______
6 ______
7 ______
8 ______
9 ______

4 Complete the sentences using an adjective formed from the word in brackets. Use the suffixes in the box and make spelling changes if necessary.

-able -al -ed -ible -ic -ish -less -y

0 You're so *bossy* ! (boss) Stop telling me what to do!
1 Robert is a very ______ (like) boy. He is always friendly and cheerful.
2 You should be more ______ (response) at your age, Ben, and look after your little sister!
3 That's a very ______ (origin) idea for a story.
4 Stop fighting! You're being really ______ (child).
5 It's just not ______ (realist) to expect everyone to like each other.
6 Molly is trying skydiving next. She is absolutely ______ (fear)!
7 What's got into you today? You're so ______ (bad temper).

5 What other adjectives do you know with the suffixes in Exercise 4?

EP **6 Complete the sentences with the adverb form of the adjective in brackets.**

1 'Leave me alone, I'm busy!' shouted Adam ______. (bad-tempered)
2 Georgia smiled ______ when she read her exam results. (happy)
3 Mathilda ______ accused her brother of eating her chocolate. (false)
4 Dr Richards spoke very ______ about the psychology of personality testing. (knowledgeable)
5 Eva is only 14, but she already plays the piano ______. (beautiful)
6 Do you think that we can ______ finish the project by the end of the week? (realistic)

7 Look at the answers to Exercise 6 and complete the rules for forming adverbs from adjectives.

1 Adjectives ending in a consonant: add ______
2 Adjectives ending in *-y*: change *y* to ______
3 Adjectives ending in *-e*: add ______
4 Adjectives ending in *-able*, *-ible* or *-le*: change the final *e* to ______
5 Adjectives ending in *-l*: add ______
6 Adjectives ending in *-ic*: add ______

8 Read the blog post below and answer the questions.

1 Does the writer recommend house-sharing?
2 What problems has she had with housemates?

9 Use the word given in capitals at the end of some of the lines to form a word that fits in the gap in the same line.

HOUSE-SHARING

Welcome to the wonderful world of the house-share. Sharing can save money and be an **(0)** *enjoyable* experience, but believe me, there are lots of pitfalls. The first time I advertised for people to share my house, I **(1)** ______ expected to find people who shared my love of tidiness and order. Elena was certainly a **(2)** ______ person – if a little too chatty – but within a month the house was absolutely **(3)** ______ and I had to ask her to leave.

(0)	ENJOY
(1)	FOOL
(2)	WONDER
(3)	FILTH

The next occupant of my spare room was Nina. When she moved in, she **(4)** ______ brought her cat Macavity with her – I had told her 'no pets allowed!' At first, I didn't mind, but soon Macavity had scratched my brand new sofa, which I was furious about, **(5)** ______, so they too had to go. 'I'll never find anyone I can live with!' I said **(6)** ______.

(4)	CHEEK
(5)	NATURE
(6)	PESSIMIST

Then I met Ida. She is great fun, with a **(7)** ______ personality. Best of all, she is one of the most caring and **(8)** ______ people I've ever met. So, stick with it! The right housemate is out there somewhere.

(7)	MAGNET
(8)	SELF

10 Think of adjectives to describe your family members and close friends. Try to write one adjective for each of these suffixes.

-able -al -ed -ful -ible -ic -ish -ive -less -y

11 Compare your ideas with a partner.

LISTENING

1 Discuss the questions with a partner.

1 Which social media accounts do you have and why?
2 Do you tend to share lots of photos and videos?
3 Do you know anyone who exaggerates or even lies on social media?

03 **2 Listen to Extract 1. You hear two friends talking about a girl called Shania and her social media use. For question 1 choose the answer (A, B or C) which fits best according to what you hear.**

1 What does the girl suggest about Shania?
  A She is being dishonest on social media.
  B She has a better life now thanks to social media.
  C She wants to have lots of followers on social media.

03 **3 Listen again and answer question 2.**

2 What point does the boy make about social media?
  A It encourages feelings of envy among people.
  B It allows people to express themselves fully.
  C It highlights some enduring human characteristics.

4 Read the part of the script relating to question 2. The words and phrases that give you the correct answer are highlighted. Underline the words and phrases that try to distract you from the correct answer.

GIRL: It does look like that, doesn't it? I saw the photos she posted a couple of weeks ago and thought, 'Wow, she's living the dream!' But then I bumped into her in town the other day and, talking to her, I got the impression that things might not be as amazing as she's making them out to be. But that's the thing, isn't it? You can be who you want to be online and create this illusion for your thousands of followers that everything's perfect.

BOY: I don't know. I mean, it's true that people show off online and make themselves look like they're really cool, popular, happy and everything, but hasn't that always been the case? I suppose that social media has made it *easier* for people to make stuff up or exaggerate aspects of their lives or personality. But then people have boasted about their fancy clothes and big houses for centuries. With today's social networks it's just more obvious.

04 **5 Now listen to Extract 2. You hear two friends discussing their teacher. Answer questions 3 and 4.**

3 What does the boy say about his previous class?
  A He enjoyed the discussions.
  B He made a lot of mistakes.
  C He was lacking in confidence.

4 What do they both think makes their teacher exceptional?
  A She has a good sense of humour.
  B She increases students' self-esteem.
  C She is a similar age to the students.

05 **6 Now listen to Extract 3. You hear two friends discussing a friend called Adrian. Answer questions 5 and 6.**

5 The speakers are worried about their friend Adrian because
  A he has problems with his girlfriend.
  B he isn't focusing on his studies.
  C he won't talk to them anymore.

6 What do the two speakers agree to do?
  A let Adrian work the problem out for himself
  B suggest ways of dealing with the situation to Adrian
  C discuss the issue with Adrian's sister

7 Discuss the questions with a partner.

1 What problems can be caused by people giving a false impression of themselves on social media?
2 What qualities do you think a teacher should have?
3 Do you think the speakers in Extract 3 made the right decision regarding their friend's behaviour? What else could they have done?

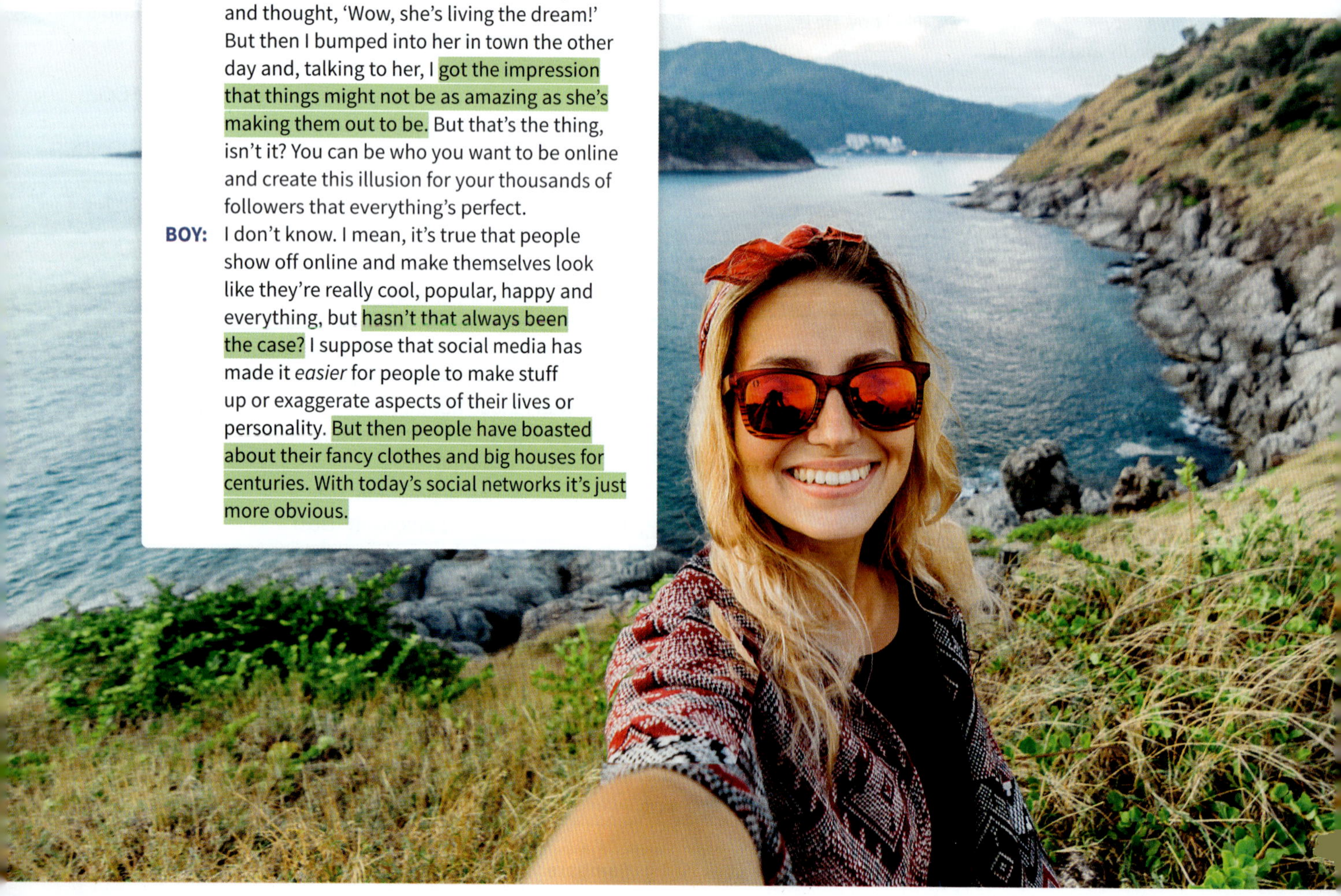

SPEAKING
PERSONAL INTERVIEW

1 **Look at the questions. Which are about the present and which are about the past? Write *present* or *past* for each.**

a Have you celebrated any special occasions recently? (What happened?)
b What kind of activities do you enjoy doing with your friends in your spare time?
c What has been your most memorable holiday?
d What did you like most about your primary school? (Why?)
e How important is it to spend time with your family? (Why?)
f What is your favourite way to communicate with friends? (Why?)
g What do you like most about the place where you live?
h Who has influenced you most in your life? (Why?)
i What was the last film you watched? (What did you think of it?)
j Do you ever wish you were famous? (Why? / Why not?)

06 **2** **Listen to two students, Hugo and Teresa, each answering two of the questions in Exercise 1. Which questions do they answer?**

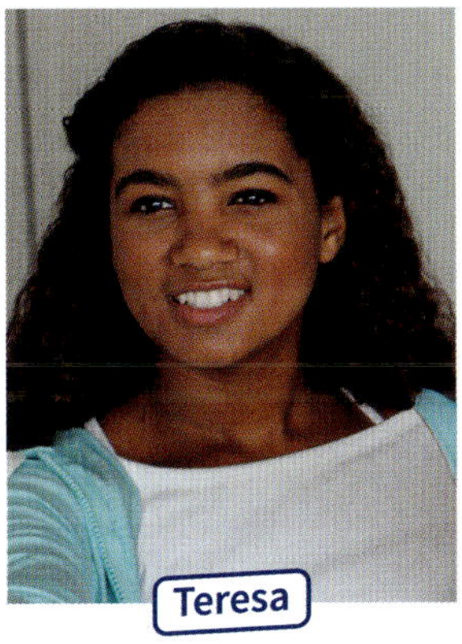

06 **3** **Listen again and answer the questions.**

1 Did the students expand their answers appropriately?
2 Did they use a range of tenses?
3 Who did the examiner ask follow-up questions to? Why?

4 **Read Teresa's first answer and underline the different past tense forms she uses.**

I suppose it would be my grandmother, since she's always been there for me. She'd look after us while our parents were working. Not only that, but she taught us good values like working hard and being polite. Plus we actually used to have a great time with her. To be honest, she could be strict, but she had a good sense of humour. She's definitely had the strongest impact on me.

06 **5** **Look at the *Prepare to speak* box. Listen again and complete the expressions.**

PREPARE TO SPEAK

Personal interview

Asking for clarification

Sorry, I didn't [1] .... Could you say it again, please?
What do you mean exactly?

Adding additional information

…, too.
And [2] .... thing is …,
Not [3] .... that, but …
Plus, …
Besides, …
…, especially …

Giving and explaining opinions

I'd rather …
I [4] .... it would be …
To be honest, …
… definitely …
I [5] .... say …
For one thing, …
But the [6] .... best thing …

6 **Look at the questions in Exercise 1. Think about how you could answer each question. What additional information could you add to each answer?**

7 **Work with a partner. Ask and answer the questions in Exercise 1 using phrases from the *Prepare to speak* box.**

2 THE BIGGER THE BETTER?

? ABOUT YOU

▶ 02 **Watch the video and then answer the questions.**

What kind of things do you think cause some cities in the world to grow so quickly?

What are the advantages and disadvantages of living in very large cities?

Should cities have some areas where cars are banned? Why? / Why not?

VOCABULARY AND READING

CITIES

EP **1 Read what five young people say about the places where they live. Who mentions**

1 tall buildings?
2 areas with trees or plants?
3 a residential area of a city?
4 ways to travel from one part of the city to another?
5 dirty and crowded parts of a city?
6 large numbers of people living in a small area?
7 something that keeps traffic away from a city centre?
8 the uncontrolled growth of a city away from its centre?
9 buildings that are neglected and in very poor condition?
10 areas where people can go on foot but not in vehicles?

ANDY, 16, SINGAPORE

Nearly 6 million people live in Singapore, a country that measures just 50 kilometres across, so it's very **densely populated**. Having said that, there are plenty of **green spaces**, where you can even go mountain biking and trekking.

IGOR, 19, RUSSIA

I live with my family on the top floor of one of the **high-rise** blocks close to Moscow's outer **ring road**, so we have an amazing view out over the city.

BEATRIZ, 18, BRAZIL

My parents grew up in **slums**, where people were squashed into **derelict** and unsafe buildings, but the area has really improved and now it's become a popular residential area, which I'm happy to call home.

HANNAH, 17, USA

Los Angeles, where I've moved to from the UK, is famous for its **urban sprawl**, and it's true the houses go on and on for miles. But on a good day, I can drive to the centre from the **suburb** where I live in about 50 minutes, so it's not too bad.

LANA, 15, SLOVENIA

There are really efficient **transport links** between where I live in Ljubljana and the centre of the city, which is largely **pedestrianised** these days, making it both clean and safe.

2 Complete the questions with a word or phrase from Exercise 1.

1 Does your town have good, affordable .... to help you get around?
2 Apart from the view from the top, what are the advantages of living in a .... building?
3 How suitable are the .... in your town for football, jogging or just hanging out with friends?
4 Is it preferable to live in a city centre or out in a ....?
5 Would you describe your town as ...., or are the buildings spread out over a large area?
6 Are there any .... buildings in your town? What do you think should happen to them?
7 Does your town have a .... to help traffic avoid the centre?
8 If you ran a shop or a café, would you want the street your business was on to become ....? Why? / Why not?
9 Is it necessarily a bad thing if a town's .... takes over the surrounding countryside as it grows?
10 Some people say that, despite the poverty, there is a strong community spirit among residents who live in ....

3 With a partner, ask and answer the questions in Exercise 2.

4 Quickly read the article on the opposite page to identify the places in the photographs. Which other places are mentioned in the text? Is the writer's opinion about the growth of these places generally positive or negative?

5 Read the first paragraph in more detail and answer the question below with a partner. Identify the parts of the text which gave you the answer.

1 What does Barcelona indicate about densely populated cities, according to the writer?
A They can be found anywhere in the world.
B There is optimum opportunity for social contact in them.
C A high quality of life is perfectly possible in them.
D Well-organised public transport is essential for them to work.

6 For questions 2–6, choose the answer (A, B, C or D) which you think fits best according to the text.

2 What does the writer say about city growth in the second paragraph?
A It is likely to threaten food supplies.
B Attempts to measure it may be very inaccurate.
C It sometimes leads to uninteresting architecture.
D Parks and woodland will disappear.

3 According to the writer, what cause of urban sprawl is specific to the United States?
A increased prosperity among the working-class
B high crime rates in inner cities
C restrictive construction regulations
D a demand for increased living space

HOW CITIES GROW, AND WHY THIS HAS TO CHANGE

07

I have just spent two days in Barcelona, one of the most densely populated urban settlements on Earth. There are 103 road intersections per square kilometre – high compared with Brasilia's 41, or Shanghai's Pudong area, which has no more than 17. And despite this high density, residents are proud to call the city home, walking or cycling short distances to work, or using the city's first-class public transport network. Visitors are charmed by the maze of pedestrianised streets that thread their way through the assortment of four to seven-storey buildings constructed over the centuries, leading to squares where people sit at café tables under the shade of large trees.

But Barcelona is the exception, rather than the rule. The dominant trend now is actually for cities to spread outwards into the surrounding countryside, rather than to become more and more densely populated. This has disturbing consequences. The total area occupied by all the cement, concrete, asphalt and green spaces of all the world's urban areas is roughly 1.5 million square kilometres. As the global urban population is expected to grow by some 50% over the next thirty years, a not unreasonable expectation is that the area occupied by the world's cities will increase by the same amount. And as by far the most productive farmland is typically located close to where the bulk of the produce is consumed, it is these areas which, rather than increasing their harvest yield to feed growing populations, will be replaced by concrete. This is simply not sustainable.

Urban sprawl is particularly common in North American cities, such as Atlanta. Economic growth is often cited as the principal cause of this. However, the attraction of cheaper land in suburban areas, which allows for larger and larger properties, plays an equally significant role, with many citizens keen to escape the congestion, crime, and noise of the city. Many of those involved in urban development, however, claim that planning laws which limit an area to one particular use such as residential, commercial or institutional, are a major reason for urban spread in the States since they discourage the development of walkable communities because homes have to be built away from shops, schools, and employment areas. Other countries, where more diverse land use is permitted, don't have this additional influence. With urban sprawl being blamed for increased energy use, pollution, and a decline in community cohesion, legislation needs to change sooner rather than later.

But this kind of destructive urban spread is not inevitable. Take one of Africa's most exciting cities, the Ethiopian capital Addis Ababa, where urbanisation is occurring more quickly than anyone thought possible. Government investment has transformed the city into a vast building site. Towering cranes are silhouetted against the African sky as the skeletons of high-rise buildings emerge in the urban core. And with funds and expertise brought in by Chinese companies, a light-rail system has been built that runs across the city, a remarkable achievement in a place where 80% of the population live in slums. This enables residents to commute easily from their high-density apartment blocks that have been shooting up across the city, and it has the added ecological benefit of lessening people's reliance on the car and thus reducing their individual footprint.

Even urban areas designed very much with cars in mind are being transformed. Perhaps the megacity that has most successfully avoided urban sprawl is Seoul, South Korea. When the mayor decided to dismantle an eight-lane highway that used to run through the centre, he said, 'Seoul is for people, not cars.' In its place is a new canal and pedestrianised walkway. No alternative road was built, and although it may seem counterintuitive, this does seem to have prompted people to abandon their cars in favour of much greener modes of mass transit. This in turn has made further government investment in transport links more viable.

The world's urban population will continue to grow. The more it grows, the more homes we will need. Housing large numbers of people in multi-centred, low-carbon, high-density cities must be a global commitment.

TALKING POINTS

Would you prefer to live in a high-rise city like Seoul, or somewhere with a low population density? Why? Do you think it is always true that larger cities are more dangerous places to live than smaller ones?

4 Which word or phrase suggests the high speed of change in Addis Ababa?

A emerge *(line 55)*
B brought in *(line 56)*
C runs *(line 57)*
D shooting up *(line 61)*

5 The removal of the highway in Seoul demonstrates

A a surprising way to reduce vehicle numbers.
B a method of lowering the cost of public transport.
C how politicians do not always fulfil their promises.
D that attempts to minimise traffic do not always succeed.

6 An idea recurring in the text is that cities of the future

A must encourage cleaner forms of transport.
B will need to develop infrastructure and avoid covering too large an area.
C may become difficult to live in if their populations become too high.
D should discourage people from building sub-standard housing and from driving.

GRAMMAR
COMPARATIVES AND SUPERLATIVES

1 Look at sentences 1–6 and find examples of the structures in the box. Some sentences have more than one example.

comparative adjective
comparative adverb
qualifier used with comparatives
superlative adjective
qualifier used with superlatives
superlative adverb
double comparative adjective (with *and*)
double comparative adverb (with *the*)

1 **By far the most productive** farmland is typically located close to cities.
2 Cheaper land in suburban areas allows for **larger and larger** properties.
3 Urbanisation is occurring **even more quickly** than anyone thought possible.
4 Perhaps the megacity that has **most successfully** avoided urban sprawl is Seoul.
5 People are abandoning their cars in favour of **much greener** modes of mass transit.
6 **The more** the population grows, **the more** homes we will need.

» GRAMMAR REFERENCE AND PRACTICE PAGE 145

2 Put the word in capitals into a suitable comparative or superlative form, adding another word or an ending if necessary.

1 Jack's family have got ________ flat I've ever seen. **AMAZING**
2 I noticed that the streets were ________ than usual, probably because everyone was at home watching the match on TV. **CROWDED**
3 The historic building I've visited ________ is Chatsworth House, in central England. I was there just last month. **RECENT**
4 The town's new ring road was constructed far ________ than anyone expected. **QUICK**
5 The Pencil Museum in Keswick, England sounds like it will be ________ museum in the world, but my young cousins loved it. **INTERESTING**
6 The multi-storey house of telecoms magnate Mukesh Ambani is by far ________ private residence in the world. **LARGE**

3 Choose the correct word or phrase to modify the comparatives and superlatives. Then decide which statements are true.

1 The Pyramid of Khafre at Giza was *far / by far* the tallest building in the world for 3,800 years.
2 A concrete beam can be made *incredibly / considerably* stronger if steel rods are placed inside it.
3 On its completion in 2019, the Tianjin CTF Finance Centre became *easily / substantially* the world's tallest skyscraper.
4 Adding solar panels to your home can make your energy bills *significantly / largely* lower.
5 In the UK, it's often *substantially / by far* more expensive to buy an old home than a new one.

4 Complete the sentences with the most suitable double comparative phrase from the box.

busier and busier | less and less efficiently | less and less frequently | louder and louder | more and more polluted

1 As we got closer to the nightclub, we could hear the music getting ________.
2 My parents decided to replace their boiler because it'd been working ________ and costing too much.
3 The growth of budget airlines has made tourist hotspots like Venice become ________ in recent years.
4 Cuts to public transport mean that trains are running ________ nowadays.
5 Air quality monitoring has shown that the city centre is becoming ________.

5 Complete the sentences so that the meaning is the same.

1 If you live further from the centre, your journey takes longer.
The further you live from the centre, the ________.
2 English gets easier when you use it more.
The ________, the easier it gets.
3 The chance of having a traffic accident increases if you're travelling quickly.
The quicker ________ you are to have an accident.
4 I get sleepier and sleepier when I stay up late.
The later ________ I get.
5 When the metro gets more crowded, I use it less frequently.
The ________ the metro gets, ________ I use it.

6 Correct any mistakes in these sentences. One is correct.

1 The building was actually completed quicklier than expected.
2 The city is more crowded during the weekends it is in the week.
3 Istanbul has far the largest population of any city in Turkey.
4 The cities currently growing the most rapidly are located in Asia and Africa.
5 The more insulation a building has inside its walls and roof, it will be warmer.
6 Simon's behaviour is becoming more and also more juvenile as he gets older.

7 » WORK IN PAIRS. TURN TO PAGE 128.

VOCABULARY
BUILDINGS AND PLACES: IDIOMS

08

1 **Listen to six conversations. Which conversation is about**

a getting very angry?
b doing something to a high standard by spending lots of money?
c feeling confident and comfortable?
d overcoming prejudice which stops someone from advancing in their career?
e meeting an obstacle and being unable to decide what to do?
f making it impossible to go back to a situation which existed before?

EP 08

2 **Match the words to make the idioms you heard. Then listen again and check. Try to work out the meaning of each idiom.**

hit	your bridges	....
break	at home	....
hit	to town	....
go	the glass ceiling	....
feel	the roof	....
burn	a brick wall	....

3 **Read the information about the six people below, then answer the questions.**

1 Who has **hit a brick wall**?
2 Who is really **going to town**?
3 Who has **burned their bridges**?
4 Who might be about to **hit the roof**?
5 Who **feels at home** in their new role?
6 Who has managed to **break a glass ceiling**?

4 **Which three people most need help and advice? What advice would you give them?**

EP **5** **Read Rupert's post. What's his problem, and what would you suggest?**

THE HOUSING BLOG

A safe space where you can share any accommodation issues you have with our community of users

Hi,

A few months ago, I had to move out of the place where I was living. I desperately needed **a roof over my head** because I didn't want to move back in with my parents. So I was pleased when I found a flatshare with three guys, and moved in that very day. The others have known each other for ages and **get on like a house on fire**. But I feel left out, and I'd like to move out. I signed a contract with them for a year, but I'm not sure if it's **set in stone** or whether I can give notice and move out early. I don't want all the money I've paid in advance to **go down the drain** because I'll need it back to find another place. Any suggestions?

Rupert

6 **Choose the correct definition of the idioms in Rupert's post.**

1 a roof over your head
  a a place to live **b** a top-floor flat
2 get on like a house on fire
  a argue loudly **b** have a great relationship
3 set in stone
  a old-fashioned **b** impossible to change
4 go down the drain
  a be wasted **b** be spent on bills

7 » **WORK IN PAIRS. TURN TO PAGE 128.**

When **Rose** started work with an engineering firm, she was the only female employee. But her career took off, and she has become the first female managing director of the company.

Mario used to be his team's top goal scorer. Now aged 33 he's started to lack the speed to keep up with younger players. But rather than quit, he's started playing as goalkeeper, which involves less running. And you know what? He absolutely loves it!

Sho and his fiancée are planning their wedding. Sho has decided to have several costumes made at a cost of several thousand dollars for both of them to wear during the wedding. It's the most important day of his life and he wants everything to be perfect.

Samantha is writing her first novel, but the story is getting very complicated and she can't work out how it's going to end. She's run out of ideas.

Joe was offered a new job by a rival company, but he turned it down because the salary was too low. He's now been made redundant by his current employer but thinks it's too late to try to get the position with the other firm.

Tina's brother borrowed her new phone without asking, and when she got it back, the screen was smashed.

WRITING
INFORMAL EMAILS OF ADVICE

1 Read the extracts from the beginning and end of emails written to friends in other countries. Which ones sound suitably friendly and which ones don't? How could the unfriendly ones be improved?

Opening an email

1 Hi Dave,
Great to hear from you – it's brilliant that you're coming to Mumbai.

2 Dear Frankie,
There are loads of cool places to hang out in Brisbane.

3 Dear Joanne,
Thank you for your email. I am delighted to hear of your plans to relocate to Moscow in the near future.

4 Hi Lucinda,
Moving to Porto, then? Nice one! Best town in the world, by the way!

Closing an email

5 I trust the suggestions outlined above will enable you to get the most out of your time visiting London.
6 Anyway, I'm sure that whatever you do, you'll have an amazing time when you come to Milan.
7 All being well, we'll meet up before long, and I'll be happy to show you some of the coolest places to hang out in Warsaw!
8 That's all I have to say about visiting São Paolo.

2 Would the following phrases be more suitable for opening or closing an email to a friend? Write *O* or *C*.

1 Say 'hi' to your parents from me.
2 Haven't heard from you in ages!
3 Anyway, looking forward to catching up properly soon.
4 Thanks for getting back in touch.
5 Don't forget to bring waterproof clothing, just in case!
6 It was a lovely surprise to get your email.
7 I was thinking about you just the other day!
8 And next time we meet, we'll be on holiday! Can't wait!

3 Some of the phrases in these messages to friends are too formal. Replace them with an informal phrase from the box.

catch them | in the next day or two | loads of us | really amazing time | ~~Shame you couldn't~~ | try and get us | 've got to let you know | well worth going to

Hi Jake, how's it going? ~~It was disappointing that you were unable to~~ *Shame you couldn't* get to the gig the other evening. There were a substantial number of people there, and we all had a most delightful evening. The band were unbelievable, and you should definitely try and attend a performance when they play again! I'll endeavour to purchase tickets next time.

Hi Marta, I wish to inform you about this new shop that's just opened on Howarth Avenue. They have some amazing stuff – easily the best in town, I'd say! The prices are pretty reasonable too. It's advisable to visit it, so what about us going together after school in the near future? Love, Sandrine XX

4 Which of these versions of the same sentence would be acceptable in an informal mail?

1 a It's fantastic news that you're coming to Jakarta!
b Fantastic news that you're coming to Jakarta!
c Fantastic that you're coming to Jakarta!
d Fantastic coming to Jakarta!

2 a I'm not sure if I'll still be here though, as I'm hoping to go and study in Salamanca.
b Not sure if I'll still be here though, as I'm hoping to go and study in Salamanca.
c Not sure if I'll still be here though, as hoping to go and study in Salamanca.
d I'm not sure I'll still be here though, as I'm hoping to go and study in Salamanca.

3 a Anyway, I'll speak to you soon.
b Anyway, I'll speak soon.
c Anyway, speak soon.
d Anyway, speak.

4 a I'm looking forward to seeing you soon.
b I'm looking forward to soon.
c Looking forward to seeing you soon.
d Look forward to seeing you soon.

5 Complete the *Prepare to write* box with phrases from Exercises 1–4.

PREPARE TO WRITE
An informal email

- When you are writing a message such as an email to a friend, remember to sound friendly.
- Start the email with a comment addressed to your reader, such as (*It was*) 1 ....
- Use informal language, such as 2 .... *for getting in touch.*
- End the email with a friendly comment about what you expect to happen next, such as 3 ....
- Consider using ellipsis (missing out words), e.g. 4 .... *to seeing you soon.*

6 Discuss the questions with a partner.

1 Moving home is thought to be one of life's most stressful experiences. Why do you think this is?
2 What do you think a family from another country would find easiest and hardest about moving to your town or city?
3 How easy would it be to make friends when you move to a new place, and what are the best ways of doing this?

7 **Read this task and complete Tomek's answer with the phrases in the box. What do all the phrases have in common?**

You have received this email from a friend overseas.

... and so, for various reasons, my family have decided to move to your city, where I'll be starting a new school next year. What's your city like for a newcomer from another country, like me? And what can you suggest I do in order to make friends and settle in?

Write your **email** in reply.

An international one presumably
Anyway, fantastic news   Great to hear from you
Looking forward to   Might just be   New jobs here
no idea why, though   No wonder really,
One tip for you   plenty of English speakers

Hi Jason,

[1] .... Brilliant that you're coming to live in Kraków with your parents. [2] ...., I guess? Anyway, you can fill me in on all that once you're here.

As for what it's going to be like, well, Kraków's one of those places that people from all over the world are drawn to, whether to visit or live in. [3] .... considering the gorgeous architecture of the Old Town! Plus, it's got a massive student population, and that includes millions of students from overseas. So [4] ...., which means you'll probably find it quite easy to make friends with other ex-pats, including those at your school. [5] ...., with the teaching in English, right? [6] .... – do take the initiative and suggest exchanging phone numbers with people, even if you don't know them all that well.

Also, I think you'll feel more at home here if you start learning the language. People often say Polish is a difficult language to learn – [7] ...., as it's no harder than English really. [8] .... because people feel intimidated when they see all the consonants in words like 'Szczyrk', but don't let that put you off, it'll be a piece of cake for you!

And why not come out with some of my friends who speak English? Once you get to know a few people, you'll feel at home.

[9] .... that you're coming!
[10] .... seeing you soon!

Tomek

8 **Find examples of the following strategies used in Tomek's email to create a friendly tone.**

1 paying Jason compliments
2 asking questions / checking details
3 using exclamation marks
4 exaggeration

9 **Which of the following ways of giving advice are used in Tomek's email?**

a first conditional
b second conditional
c positive imperative
d negative imperative
e *Why not* + infinitive
f *You might want to ...*
g *You could consider -ing*
h *How about -ing?*
i *What I'd do is ...*

10 **Discuss the following quotations, saying whether you agree with them and why.**

1 'I'd have the time of my life if I moved into a flat with a few of my mates.'
2 'It's best to live at home until you get married.'
3 'The whole point of moving out of home is to gain independence, and so it makes more sense to live on your own than to share a flat with friends.'
4 'The cost of renting a flat is so high that moving out of the family home is simply unaffordable for most young people.'

11 **Read this task and reply to the email.**

You have received this email from a friend overseas.

... I'm thinking of moving out of my family home and into an apartment with my university friends, but I'm not sure if it'd be a wise move. What would you do? And how should I decide whether it's the right thing to do?

Write your **email** in reply.

- Use friendly language.
- Consider using ellipsis.
- Use a range of different structures to give advice.
- Make your email friendly and interactive.
- End some sentences with exclamation marks and question marks.
- Make sure that you answer any questions in your friend's email.

LIFE SKILLS COMMUNICATION

NEGOTIATING CONFLICT

LIFE SKILLS

Dealing with conflict

Throughout our lives, we may find ourselves in conflict with friends, family or others. In order to maintain and deepen good relationships, it's important to be able to resolve conflicts in a way that is calm, respectful and acceptable to both sides. Learning how to negotiate conflict constructively can help us to do this.

1 **Read three situations where people are in conflict. With a partner, answer the question in bold at the end of each one.**

A James is getting angry with his friends Tom and Mark because they keep dictating what to do at the weekend. Tom and Mark think they have to take the initiative because James only ever wants to hang out at home and watch TV, which can get tedious. The situation is making everyone frustrated.

How can the three boys avoid falling out permanently?

B Adam and his sister Lucy both have to help with the household chores as their parents work long hours. Adam thinks he should do less because he's revising for his final exams and doesn't have much time. Lucy thinks she should do less because she's training for an important basketball tournament and isn't at home very much. This is causing them to quarrel.

How can they resolve the issue?

C Alesha and her brother Jamal share a laptop to do their school projects, but they each think they should have priority. What's more, Alesha knows Jamal often plays games instead of doing schoolwork, while Jamal is sure Alesha wastes time chatting with her friends online. They are both getting angry but neither has said anything yet.

How should they deal with the problem?

2 **Have you experienced anything similar? If so, how did you deal with the conflict?**

3 **Read the article about negotiating conflict constructively. Does it mention any of your ideas from Exercise 1?**

4 **Read the text again. In your own words, why should you avoid doing these things when you're in conflict with someone?**

1 losing your temper with the other person
2 interrupting the other person
3 mentioning something that the other person did or said before
4 using phrases like 'hate' or 'can't stand'
5 trying to get exactly what you want

09 **5** **Listen to two conversations. Which conversation is from one of the situations in Exercise 1?**

09 **6** **Listen again. Based on the advice in the article**

1 what did Petra and Tamsin do right?
2 what did Adam and Lucy do wrong?

WE CAN WORK IT OUT

10

We've all had arguments with people we care about, sometimes about important issues, but also over things that later seem trivial. We've all been in situations where we feel the other person doesn't understand our point of view. Conflict is a part of life, and conflict with friends or siblings is especially common during our teenage years. It can make us feel uncomfortable, let down, isolated, or even unloved. If we don't handle conflict well, it can damage the relationship we have with the other person, sometimes permanently. On the other hand, if we work together to resolve the issue in a healthy way, it can strengthen that relationship by increasing our understanding of one another and building mutual trust. What, then, are the key strategies for negotiating conflict constructively?

1 TALK, BUT DON'T SHOUT

When conflict arises, it's important not to ignore it. Unless you confront it, things will only get worse, especially if both sides feel angry about the situation but don't say anything. More than likely, one of you will eventually snap, but remember: conflict can never be resolved by shouting. Instead, find a good time and a quiet spot to sit down with the other person and say, *'Listen, can we talk about …'* That way, you start a conversation rather than an argument.

2 LISTEN ACTIVELY

When you're describing how you feel or saying what you'd like to happen, you want the other person to listen to you. In the same way, when the other person is talking, it's important not to interrupt but to pay attention, otherwise you'll never understand their point of view. You should also acknowledge how they feel, even if *you* feel very differently. Phrases such as *'I didn't realise that was how you felt'* or *'I understand what you're saying'* can be really effective here.

3 KEEP TO THE CURRENT SITUATION

It might not be the first time you and your friend or your brother or sister have been in conflict. If that's the case, it can be tempting to bring up past experiences or other issues you might be having. However, this is unfair and will only make matters worse. In fact, you may well end up saying nasty things you'll regret. If that starts to happen, saying something like *'Hold on, let's just focus on …'* can help you stick to the issue at hand.

4 USE MODERATE LANGUAGE

You might be furious with the other person, but how you express that anger can make a big difference. Rather than telling them you can't stand the way they treat you or hate the things they're doing, which will simply create more anger, use more diplomatic language such as *'I'd prefer it if you did/didn't …'* and *'Could you try (not) to …'* What's more, don't forget to explain why you feel the way you do. Unexplained anger can be confusing and distressing for the other person.

5 SEEK COMPROMISE

Negotiating conflict isn't about one person winning and the other losing. It's about finding a solution that's acceptable to both sides. If you both insist on getting your own way completely, either the conflict will continue or you'll end up falling out. Instead, accept that you'll need to compromise and work together to find a middle ground. Using phrases such as *'Why don't we …?'*, *'Let's both try to …'* and *'That works for me'* will help you achieve this.

Project

Role play: resolving conflict

In pairs, role-play a situation where two people are in conflict. Use the advice and the phrases in the article to try to resolve it in a way that is acceptable to everyone.

1 DECIDE

Choose one of the situations in Exercise 1 or think of a different situation.

2 THINK

Add some details to make it more interesting. For example:

A This weekend is the birthday of one of the boys.

B One of the siblings is much untidier than the other.

C Both siblings have an important end of year project to hand in next week.

3 PLAN

Plan and rehearse what you're going to say. Make sure you include some of the phrases in italics from the article.

4 PRESENT

Present your role play to another pair.

5 FEEDBACK

Listen to the role play of the other pair and give feedback. Did the speakers

- resolve the conflict well?
- use phrases from the article?
- add details to make it more interesting?

3 ALL IN ONE PIECE

ABOUT YOU

▶ 03 **Watch the video and answer the questions.**
Is it important to know about health and the body, or should this just be left to medical professionals?
Would you be interested in working in healthcare? Why? / Why not?
What do you consider to be the single greatest danger to people's health?

VOCABULARY AND READING

THE HUMAN BODY

EP **1 Read these statements about the body and check the meaning of the words. Then decide if the statements are true or false.**

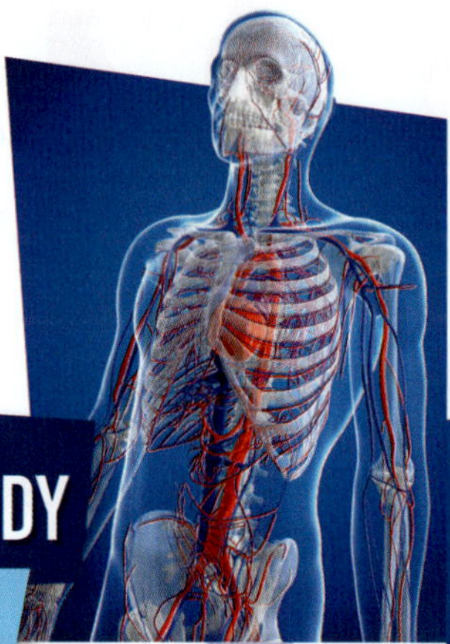

The AMAZING HUMAN BODY – fact or myth?

1. Adults **inhale** and **exhale** an average of 80,000 times per day.
2. Putting too much food in the mouth can cause a person to **choke**, which can sometimes be fatal.
3. It's possible for people to control a robotic **limb** using their brain and muscles.
4. In humans, the right **lung** is bigger than the left because of the space taken up by the heart.
5. An average person produces around 100 millilitres of **sweat** per hour during exercise.
6. When you wear headphones, the number of **germs** (viruses and bacteria) in your ear increases by 700 times.
7. Your **spine** gets shorter while you are asleep.
8. People who sleep less than seven hours a night are less likely to become **poorly** than those who sleep more.
9. Sitting with crossed legs for a prolonged period can make them feel **numb** because their blood flow is restricted.
10. There are approximately 6,000 kilometres of **nerves** in the human body.
11. The **joint** you're most likely to injure playing sport is your knee.
12. Children who are **left-handed** may find it more difficult to learn to write.

2 Complete the questions with words from Exercise 1.

1. Is it possible to __________ on your tongue?
2. Roughly what proportion of the air you __________ is oxygen? And in the air that you __________?
3. Where is the __________ which you can press in order to prevent a sneeze?
4. Which would you expect to contain more __________ – a mobile phone or a toilet seat?
5. Are there more species of vertebrates (i.e. those that have a __________) or invertebrates in the world?
6. Do you think people who are physically active get __________ less frequently than those who don't?
7. Do you ever get __________ on the palms of your hands when you're nervous?
8. Have you ever felt part of your body going __________? What might have caused this?
9. Is it true that the axolotl can regrow any of its __________ and even its eyes if it loses them? And do you think it will ever be possible for people to do this?
10. What proportion of the population are __________?
11. Most human __________, such as the shoulder, allow movement, but some don't. Whereabouts in the body are the ones that don't?
12. What else do we use our __________ for apart from breathing?

3 Answer the questions in Exercise 2 with a partner.

4 Read the article opposite quickly and identify the points which photos A–C are illustrating.

5 Read the article again and answer the questions.

1. What does the writer say about the human body in the first paragraph?
   A It's less impressive than people think.
   B It has evolved more quickly than people think.
   C It can keep going for longer than people think.
2. The writer argues that the 'funny bone'
   A should be renamed.
   B is poorly protected.
   C may be in the wrong place.
3. What point does Lucy Brantwood make about the shape of the human spine?
   A It is not suited to walking on two legs.
   B It caused our ancestors a lot of pain.
   C It is superior to the spine of other species.
4. Why does the writer compare humans to whales in the last paragraph?
   A Humans and whales have both devised unique methods of communication.
   B Whales have adapted to their environment in similar ways to humans.
   C Whales avoid a problem that humans experience.
5. What is the author's main purpose in the article?
   A to discuss some flaws of the human body in a light-hearted way
   B to offer practical suggestions for when something goes wrong with your body
   C to argue that medical professionals have failed to explain some common symptoms

A

Is the human body really as AMAZING as we're led to believe?

by Jack Ashford, Science Correspondent

We're frequently told what an incredibly sophisticated piece of equipment the human body is. It can do anything: it can heal itself, it can fight germs, regulate temperature by sweating, and with good maintenance, it can last up to as much as a century, as we all know. But the view of the body as some sort of perfect well-oiled machine is a myth. In fact, I'll go further, and say it's nonsense. We've ended up in the shape we're in through gradual evolution over millions of years. And evolution doesn't produce perfection, it simply helps the species to adapt in order to survive in the environment it has to endure. With this in mind, I surveyed anatomists, medics and biologists to get a view on the general state of the human body. And believe me, it's a less than perfect picture.

For a start, do we really need to be right- or left-handed? Couldn't we have two hands that both work equally well? The same goes for feet – just think how many more goals would be scored if footballers could use both of them equally well! And do you know where your so-called 'funny bone' is? It's that spot just above your elbow that, if hit by mistake, sends a weird painful sensation shooting through your arm, and can leave the whole limb feeling numb for several minutes. In fact, it's not a bone at all, but rather the ulnar nerve that runs from your neck all the way down to your hand. For almost all of its length it's surrounded by the bones and muscles in your arm. However, at the elbow joint, the only thing separating this sensitive nerve from the sharp edge of your table is a thin layer of skin and fat. That can't be a good idea, can it? Clearly, a bit of rewiring is needed here.

C

And then there's the spine. It's a wonder we can even walk at all, according to Professor Lucy Brantwood. The posture of our early ancestors was radically different from ours – they walked on all fours. So their spine was arched in shape, in order to withstand the weight of the lungs and other organs below. But then humans stood up and started walking around on two legs instead of four. So now the lower spine curves forward, and the upper spine curves the opposite way, putting tremendous pressure on the spine overall. It's no wonder then that some 80% of adults experience back pain. 'Think of your dog on the other hand,' says Brantwood. 'Its spine is one single curve. That's a great system. Simple, strong and pain-free.' Surely there must be a solution to humanity's problem of chronic back pain? Well there is – we just need to return to all fours.

B

While some parts of the body are left vulnerable, others seem to be in the wrong place. Your foodpipe (which takes food and liquid from your throat to your stomach when you swallow) opens into the same place as your windpipe (which leads air between your throat and lungs when you inhale and exhale). To stop food going down the wrong way into the windpipe, there's a little flap called the epiglottis. This should move to cover the opening to the windpipe whenever food is swallowed, but sometimes it isn't quick enough. When you are talking or laughing while eating, there is a chance that food may slip into the windpipe, causing you to choke. Here it's interesting to compare humans with our fellow mammals, whales, who might be able to teach us a thing or two. Whales breathe through their blowholes on the top of their head, whereas they feed as we do, via the mouth. So all we'd have to do is follow their example by moving our windpipe into our nose, and away from the foodpipe. Sure, we'd lose the ability to talk. But perhaps we could communicate through song as whales do …

TALKING POINTS

Which creatures do you think are especially well adapted to their environment?
What other parts of the human body could you argue are badly designed?
How do you think the human body might continue to evolve in the future?

GRAMMAR
MODALS: SPECULATION AND DEDUCTION

1 Match extracts 1–3 to explanations i–iii.

1 There is a chance that food **may** slip into the windpipe.
2 Surely there **must** be a solution to humanity's problem of chronic back pain?
3 That **can't** be a good idea, can it?

> **i** a suggestion about what is probably true
> **ii** a suggestion that something isn't true
> **iii** something that is possible

» **GRAMMAR REFERENCE AND PRACTICE PAGE 146**

2 Complete sentences 1–7 with endings a–g. Then decide which explanation in Exercise 1 applies to the modal verb in each sentence.

1 Life expectancy in Japan is very high,
2 If you have a very high temperature, seek medical advice,
3 Don't look up your symptoms on the internet
4 It's worth getting dental check-ups,
5 Some people find they get tired very easily,
6 Minor symptoms **might be** the first sign of a serious illness,
7 Painkillers sold in supermarkets **can't** really **be** effective,

a since it **could indicate** that you have an infection.
b as you **could have** a problem with your mouth that you're unaware of.
c or you'll think you **must have** a terrible disease!
d so it's worth making an appointment to see the doctor.
e which **may be caused** by a lack of vitamins.
f and it is thought that the population's fish-based diet **must be contributing** to this.
g because they're too cheap to be good quality.

3 With a partner, say which of the statements in Exercise 2 you agree with, and why.

MODALS: PERMISSION, OBLIGATION AND ADVICE

4 Look at the signs from a hospital. Why do you think it's important to follow each piece of advice?

1 You **cannot** bring hot food into the hospital. Thank you.

2 Remember! To stay healthy you **should** cut down on fatty foods.

3 VISITORS TO THE HOSPITAL **DON'T HAVE TO** MAKE AN APPOINTMENT.

4 You **must not** enter the hospital as a visitor if you think you are ill.

5 All visitors **must** wash their hands before visiting patients.

6 Up to three visitors **may** visit an in-patient at any one time.

7 All children **need to** be accompanied by an adult.

8 REMEMBER! WE ALL **OUGHT TO** EXERCISE AT LEAST THREE TIMES A WEEK!

5 Match the modal verbs in Exercise 4 to functions a–e.

> **a** giving advice
> **b** saying what is allowed
> **c** saying what is prohibited
> **d** saying what people are obliged to do
> **e** saying what is not necessary

» **GRAMMAR REFERENCE AND PRACTICE PAGE 146**

6 » **TURN TO PAGE 128.**

7 Scan the responses below to identify which two posts in Exercise 6 they are replies to. Ignore the gaps.

A First of all, it's obvious that you are highly motivated, so good on you! I'm sure your employer [1] .... that in you – in fact, it [2] .... why you got the job in the first place. But I just wonder whether you [3] .... an obsession with work. You [4] .... things in perspective, and remember that you [5] .... that you have a decent work–life balance. At the end of the day, it's just a job, and you [6] .... it rule your life.

B I understand that you feel that using your device [7] .... you feel drowsy, and this is why you use it at bedtime. But it [8] .... the case that your device is actually doing the opposite, because of the blue light, which [9] .... it more difficult for you to get to sleep. If you want to get to sleep quicker, I really do think that you [10] .... screens from your bedroom altogether. Good luck!

8 Complete the responses in Exercise 7 with the verb phrases in the box. Use each phrase only once.

> could be   may even explain   may make
> might actually have   must ensure   must recognise
> need to keep   ought to help   should get rid of
> shouldn't let

9 Correct the mistakes in these sentences.

1 You mustn't join an expensive gym if you want to keep fit. You can work out at home.
2 By law, employers ought to make sure that their workplace is safe for everyone.
3 If taking a shower gives your skin a rash, you can be allergic to your soap, shampoo or shower gel.
4 You really could take these pills if you want the infection to clear up.
5 If you have a headache, you ought to be dehydrated.
6 He mustn't have broken his arm in the accident. He's back at work already.

10 » **WORK IN PAIRS. TURN TO PAGE 129.**

VOCABULARY

HEALTH: PHRASAL VERBS AND EXPRESSIONS

12

1 **You will hear four people talking about their health. Which person**

- **a** is feeling exhausted?
- **b** lost consciousness unexpectedly?
- **c** had thought they might be seriously ill?
- **d** has concerns over how their condition affects others?

EP 12

2 **Listen again. Complete the extracts by writing one word in each gap. Ignore phrases A and B for now.**

Speaker 1

1 I went to sit down in a chair, then just ________ out.
  a became unconscious **b** began feeling tired

2 When I came ________, the first thing I was aware of was my mum standing over me …
  a changed my mind **b** became conscious

3 And I freaked ________. I was like, what was that, am I OK?
  a was surprised **b** panicked

Speaker 2

4 I just ________ out in a sweat.
  a started sweating suddenly **b** became hot enough to sweat

5 She'd probably ________ something on to me.
  a given me an illness **b** explained something to me

6 I managed to fight it ________ really effectively.
  a resist an illness **b** identify an illness

Speaker 3

7 I think my body's telling me I overdid it. I'm absolutely burned ________.
  a too hot **b** exhausted

8 So I'm going to go and sleep it ________ and get up again in a couple of hours.
  a sleep in order to feel better **b** go to sleep earlier than usual

Speaker 4

9 And I have these episodes where I'm sitting with someone and then I just ________ off.
  a start feeling ill **b** fall asleep

10 I mean one minute I'm fine, and then suddenly I look as though I've passed ________!
  a died **b** fallen asleep

3 **Choose the correct definition, a or b, for each of the phrasal verbs in Exercise 2.**

4 **Ask and answer the questions with a partner.**

1. Do you know anyone who's blacked out, and if so, how long was it before they came round?
2. When you feel poorly, is it better to take medication, or just sleep it off?
3. Have you ever felt burned out? When?
4. Have you or has anyone you know ever nodded off at a really inappropriate moment?

EP

5 **Match statements 1–6 to responses a–f. Then work out the meaning of the expressions.**

1. I didn't sleep a wink last night.
2. How are you feeling this morning?
3. I heard your dad had a kidney infection. How is he now?
4. Rosa fell off her mountain bike, but she's all in one piece.
5. Apparently there's a bug in school that's spreading quickly.
6. Are you OK? You look a bit under the weather.

- **a** I'm as right as rain! In fact, I've never felt better!
- **b** She's lucky – she could have been badly injured.
- **c** Why ever not? Is something worrying you?
- **d** He's definitely on the mend, and feeling better than he was.
- **e** Oh dear, that's a cause for concern. I hope you don't catch it.
- **f** I am, actually. I've got a sore throat and a headache. I'll be alright in a day or two.

6 **The phrasal verbs and expressions in three of these sentences are used incorrectly. Identify the sentences and suggest how they could be corrected.**

1. The increasing amount of graffiti in some areas is a cause for concern for the city authorities.
2. I was drowsy, so I decided to sleep a wink before lunch.
3. I'm feeling right as rain this morning; I must be coming down with something.
4. He's got some cuts and bruises after the accident, but he's all in one piece.
5. The hospital are going to do some tests to confirm whether or not I'm under the weather.
6. Duncan is recuperating at home after an operation, and he's definitely on the mend now.

7 **Complete the questions with your own ideas. Then ask and answer them in small groups.**

1. Do you think it's harder for your body to fight off an infection when …
2. How freaked out would your classmates be if …?
3. Would you say it's a cause for concern that …?
4. After not sleeping a wink all night, do you think you …?
5. Have you ever felt right as rain one minute, but then …?
6. Do you think that the best thing to do when you're feeling under the weather is to …?
7. If you broke out in a fever before an exam, would you …?
8. If you thought that you had passed on an illness to someone, would you …?

LISTENING

1 Discuss the questions with a partner.

1 Have you ever been given any advice about your future career choice, and if so, what was it?
2 At what age should young people begin considering their future choice of career, and how should they go about doing this?

2 Read the email Katrina has received and answer the questions.

Dear Katrina,

I can't believe it's already seven years since you left us at Moorbrook High School and went on to medical school – doesn't time fly? Now that you've got a few months as a junior hospital doctor under your belt, I wanted to ask you a favour. A lot of our pupils here have expressed an interest in embarking on higher education courses in medicine. So I was wondering if you might be willing to come and give a talk to the Year 12 and 13 students about what it's actually like to study medicine and work as a doctor. Knowing you, I'm sure you'll tell it like it really is, which I know the students would appreciate!

Perhaps I could give you a call so we can discuss the details?

Best wishes,

Pippa (There's no need to call me Mrs Shantington any more!)

1 How do Pippa and Katrina know each other?
2 What does Pippa want Katrina to do?
3 Why does Pippa think Katrina would be suitable for this?

3 Make a list of the advantages and disadvantages of being a doctor.

13
4 Now listen to Katrina's talk to the pupils at Moorbrook High School. Does she mention any of your ideas from Exercise 3?

5 Look at the task in Exercise 6 and identify what kind of word (e.g. singular noun phrase, verb phrase) could go in each gap. Suggest one possible word or phrase which could complete each sentence.

13
6 Listen again. You will hear a young doctor called Katrina Davis speaking to a group of school students about careers in healthcare. For questions 1–8, complete the sentences with a word or short phrase.

1 Katrina suggests working for a .... as an alternative to jobs in healthcare.
2 Katrina recommends that the students attend .... to learn about different areas of work.
3 Katrina uses the word '....................' to describe the way she intends to talk about working in healthcare.
4 Many medical professionals report that they have a worse .... than most people.
5 When discussing doctors' earnings, Katrina says that .... is an issue for most newly qualified doctors.
6 Katrina considers .... to be the hardest part of her job.
7 Katrina believes that .... is the most important quality that doctors should demonstrate.
8 Working in healthcare provides doctors with plenty of opportunities for more .... as part of their career development.

13
7 For question 6, Katrina mentions two disadvantages and two advantages of working in medicine. Which of the highlighted phrases is the correct answer to question 6? Underline the words in the question and the words in the script that lead you to the correct answer.

Do be prepared for the ups and downs. You'll experience burnout – working nights is standard for junior doctors, so you soon accept tiredness as an inevitable part of the job. But you bounce back quickly enough. What's tougher than anything else, especially after spending time with a patient, is breaking bad news, and some colleagues say it never gets easier. But then there's nothing better than the satisfaction of seeing a very ill patient recover, and the gratitude of their family.

8 Does Katrina's advice make you more likely or less likely to consider studying medicine, or does it not make any difference?

9 In groups, discuss what factors you would consider the most important when choosing your future career.

SPEAKING
SPECULATING AND DESCRIBING PICTURES

1 **With a partner, say if you agree or disagree with these statements and say why.**

1 Life's too short to worry about health; it's more important to have fun.
2 Regular exercise is the best thing for both your physical and mental wellbeing.
3 People should be free to make their own choices, not lectured about nutritious diets and active lifestyles.
4 People don't have to spend money to keep fit.

14 **2** **Listen to Paola doing an exam task. Which two of the three photos does she talk about, and why did she choose them?**

A

B

C

3 **Discuss the questions with a partner.**

1 Do you think that Paola understands what she has been asked to do?
2 Is everything Paola says relevant to the task?
3 Does she talk about the pictures separately or together?
4 Do you feel that she answers both questions fully about both pictures?

4 **Put the headings in the correct place in the *Prepare to speak* box.**

Certainty Doubt / Lack of certainty
Possibility Probability

PREPARE TO SPEAK

Speculating

1 ....
It's certainly the case that …
What's happening is that …
Judging by …, it's pretty clear that …

2 ....
I'm (pretty) sure they can't …
I suppose that he/she must …
As far as I can tell, …
They must surely …
It looks as though …
It seems to be the case that …

3 ....
One interpretation is that …
What might be happening is that …

4 ....
I don't have a clue what/why/whether …
It's hard to say where/what/why …

14 **5** **Listen again. Which of the phrases from the *Prepare to speak* box does Paola use?**

6 **With a partner, take turns to do the same task. Use a different pair of pictures. Use some of the phrases from the *Prepare to speak* box.**

- What might the people who are working find rewarding about their jobs?
- In what ways do they make a difference to the lives of the people they help?

7 » **WORK IN PAIRS. TURN TO PAGE 129.**

4 MAKING YOUR MIND UP

? ABOUT YOU

▶ 04 **Watch the video and then answer the questions.**
What important decisions have you had to make recently?
How did you make them?
Who do you ask for advice before making a decision?

VOCABULARY AND READING
MAKING DECISIONS

EP **1 Read the conversation and match the phrases to the meanings, A or B.**

Lucas: I'm still undecided about what course to do at college. I'd made up my mind to do architecture, but as the time to decide gets closer, I'm in two minds about it.
Ava: What are you unsure about?
Lucas: Well, I do love the subject but I'm in doubt about whether I've actually got the commitment to study it for five years.
Ava: Why don't you seek advice from someone? Do you know any architects?
Lucas: Apart from my mum, you mean? Yes, several. I guess I could have a chat to them and think through whether it's right for me.
Ava: Yes, and then you can do the traditional decision-making thing of weighing up the pros and cons. And at the same time, you can consider your other options. Just take a piece of paper and brainstorm ideas about your interests, skills and all that kind of thing. That usually helps me come to a decision.
Lucas: Good idea. And whatever I decide, it's not the end of the world. If I'm not happy with my choice, I can always reconsider it later.

A Phrases meaning 'not decided'	B Activities in the decision-making process

2 Find and correct eight mistakes in this extract from a blog.

For the whole of last year, I was in a few minds about taking a gap year. I sought advise from my teachers and parents, but I really couldn't make my mind. I was indecided about whether it would do my university application more harm than good. I was also on doubt about whether it would leave me in debt. As I'd been taught at school, I brainstormed ideas and weighed up the cons and pros. They seemed to be about equal, so I spent a lot of time thinking all my options. Finally, I came to the decision. I'm planning a gap year, but I still have time to reconsider if necessary. I'd advise anyone thinking about a gap year to consider all their options carefully. If you're still unsure about it, I'd say be brave and go for it!

3 Discuss the questions with a partner.

1 Is it common for young people in your country to take a gap year?
2 Do you know anyone who has taken a gap year?
3 What are the pros and cons of gap years?
4 How would you make up your mind about whether to do a gap year?

4 Read the four paragraphs opposite, in which university admissions tutors give their views on taking a gap year. What is each tutor's view?

- more in favour of gap years
- for or against depending on the individual
- more against gap years

5 Look at question 1. Identify the key words in the question.

1 Which tutor has a different view from the others on the value of the poorly paid work some students do on a gap year?

6 The views of tutors A–D relating to poorly paid work are highlighted in the paragraphs opposite. Which tutor has a different view from the others? In what way does their opinion differ?

7 Now read questions 2–4 and highlight all parts of the paragraphs which may be relevant. Then use your highlighted text to answer the questions.

Which tutor

2 has a similar view to B on the type of student who will benefit most from a gap year?
3 shares A's opinion on the importance for students of planning what they are going to do in a gap year?
4 has a different view from C about how a gap year should be funded?

GAP YEARS:

what do university tutors think of them?

A

If you are undecided whether or not to take a gap year, ask yourself 'If I went straight to university, would I always be in doubt about whether I should have had a year out?' Having said that, I'd also say that all students should think through their decision carefully and only do the gap year if they can finance it through work or savings. Unless you work everything out in advance, you could end up wasting time and money. I've seen bright young people fritter away their precious gap year doing a low-skilled low-waged job which won't help their future. But if you have a specific career goal in mind, a gap year in that field could help you make your mind up one way or the other. If it's not for you, better to discover sooner rather than later.

B

When students come to me seeking advice about gap years, I avoid telling them what they should do as there are so many variables. A student who is unsure about a subject like medicine, for example, would do well to spend a year volunteering in a hospital. They will experience all sides of their chosen career and can really weigh up the pros and cons and decide whether it is right for them. Working in a minimum-wage job, on the other hand, may not be very beneficial in the long run. It also depends on finance. I read one article that said parents were generally supportive of gap years, and those who could afford to helped to fund them, which is great. That's probably because the vast majority of students – 86%, according to one study – feel that their gap year made them more employable.

C

I think most students are in two minds about doing a gap year at some point, which is a good thing. It means they are taking their futures seriously and considering all their options. It's the ones who come to a decision too easily that I'd be more worried about. I'm broadly in favour of gap years, mainly because I had to go straight from school to university. However, a few conditions must be met. The main one is that it must make a positive contribution both to the individual and the community. It's fine to accept parental support and volunteer if that is an option. If not, students will need to generate income for themselves. Young people tend to be idealistic and want to spend their gap year building schools in developing countries. However, working at a local cafe or shop can also give them valuable skills and life lessons even if the wages are far from impressive.

D

When a student tells me they intend to take a gap year, my first reaction is to suggest they reconsider. I even told my own children they couldn't do one. Some people argue gap years are good for those doing vocational courses. The evidence is far from conclusive, but students who are determined to take a break from their studies should sit down and brainstorm ideas about what they could do during the year and how it would help their future career. They should consider also what they will live off; will they earn their own keep or rely on their parents? It's been said that 66% of students who have done a gap year take their studies more seriously than those who haven't, though in my view this can't have been a serious piece of research. I know many people who took 'a gap year', found low-wage employment and remained there without ever going to university. Where are they in the statistics?

TALKING POINTS

If you took a gap year, how would you spend it?
Would you prefer to go on an organised gap year or plan it yourself?
Should parents fund gap years if they can?

GRAMMAR
MODALS IN THE PAST

1 Read extracts 1–5 from the article and choose the option, a or b, with the closest meaning.

1 You'll always be in doubt about whether you **should have had** a year out.
  a You didn't take a gap year and may regret it.
  b You were advised to have a gap year but didn't.

2 Parents were generally supportive of gap years, and those who **could afford to** helped to fund them.
  a Parents who had the ability to pay for the gap year did so.
  b Parents who supported gap years helped to pay for them.

3 ... though this **can't have been** a serious piece of research.
  a Serious research was not really possible at that time.
  b The writer strongly believes the research was not serious.

4 I **had to go** straight from school to university.
  a I decided to go straight from school to university.
  b I had no choice about going straight from school to university.

5 I even told my own children they **couldn't do** one.
  a His children didn't have the ability to do a gap year.
  b He didn't give his children permission to do a gap year.

2 Match the modals in Exercise 1 to five of the functions in the box. There is one function you do not need.

(lack of) ability advice (lack of) obligation
(lack of) permission regret speculation/deduction

3 Which of the functions in Exercise 2 do these examples belong to?

1 I **needn't have worried** about my daughter's gap year. She had a great time in the end.
2 I **wasn't allowed to take** a gap year, so I was keen to encourage my son to take one.
3 Theo **was able to fund** his gap year by taking fruit-picking jobs in different countries.
4 You **ought to have made** a better plan. You wouldn't have wasted so much time.
5 Lorena got a place in Pompeu Fabra University in Barcelona. She **must have got** very good exam results.
6 I **didn't need** a visa for my trip as I was only travelling around Europe.
7 Mark's started planning his gap year. He **might have booked** his flight by now.

» GRAMMAR REFERENCE AND PRACTICE PAGE 147

4 Choose the correct option.

1 At my school, we *must have* / *had to* study Biology.
2 Amanda was a clever child – by the time she was two, she *could talk* / *could have talked* perfectly.
3 That restaurant has gone out of business already. There *couldn't be* / *can't have been* enough customers.
4 I'm not sure, but I think I *might have* / *must have* made a mistake in my calculations.
5 We *might* / *ought to* have made a reservation – I didn't realise it would be so busy.
6 I *mustn't* / *wasn't allowed to* go to sleepovers when I was a child.

5 Complete the sentence with an appropriate modal, which may be in the negative form.

1 We ________ have rushed. The meeting started half an hour late.
2 You ________ to have had some coaching. You would have done better in the match if you had.
3 Unfortunately, Jack ________ get on the same flight as us, so he'll arrive a bit later.
4 Ashley's gloves aren't in the house or car. She ________ have lost them somewhere else.
5 My parents said you ________ come on holiday with our family! I'm so excited!
6 Sorry I'm late. I ________ to finish an essay.
7 You ________ have won the competition. You'll never know because you didn't enter.
8 We didn't ________ to take our own towels to the pool. They were supplied by the hotel.

6 Correct any mistakes in these sentences. One is correct.

1 When we were at school, we must choose our subjects at the age of 14.
2 We couldn't have dropped maths as it was compulsory.
3 Laura must tell Kevin about the accident because nobody else knew about it.
4 Tim couldn't moved that heavy box – he was there alone.
5 I might have be rich if I'd studied law.
6 You shouldn't have done that. It's not right!
7 You may seen the message. It was marked as read.
8 When I was a child, I allowed to stay up late at weekends.

7 Complete the second sentence so that it has a similar meaning to the first sentence, using the word given. You must use between three and six words, including the word given.

1 I regret not listening more carefully to my parents' advice. **ATTENTION**
I should ________ my parents advised me to do.
2 The bag was full of books so I'm sure it was heavy. **HAVE**
The bag was full of books so it ________ a lot.
3 Participation in sports lessons was compulsory at my school. **HAD**
We ________ part in sports lessons at my school.
4 Ruby doesn't like sweet things, so there's no way she ate all the chocolate. **BEEN**
Ruby doesn't like sweet things, so it ________ who ate all the chocolate.
5 The art gallery refused to allow us to take photos of the exhibits. **GET**
We ________ to photograph the exhibits in the art gallery.
6 I managed to finish my painting in time for the exhibition. **ABLE**
I ________ my painting finished in time for the exhibition.

8 » WORK IN PAIRS. TURN TO PAGE 129.

VOCABULARY

LIFE EVENTS: VERB AND NOUN COLLOCATIONS

1 **What life event do you think is happening in the photo?**

16 **2** **You will hear part of a radio programme in which a psychologist gives advice to the families of students who have recently done their exams. Answer the questions.**

1 What decisions facing young people does she mention?
2 What advice does she give to the families of school leavers?

EP 16 **3** **Complete the extracts from the recording with a verb and/or a noun from the boxes in the correct form. Each word may be used only once. Then listen again and check.**

Verbs	**Nouns**
accept, apply for, fail, follow, get into, graduate, leave, pass, resit, take (x2)	apprenticeships, exams, grades, path, place, step

1 Thousands of students have been ______ ______ in the last few weeks.
2 … whether they ______ or ______ their exams, it's time for all of them to make some vital decisions.
3 … they'll have to decide whether to ______ the exams later in the year or start ______ jobs.
4 Those who manage to get good ______ have to try to ______ the best possible university.
5 … decide whether to ______ the ______ they are offered immediately or ______ a gap year.
6 … avoid putting pressure on the student to choose a specific ______.
7 Everyone involved should remember that ______ school is a huge ______.
8 ______ from university may be a goal for many, …
9 Each young person should ______ the path that is right for them.
10 Increased numbers of young people are choosing to do ______ or 'learn on the job'.

4 **Identify the incorrect or least likely option.**

1 Leaving *home* / *college* / *job* can be very stressful.
2 Dominic did *a course* / *a scholarship* / *an apprenticeship*, which he really enjoyed.
3 My brother will be taking *an exam* / *a gap year* / *a university* next year.
4 Luca has been offered *an exam* / *a job* / *a place* at university.
5 The teacher *sat* / *marked* / *set* the exam.
6 Holly has been applying for *jobs* / *a gap year* / *apprenticeships*.
7 Young people should ask for advice before deciding on *a career* / *a path* / *a step*.
8 It can be difficult to get into *university* / *a job* / *some schools*.

ADJECTIVE AND NOUN COLLOCATIONS

17 **5** **You will hear a young man called Darren talking about the decisions he made after leaving school.**

1 What did he decide to do in the end?
2 What influenced his decision?

EP 17 **6** **Listen again and complete what Darren says using adjectives from the box.**

big	clear	deciding	immediate
major	mixed	strong	vital

I was at the same school from the age of four, so you can imagine what a [1] ______ change it was for me to leave. It was also something I had [2] ______ feelings about. I was delighted to be free, but I was also terrified about my [3] ______ future. Both my elder sisters were at university and it was kind of expected that I'd do the same. So the [4] ______ decision for me was whether to do that or not.

My uncle had always been a [5] ______ influence in my life and he told me to follow my instincts and not just do what everyone else did. His advice actually played a [6] ______ role in my decision to take a year to think about what I really wanted to do in life. During that year, I kept changing my mind but, in the end, money was the [7] ______ factor. I loved getting my wages and the thought of having to pay off a student loan put me off. For the moment I'm very happy with the path I've chosen. I don't think some young people have a [8] ______ understanding of all the options open to them, including work and apprenticeships.

7 **Identify the incorrect option.**

1 I have *big* / *strong* / *mixed* feelings about the importance of a university education.
2 In my view, grandparents have a *major* / *strong* / *vital* role to play in bringing up children.
3 I think money is often the *deciding* / *strong* / *vital* factor in career-related decisions.
4 Many young people face *big* / *major* / *deciding* changes at the age of 18.
5 I'm not planning to make any decisions in the *clear* / *immediate* / *near* future.

8 » **WORK IN PAIRS.** **TURN TO PAGE 129.**

WRITING AN ESSAY

1 **Work with a partner. What factors would you consider in deciding which college or university to go to?**

2 **Read the task and answer the questions.**

1. How many factors do you have to write about? Is it OK to write about more?
2. What do you have to give your opinion on?
3. Do you have to use the quotes from the discussion?
4. How many words should you write? Are you allowed to write more?
5. What is meant by 'an appropriate style'?

Your class has attended a talk on some of the factors to consider when choosing a college or university course. You have made the notes below:

Factors to consider when choosing a course
- reputation
- location
- job prospects

Some opinions expressed in the discussion:
"Ask other people what they think of the college."
"I'd like a college in my home town."
"I want a course that will prepare me for work."

Write an essay discussing **two** of the factors in your notes. You should **explain which factor you consider to be more important, giving reasons** in support of your answer.

You may, if you wish, make use of the opinions expressed in the discussion, but you should use your own words as far as possible.

Write your answer in **220–260 words** in an appropriate style.

3 **Read the sample essay and answer the questions.**

1. Which factors has the student discussed?
2. Has the student fulfilled the task in all respects?

While many young people dream of graduating from university, the choice of courses on offer can be overwhelming. **Although** students need to consider many factors when making their choice, two of the main ones are, in my opinion, the reputation of the university and a graduate's chances of getting a job. (1)

Nowadays, there are several different scales to assess the quality of universities overall, as well as specific courses. **However**, parents and students need to know how to interpret them and then decide what matters most to them. A university with lower status may, in fact, have the best course in a given subject. For me, what current and former students say about the university gives you a better indication of what it will be like.

The second factor that I would like to discuss is the likelihood of students finding a job after they graduate. It is undeniable that certain degrees are more likely to result in steady, well-paid jobs in areas such as medicine, engineering or accountancy. **In spite of** this, many students choose courses because they love the subject, which is important if you are going to spend three or more years studying it. (2)

In conclusion, choosing a university course is a life-changing decision and it's important to consider all aspects when making your choice. I believe that the reputation of the institution and the employability of graduates are the two most important factors to take into account. (3)

4 **The following sentences could be added to the essay to ensure the question was fully answered. Where would you add them? Write *1*, *2* or *3*.**

a Nevertheless, they should not neglect the most important consideration, which is obtaining employment after graduation.
b Of these, the latter should be every student's primary consideration.

5 Put the words in bold in the essay and in Exercise 4 under the correct headings in the *Prepare to write* box.

PREPARE TO WRITE

Contrast linkers

Followed by subject + verb (two ideas in the same sentence)
Even though, while, [1] ...., but

Followed by subject + verb (two ideas in different sentences)
In contrast, [2] ...., [3] ....

Followed by gerund, noun or pronoun (two ideas in the same sentence)
Despite, [4] ....

6 Put the linker in brackets into the correct position. Make any necessary changes to punctuation.

0 Katie studied medicine at university her sister went straight from school to a job. (in contrast)
Katie studied medicine at university. In contrast, her sister went straight from school to a job.
1 Jacob is a few years older than the others he gets on well with them all. (even though)
2 Natasha was offered a well-paid job she decided to stay on at college. (however)
3 Having been offered a place at a top university, Gemma decided to do an apprenticeship. (despite)
4 I was invited to their wedding I couldn't go. (but)
5 I chose engineering it is one of the most challenging subjects. (although)
6 All my friends told me I should stay in university accommodation I decided to rent a flat. (nevertheless)
7 Medicine is definitely an interesting career it's not for me. (while)
8 Many people attended the party the short notice. (in spite of)

7 Complete the sentences with a suitable contrast linker.

1 .... there were a large number of disadvantages, they still opted to go ahead.
2 We planned to attend the event. ...., in the end we were not able to.
3 .... being the younger of the two brothers, Ethan graduated first.
4 Twenty people started the course; ...., only a few qualified as paramedics.
5 Jemima won the competition .... nobody expected her to.
6 .... sport plays a vital role in a healthy lifestyle, fewer young people than ever take part in team games.
7 Megan got a place at a top university .... the stiff competition.
8 In the UK, the number of females studying biology is higher than the number of males. ...., in engineering, the number of males is greater.

8 Read the essay question. Identify the things you have to write about.

Your class has been discussing who to seek advice from when making important life decisions. You have made the notes below:

Who to seek advice from
- family
- friends
- professionals

Some opinions expressed in the discussion:
"Your parents have your best interests at heart."
"Friends don't have any more experience than you do."
"Counsellors are specially trained to guide you to a decision."

Write an essay discussing **two** of the groups to seek advice from when making important life decisions. You should **explain whose advice you think is more valuable**, giving reasons in support of your answer.

You may, if you wish, make use of the opinions expressed in the discussion, but you should use your own words as far as possible.

9 Work in pairs. Complete the table below with the pros and cons of seeking advice from the three groups of people mentioned in the essay question. Then decide which two groups you are going to focus on.

	Pros	Cons
family	*your parents might have made similar decisions in the past*	
friends		
professionals		*professionals don't know you personally*

10 Write your essay in 220–260 words. Use linkers from the *Prepare to write* box where appropriate.

LIFE DECISIONS

LIFE SKILLS

Making good life decisions

In the next few years, you will probably have to make some major decisions to do with your studies, your career or other areas of your life. What you decide may shape your future. Knowing how to approach such decisions in a careful way can help to ensure that you make the right ones.

1 **Discuss the questions with a partner.**

1. What major decisions will you have to make in the next five to ten years?
2. Which ones do you think will be the most difficult to make?
3. Whose advice might you ask before making them?

2 **Listen to Ellie, Marcus and Jacob talking about making decisions. Who**

1. is/was happy with their decision?
2. has/had to decide something quickly?
3. is/was unhappy with their decision?

3 **Listen again and answer the questions.**

1. Why is this year an important one for Ellie's basketball team?
2. Why was Ellie's brother's advice not helpful?
3. What did Marcus decide not to do?
4. In what way was Marcus impulsive?
5. Why did Jacob's parents say yes to the chance to work abroad?
6. What was the general opinion of Jacob's teachers?

4 **Read the introduction to Jenny's blog and the two requests for advice. Tick the correct box.**

	Alex	Jackson	Both
Who…			
a … is thinking about employment?			
b … has recently been given an opportunity?			
c … has a clear idea about what they want to do?			
d … is worried about the feelings of others?			

5 **Work with a partner. What advice would you give to Alex and Jackson?**

6 **Read Jenny's advice. Is it similar to yours?**

7 **According to Jenny, why should you**

1. avoid basing your decision on what others decide?
2. wait until you know all your options?
3. speak to somebody who has made a similar decision?
4. make a list of pros and cons?
5. avoid deciding impulsively?

8 **Work with a partner. Look at the advice Jenny gives in bold and discuss which ideas would be the most useful for making the decisions you talked about in Exercise 1.**

ASK JENNY *ANYTHING*

The place to go for the best advice

Alex from London writes:

"Hi Jenny! I'm in my final year at school. My grades are probably going to be good enough to go to university and there are lots of subjects that interest me, but what I really want to do in life is start my own fashion business, so I think it would be better to get into the world of work as soon as possible so that I can learn from experience. However, most of my friends are going to university and they keep telling me not to waste the opportunity. Any advice is welcome!"

Jenny replies …

First of all, **don't decide to do something just because other people are doing it**. It's your life, not your friends'. It's true that university can be a great experience, but it's not the only path to success in the world, and maybe starting work immediately would be better for you in the long run. However, I would also recommend that you **do some research**. Take your time. There are university courses in business studies and even in fashion design that could help your career. **Make sure you consider all your options before making a decision**. There might be more than you think! Also, instead of listening to your friends, who haven't even been to university yet, why don't you **speak to somebody who has experience** of starting a business? The advice of someone who's already gone down that route might be well worth listening to.

Hi readers! Some of you have written to me asking for advice about some major life choices you're facing, so this week's topic is how to make big life decisions – you know, not the little things like whether to have pizza or pasta for lunch (pizza – always!) or what to wear to a friend's birthday party (although that's a pretty big decision!), but things that really impact on our future. I'm going to answer two of them, but hopefully this will be valuable advice for everyone.

Jackson from Yorkshire writes:

"I need some help, please, Jenny. My parents run a small farm. It's been in our family for generations, and as the older of two children (I'm 19, my sister's 17), my parents want me to take it over eventually. I enjoy working on the farm, but I've just had a very tempting offer of a job in the city that I really want to do and I'm thinking of accepting it. My parents want me to be happy but I also don't want them to feel I've let them down. What would you do?"

Jenny replies …

What I would do is **make a list of pros and cons**. You've already mentioned some: one pro is that you really want to do this job, a con is that you don't want to let your parents down. Think of all the others. What are the possible consequences – good and bad – of accepting the job? Maybe it will be the start of a great career. Maybe you'll find you aren't suited to city life. A list like that will clarify everything for you. Whatever you do, **don't make the decision in the heat of the moment**. We can often get carried away by the excitement of new ventures and jump right in, but being rational rather than emotional is likely to help us make a wiser choice. And remember, **a bad decision is not the end of the world** – it's a chance to learn.

Project
A research interview

You are each going to interview an older person about how they made a big life decision and how they feel about it now.

1 DECIDE

Decide who you each want to interview.

2 PLAN

Look at this list of interview questions. With a partner, add four or five more.

- How old were you when you made the decision?
- Who did you ask for advice?
- Did you know all your options before deciding?
- What advice would you give to someone making the same decision now?

3 INTERVIEW

Each speak to your interviewee separately.

4 PRESENT

Report back to your class what you learned.

5 FEEDBACK

Listen to your classmates' reports. Whose interviewee:

- had the toughest decision to make?
- asked the most people for advice?
- seems happiest with their decision?
- made a decision you would never have made?

REVIEW 1 UNITS 1–4

VOCABULARY

1 Match the sentence halves.

1 When the ring road was built,
2 The council has pedestrianised the city centre
3 High-rise buildings were designed
4 Green spaces are important
5 In densely populated areas,
6 Due to urban sprawl,
7 Most slums have been demolished
8 The mansion is derelict

a as the owners couldn't afford to maintain it.
b diseases tend to spread more easily.
c cities have become much bigger.
d to give residents access to nature.
e it really cut down our travel time.
f to make room for new houses.
g to make it safer for shoppers.
h to save space in city centres.

2 Complete the extract from Arianna's email to her friend Sam. The beginning of each word has been given. Put any verbs in the correct form.

I met my best friend Laura at a party. The first thing I noticed was that she appeared to be very [1]ext ______ as she was surrounded by lots of friends and seemed to be holding several conversations at once. As you know, I'm not at all like that. I think you'll agree that I'm a naturally quiet person – [2]in ______, in fact, so I usually gravitate towards other shy people. I didn't know anyone at the party and was [3]f ______ l ______ out, standing on my own. Suddenly, Laura broke away from the group she was with and started walking towards me. At first, I was very [4]s ______ -c ______, wondering what she would think of me. I needn't have worried. She made me feel at ease and once I got to know her, I realised that while she [5]c ______ a ______ as very confident, she actually isn't. She's become a really close friend – someone I can [6]r ______ to as we have similar interests and problems. Laura's very [7]o ______ -m ______, so I can talk to her about anything at all and she's never [8]ju ______.

3 Correct the idioms in these sentences.

1 Lots of women have done exceptionally well in their careers, **breaking the glass floor**.
2 I was doing so well with my research but I can't find out anything about the church – I've **hit a wooden wall**.
3 It's possible to make changes to the agenda during the meeting – it isn't **set in rock**.
4 I mustn't get home late – or my dad will **hit the ceiling**.
5 The party was great – they'd really **moved to town on** the decorations.
6 In today's world, it can be a real struggle to keep **a house over your head**.
7 Oh no! My computer's crashed. All that hard work has **gone down the pipes**!
8 I'd never met Jaime's sister before but we **got on like a home on fire**.

4 Choose the correct option.

1 I've got *mixed* / *major* feelings about *following* / *taking* a gap year.
2 In the end the *deciding* / *strong* factor in my decision to *pass* / *do* an apprenticeship was the need to earn money.
3 Our teachers have always given us a *near* / *clear* understanding of the need to *get* / *take* good grades.
4 Fortunately, I don't have to *take* / *pass* any exams in the *clear* / *immediate* future.
5 Family support plays a *vital* / *deciding* role in students' chances of *passing* / *graduating* from university.
6 My father had a *deciding* / *strong* influence on my decision to *follow* / *accept* this particular career path.

5 Complete the conversation with words and phrases from the box.

blacked out	breaking out	burned out	
came round	cause for concern	joints	lungs
on the mend	poorly	sleep a wink	

Alice: Hi Jusef. I heard you'd been [1] ______. Are you feeling better?
Jusef: Well, I'm [2] ______ but I'm not 100% yet. I've still got a lot of pain in my [3] ______, especially when I try to bend my knees. I didn't [4] ______ last night, and I keep [5] ______ in a sweat. Anyway, how are you?
Alice: I haven't been too well either. Last week, I [6] ______ when I was travelling home on the train. I was only unconscious for a few minutes but I really freaked out. When I [7] ______, I felt awful. My limbs felt numb and I couldn't breathe properly. It was as if my [8] ______ had stopped working.
Jusef: That sounds terrible! Did you go to the doctor?
Alice: Yes. She didn't think it was a particular [9] ______. She asked me lots of questions about work and stress levels. In the end, she thought I was probably just [10] ______.

GRAMMAR

1 Decide if the verb forms in bold are correct or not. Correct those that are incorrect.

The other day I [1]**enjoyed** a nice lunch in a restaurant with my friends, Danny and Rosie, when suddenly I started choking. A piece of carrot [2]**was becoming** stuck in my throat and I couldn't breathe. I was coughing and Danny [3]**had hit** me hard on the back but it wasn't working. Rosie stood up and [4]**has yelled** at the top of her voice, 'Is there a doctor here?' A woman ran over to us and said, 'I [5]**used to be** a nurse.' She took hold of me from behind and performed the Heimlich manoeuvre on me. The piece of carrot [6]**shooting** across the table. '[7]I always **wanted** to do that,' the woman said. 'It looks so cool in the movies.' While all this [8]**happened**, all the other diners had gone silent and were staring at our table, where all the action was taking place. I thanked the lady very much, and as she [9]**was returning** to her table, a round of applause [10]**was breaking out**. I honestly don't think I've ever been so embarrassed.

2 Identify the incorrect or least likely option.

1 You *ought to* / *should* / *might* go to the optician if you are having trouble reading.
2 I'm worried about introducing Liam to my dad – I think they *might* / *may* / *must* clash.
3 At our school we *don't have to* / *mustn't* / *needn't* wear a uniform.
4 My parents say I *don't need to* / *can* / *am allowed to* stay out later at weekends.
5 It *can't* / *mustn't* / *couldn't* be true that the old town hall is going to be demolished. It's such a beautiful building.
6 I really *must* / *have to* / *may* start going to the gym. I'm so unfit!
7 People *oughtn't to* / *couldn't* / *shouldn't* drop litter. Why can't they just put it in the bin?

3 Complete the conversation with the phrases in the box.

by far the hardest | considerably better than | further | much more energy | noticeably more | not nearly as difficult | the fittest

Alex: So, how is your new fitness regime going, Holly?
Holly: Well, actually, it's going [1] ______ expected. I'm able to run [2] ______ and further every day and my joints are [3] ______ flexible than they used to be.
Alex: I know what you mean. I'm probably [4] ______ I've ever been at the moment. Getting started with the programme was [5] ______ thing I've ever done but there are so many benefits. I'm sleeping much better for one thing.
Holly: Me too. It's [6] ______ to fall asleep at night and I have [7] ______ than before. I've actually never followed an exercise programme like this before.

4 Complete the second sentence so that it has a similar meaning to the first sentence, using the word given. Do not change the word given. You must use between three and six words, including the word given.

1 There are far fewer cars on the roads than there used to be. **NEARLY**
There ______ as there used to be on the roads.
2 I think it was a bad idea to hold the marathon in the middle of winter. **SHOULD**
I don't think they ______ the marathon in the middle of winter.
3 The police started investigating the crime a month before they found their first clue. **LOOKING**
The police ______ the crime for a month when they found their first clue.
4 Toby went to pick up his sister but she had gone home by bus. **HAVE**
Toby ______ to pick up his sister because she had gone home by bus.
5 The number of single-person households has reached an all-time high. **THE**
The number of single-person households is ______ been.
6 I'm sure someone can explain the missing jewellery. **EXPLANATION**
There ______ the missing jewellery.

5 Read the text below. Use the word given in capitals at the end of some of the lines to form a word that fits in the gap in the same line.

UNDERSTANDING **INTROVERSION**

Due to their very nature, introverts are more likely to be **(0)** *misunderstood* than their more extroverted friends. UNDERSTAND
Since extroverts are usually very **(1)** ______, they share information about themselves freely. CHAT
Introverts, on the other hand, are, quite **(2)** ______, more cautious about who they reveal themselves to. SENSIBLE
This sometimes causes more open and self-confident types to be **(3)** ______ towards introverts. JUDGE
Their quietness can be taken as a lack of **(4)** ______, which is generally not the case. ENTHUSE

Similarly, an introvert's reluctance to offer opinions in a discussion is frequently interpreted as them not being **(5)** ______ enough to contribute. KNOW
They are, of course, no less likely to be informed on a given topic but they are often more hesitant to join in for fear of looking **(6)** ______. FOOL

Introverts tend to be loyal and very **(7)** ______ friends. SUPPORT
If you have a problem, go and talk to one of your more introverted acquaintances as they are likely to listen **(8)** ______ and offer carefully considered advice. SYMPATHY

5 LOOKING AHEAD

? ABOUT YOU

▶ 05 **Watch the video and then answer the questions.**
How would your life be different if smartphones hadn't been invented?
Which labour-saving household gadget do you think saves families the most time?
What do you think will be the next major invention that will transform the way we live?

VOCABULARY AND READING
TECHNOLOGY AND PROGRESS

EP **1 You are going to read a blog post about the launch of the iPhone. What do you think these numbers refer to?**

500 200 million 2007

2 Quickly read the blog post and check your answers.

I'm old enough (just!) to remember when Apple **launched** their first iPhone back in 2007, although Steve Jobs and the Apple team had been working on the **prototype** for years. Apple **marketed** it as a major **breakthrough** in the mobile phone market, saying that customers could for the first time have a device as powerful as a computer in their pocket. In actual fact, it wasn't really as **radical** as all that, as there were already other phones available with similar features such as apps and touchscreens which did away with tiny keypads. But what made the iPhone such an important **development** in the smartphone market was its use of multi-touch technology, which allowed users to zoom in and out. This was considered **cutting edge** at the time, as it had never been done before. The technological **advances** that made the iPhone possible made older models of phone, with keypads and tiny keys, **obsolete** almost overnight. The main **drawback** of the iPhone was its high price; at $500, it was over double the price of comparable smartphones on the market at the time. But it soon became apparent that customers were more than willing to pay this. The phone of the future had arrived, **triggering** a major shift in the smartphone market, and the iPhone caught on in no time at all, with some 200 million now being sold each year.

3 Use the context to work out the meaning of the words in Exercise 2. Look them up if necessary.

4 Match 1–10 to a–j to make sentences.

1 My sister's launching her
2 Self-healing concrete is one of the most exciting developments
3 The growth in the smartphone market triggered
4 Companies usually make a prototype of
5 Advances in medical care have significantly increased
6 Some people feel that DVD players have become obsolete
7 Our firm is well known for its cutting-edge designs,
8 The leaders of the two countries announced a breakthrough in
9 The proposal to build a new airport has so many drawbacks that I
10 With effective marketing,

a am definitely not in favour of it.
b that the architectural world has seen for many years.
c life expectancy all over the globe.
d own consultancy business next year.
e huge interest in the apps that could be used with them.
f a new product before they mass-produce it.
g producing furniture of a type that no firm has ever made before.
h their trade talks and hope to reach an agreement soon.
i due to the ease and convenience of streaming content instead.
j it should be possible to increase our sales figures.

5 Look at the images of innovative transport designs from the mid-twentieth century. Discuss these questions.

1 What problem was the innovation attempting to solve?
2 How relevant could it be to contemporary problems?
3 What adaptations would be necessary if the innovation were to be relaunched today?

6 Quickly read through the article on the opposite page and choose the best answer.

Overall, the writer is

A nostalgic for a time when vehicle designers were more creative than they are nowadays.
B optimistic that the vehicle designs of the past are providing inspiration for those of the future.
C doubtful whether new vehicles will be able to cope with the demands of transport in the future.
D confident that today's vehicle designers are learning from the mistakes made by those of the past.

THE FUTURE'S HERE

The look and feel of the vehicles we travel in has changed over the past 100 years, but the way we travel in them hasn't. We still fill up our vehicles with dirty fuel, and drive them along roads that are crowded, unsafe and polluted. However, all that is about to be transformed, and the next decade will see a more radical shift in what we do with our vehicles than has occurred in the last century. And while the transport solutions which engineers are currently developing may seem futuristic, many of these developments have been on the drawing board for longer than you might think.

20

In the not-too-distant future, cars probably won't be restricted to the crowded roads of the world's towns and cities. One solution is for road vehicles to have the ability to take off and fly. The idea has been around since the 1940s, when many were confident that in the near future people would commute to work by air, not by land-based transport. Various flying cars were designed – and some prototypes were even built, but the idea never really caught on, largely due to the manufacturers' failure to market them effectively.

But now this concept has re-emerged and various companies around the world are working on a 'multicopter', basically a cross between a car and a helicopter. The Japanese electronics giant NEC has successfully tested one in front of assembled journalists. Though it was unmanned, the flight was considered a success, albeit a wobbly one, so it's likely we'll be seeing them around in the near future. The US firm Skai VTOL has already built a five-seater multicopter, which was largely made possible by breakthroughs in the development of hydrogen fuel cells as an alternative to the much heavier lithium batteries. With its cleaner fuel and potential for reducing congestion on land, it's certainly a step in the right direction.

It's likely that in the future cars will take on forms quite unlike anything that we see at present. With the move to cleaner forms of energy, the large front grills, whose purpose is to allow air in to cool the engine, will become a thing of the past. Wing mirrors too will become obsolete and will be replaced by sensors and cameras. Designers may decide either to do away with large windows, to allow more privacy, or enlarge them so that passengers can enjoy a better view while in transit.

The coming revolution isn't just confined to private transport, of course. Public transport vehicles are likely to receive an overhaul too. One such recent design was for a giant bus which straddled two lanes of traffic, allowing smaller vehicles to occupy the road beneath it, and letting it stop and allow passengers on and off without blocking the road. The idea was that users of public transport and private transport would all benefit – a win–win situation. Like anything, the concept had drawbacks which needed to be overcome; the giant bus, which was going to be launched in the Chinese city of Qinhuangdao, was eventually abandoned. But given the huge global interest triggered by the Chinese project, it's likely that in 50 years' time this and other of today's futuristic designs will have become reality.

7 Read the article again and decide whether these statements are true (T), false (F), or not stated (NS – there is no information about whether they are true or false).

1. The way people use vehicles is likely to change soon.
2. The ideas for some future transport solutions have been around for a long time.
3. The main reason for the failure of flying cars was their poor design.
4. Flying cars have a greater chance of becoming popular now than when they were first proposed.
5. The use of alternative forms of energy will lead to cars looking different from how they do now.
6. The writer believes that the giant bus will be a failure.

TALKING POINTS

Can you envisage the giant bus being successful in your city? Why? / Why not?
If you were invited to be a passenger in a flying car, would you accept?
Instead of inventing lots of new forms of transport, should we all just travel less?
'Banning all cars from city centres during the day would be a win–win situation, as people and the environment would both benefit.' To what extent do you agree?

GRAMMAR
THE FUTURE

1 Match extracts 1–6 from the article to the future structures in the box.

be about to + infinitive	future continuous
future perfect	*was/were going to* + infinitive
will + infinitive	*would* + infinitive

1 The next decade **will see** a more radical shift in what we do with our vehicles.
2 It's likely that in 50 years' time this and other of today's futuristic designs **will have become** reality.
3 In the 1940s, many were confident that in the near future people **would commute** to work by air.
4 The giant bus, which **was going to be launched** in the Chinese city of Qinhuangdao, was eventually abandoned.
5 However, all that **is about to be transformed**.
6 It's likely we'**ll be seeing** them around in the near future.

2 Complete the rules with the tenses in Exercise 1.

We use
present simple to talk about future events that are scheduled.
present continuous to talk about fixed future arrangements.
going to to talk about intentions and plans.
a ________ to predict what seems likely in the future.
b ________ to talk about something we expect to happen very soon.
c ________ to predict an activity that will be in progress in the future.
d ________ to predict an action that will already be completed in the future.
e ________ and ________ to talk about a prediction made in the past.
f ________ for a plan made in the past that didn't happen.

» **GRAMMAR REFERENCE AND PRACTICE PAGE 148**

21 **3 Choose the most suitable response in these conversations. Then listen and check.**

1 **A:** I'm considering getting an electric bike.
B: Really? They're very expensive, and you *won't get / won't be getting* fit on one of those!

2 **A:** Do you fancy coming to the beach this afternoon?
B: Mm, *I'm going to go running / I was going to go running*, but it's quite hot for that. OK, I'll come.

3 **A:** Shall I phone you this evening around seven?
B: *I'll be having / I'll have had* my guitar lesson then. Better make it eight.

4 **A:** Any plans for the summer holidays?
B: *I'm going to go / I'll have gone* camping with friends.

5 **A:** This queue is so long, isn't it?
B: I know. We may as well give up. I reckon *they'll be selling out / they'll have sold out* of tickets by the time we get to the front.

4 Complete the pairs of sentences with the verbs given, using one of the future tenses in the box. Use the same tense for both sentences.

future continuous	future perfect	*going to*
present continuous	*would*	

1 not come / see
a Everyone agrees that we ________ more extreme weather in the coming years.
b I'm afraid my sister ________ to school today, because she has a migraine.

2 be / do
a Have you decided what you ________ after you leave school?
b Some experts fear there ________ food shortages if the world's population continues to grow.

3 bring out / invite
a I ________ a few friends round next Saturday. Would you like to come?
b The firm ________ a new electric sports car next spring.

4 become / be
a Next June, my parents ________ married for 20 years.
b I predict that mobile phones ________ obsolete by the time I reach 50.

5 come / happen
a Many people didn't expect that global warming ________ so quickly.
b I didn't realise that all my friends ________ to meet me at the airport.

5 Complete the sentences with *was/were (not) going to* or *would (not)*. In which could either form be used?

1 Mark and Amy ________ initially ________ get married in March, but then they decided on a summer wedding.
2 In 1999, Microsoft founder Bill Gates argued that people ________ (soon) be using small portable electronic devices for business and socialising.
3 Andrea is studying biochemistry, although she had said she ________ do a degree in zoology.
4 In 2019, climate activist Greta Thunberg warned that the human race ________ survive if harmful emissions were not stopped.
5 Apple ________ originally ________ call their new tablet the iSlate, but then chose iPad instead.

6 Correct any mistakes in these sentences. Two are correct.

1 If you don't get into university next year, what do you do?
2 I very much doubt that space rockets will ever be electrically powered.
3 We would go to the cinema this evening, but we've changed our mind.
4 In 100 years' time our lifestyle has changed considerably.
5 I'm not sure what kind of transport we'd be using in the next century.
6 I wasn't going tell you about the party because I wanted it to be a complete surprise.

7 » **WORK IN PAIRS. TURN TO PAGE 129.**

VOCABULARY

ADJECTIVES AND DEPENDENT PREPOSITIONS

EP **1 Match the words to the definitions in the box.**

angry and unfriendly aware easily hurt
famous (for doing something bad) lower quality
obvious poisonous suitable

1 She claims to be a business executive, but she's actually a **notorious** fraudster wanted by the police.
2 It's all too **apparent** that industries need to find ways to reduce emissions of **toxic** gases such as carbon monoxide.
3 As a cyclist, I'm always **conscious** that the number of large vehicles travelling close to me make me extremely **vulnerable**, so I always take great care.
4 The referee got a very **hostile** reaction when he spoke to some supporters who'd made remarks that weren't **appropriate**.
5 The VX400 laptop costs less than the Notebook6000, but that doesn't mean it's **inferior** by any means.

2 Put the lines of text about Thomas Midgley Junior in the correct order.

1 b

An inventor with a DANGEROUS LEGACY

Chemical engineer Thomas Midgley Junior (1889–1944) is notorious

a to exposure to lead paint, but the product caught on. Today, approximately 35% of US homes still contain lead paint, although its presence may not be apparent

b for his deadly inventions, which have contributed greatly to the environmental problems we face today. When working for a car manufacturer, he had the dreadful idea of putting lead, which is highly toxic

c to the property owners. Even though contemporary popular opinion is hostile

d of the dangers of lead, and so in order to demonstrate otherwise, he publicly inhaled leaded gas for 60 seconds. Midgley also considered lead appropriate

e to humans, in car petrol. Unfortunately, his innovation caught on, despite leaded petrol being inferior

f to cleaner forms of the fuel. Midgley was conscious

g for household paint, despite the health risks. Children and pregnant women were particularly vulnerable

h towards Midgley and his poisonous legacy, he was, in his day, considered a brilliant innovator.

3 Which prepositions are used after the highlighted adjectives in Exercise 1?

0 notorious	*for*	**4** appropriate	....
1 toxic	....	**5** vulnerable	....
2 inferior	....	**6** apparent	....
3 conscious	....	**7** hostile	....

PHRASAL VERBS

22 **4 Listen to a young climate activist speaking to students. What does she want the students to do? How persuasive do you think she is?**

EP 22 **5 Listen again and complete the summary of the talk by writing the missing part of the phrasal verb in the gaps.**

Difficult times [1] **lie** .... for everyone unless more is done to help the environment. People shouldn't [2] .... **upon** helping the environment as some sort of extra, but it should be central to their lives. Most vehicles still [3] .... **on** petrol or diesel; and although the idea of electric vehicles [4] .... **on**, it's happening too slowly, and many people feel they don't want to [5] **rush** .... buying an electric car just yet. But that's what they should do. Everyone who owns a fossil fuel car should [6] .... **with** it immediately. As manufacturers of electric vehicles now [7] **cater** .... all customers, rich or poor, students are urged to persuade their parents to [8] .... **out** the range of electric cars that would be suitable for their budget.

6 » **WORK IN PAIRS.** **TURN TO PAGE 130.**

7 Read the text below and think of the word which best fits each gap. Use only one word in each gap.

How do I plan my career?

If you're in your teens, **(0)** *it* might not yet be apparent **(1)** .... you what you're going to study after school, or what career lies **(2)** .... after that. Of course, choosing a career is a massive decision, and it's not something anyone should rush **(3)** .... So before you make **(4)** .... your mind, you might like to think about STEM subjects (as distinct from Arts subjects).

What's STEM?

STEM stands for Science, Technology, Engineering and Maths. Degrees in STEM subjects are looked **(5)** .... as highly desirable by employers and can be a gateway to a range of career paths. With an Engineering degree, you could be eligible for a job in software design, car manufacturing or logistics, to name but a few.

So now what?

If you're stuck for ideas, it's worth looking online to check **(6)** .... the STEM courses running in your area. Then you can sit back and weigh **(7)** .... the pros and cons. Many colleges and universities cater mainly **(8)** .... students who want to study STEM subjects.

8 » **WORK IN PAIRS.** **TURN TO PAGE 130.**

LISTENING

1 **Look at the four photos of a building in Svalbard, Norway and what happens there. What do you think the building is for? Why do you think it exists? Why do you think its location is important?**

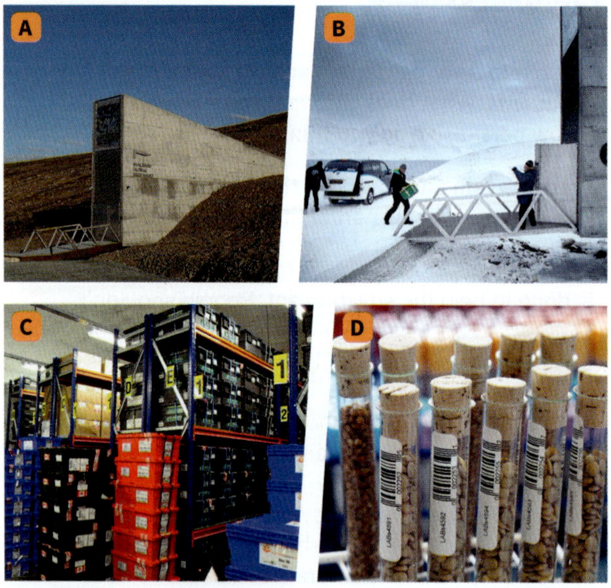

23 **2** **Listen to the first part of an interview and see if you were correct.**

23 **3** **You will hear an interview in which two scientists called Diana Morgan and Jonas Thorsby talk about a seed bank in the Arctic. Listen again and choose the answer (A, B, C or D) which best fits according to what you hear.**

1 Jonas explains that the seed bank in Svalbard is of prime importance because
- **A** it is entirely paid for by just one country.
- **B** it is the one that similar institutions rely on.
- **C** its location makes it so easily accessible.
- **D** it contains crops that are extinct elsewhere.

Tip – what does Jonas say about a *backup*?

Remember – some of the statements in the options may be true by themselves. But only one of them makes a true statement with the stem (*Jonas explains that the seed bank in Svalbard is of prime importance because …*)

4 **Now listen to the whole interview and answer questions 2–6.** 24

2 Diana Morgan provides some statistics in order to make the point that
- **A** food production is more at risk now than it was in the past.
- **B** it is important to understand which crops are profitable and why.
- **C** greater amounts of food are needed to feed people than ever before.
- **D** the need for food crops is growing faster in some countries than in others.

3 The Svalbard seed bank needs to store a wide range of seeds in order to
- **A** provide a large enough quantity of a particular crop if needed.
- **B** be prepared in case some of the seeds kept there die.
- **C** meet the needs of the world's population for as long as possible.
- **D** have the most suitable type of a specific crop for a changing environment.

4 Why does Diana consider the 2017 incident at Svalbard to be ironic?
- **A** A massive change in temperature caused very little harm.
- **B** Seeds that are worth little now could become valuable in the future.
- **C** A machine to keep the vault cold actually heated the vault.
- **D** The site was threatened by the same danger which it is supposed to protect against.

5 Jonas considers the incident in 2017 to be a 'successful failure' because
- **A** no seeds were damaged by the water.
- **B** the seed bank's international profile was raised.
- **C** video surveillance quickly identified the leak.
- **D** it showed that the seed bank doesn't need on-site staff.

6 Diana and Jonas agree that it will be a long time before the seed bank is full because
- **A** shipping seeds there is difficult and complicated.
- **B** the building is large enough to contain an enormous number of seeds.
- **C** some people want to wait and see if the project is successful before using it.
- **D** countries build up their own supplies before storing seeds there.

5 **Work with a partner. Imagine that you work for an international humanitarian organisation and you have been asked to suggest measures to protect the world's future food supply in case of a global catastrophe. Apart from seed banks, what other measures would you propose?**

SPEAKING
A DISCUSSION

1 Discuss the questions about the pictures.

1 Why do you think the people are using their devices in these situations?'
2 Are there any drawbacks to using devices in these ways?
3 Do you use your own devices in these ways? Why? / Why not?

2 Look at this task with a partner. Do any of the things you talked about in Exercise 1 relate to the five ideas in the diagram?

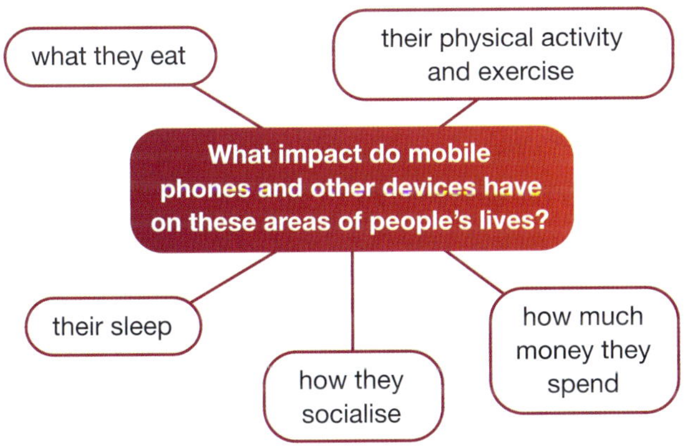

25 **3 Listen to Maya and Lucas doing the task in Exercise 2. How well do you think they complete the task?**

4 Which of the following statements are true?

1 Maya asks Lucas questions.
2 They both speak for a similar length of time.
3 Lucas responds to the points that Maya makes.
4 Both speakers make several grammar mistakes.
5 All their comments are relevant to the task.
6 Maya responds to the points that Lucas makes.
7 They discuss all five topics.
8 Lucas tries to give Maya opportunities to speak.

5 Which of these expressions sound impolite?

a Would you like to start?
b Start speaking please.
c In what ways, do you think?
d Is that what you're saying?
e So what?
f … if that's OK with you.
g Enough about me.
h Is that all you have to say?
i Have you ever had a similar experience?
j You haven't said enough.
k Tell me more.
l What's your take on this one?
m What are you talking about?
n But you could argue that …
o Is that something you'd agree with?

25 **6 Listen again and tick the expressions which Lucas says in order to involve Maya in the conversation.**

PREPARE TO SPEAK

Involving your partner in a discussion

Starting

a Would you like to start?
b Who's going to kick off then? (*informal*)
c Shall I go first?
d Perhaps we could start with …

Responding to your partner's comments

e Good point!
f That's interesting. In what ways, do you think?
g I know what you mean, but don't you think …?
h Well, I guess that's true, but …
i So what you're saying is …
j Exactly what I think!
k My idea/thought/opinion exactly.
l Exactly! / Precisely! / Absolutely!
m I hadn't thought of that actually.
n But you could argue that …
o No way!

Encouraging your partner to speak

p What's your take on this one?
q In what ways, do you think?
r Anyway, enough from me. Have you …?
s Would you agree that …?
t Is that something you'd agree with?
u Do you think it's fair to say that …?
v What do you mean exactly?
w How do you mean?
x Like what, for example?
y Why do you say/think that?
z What makes you feel (like) that?

7 In one minute, note down

- one thing that would make the world a better place.
- one thing that you would like to happen in your lifetime, but which probably won't.
- one thing that you don't want to happen, but which is inevitable.

8 » WORK IN PAIRS. **TURN TO PAGE 130.**

6 BLOCKBUSTERS AND BESTSELLERS

? ABOUT YOU

▶ 06 **Watch the video and then answer the questions.**
How often do you watch films and read books?
What genre of films or books do you like best?
What is the last film you saw and the last book you read?

VOCABULARY AND READING
FILMS AND BOOKS

EP **1 Are the words in the box associated only with films or with books and films?**

blockbuster	blurb	box-office flop	cinemagoer
instalment	main character	masterpiece	
remake	revenue	sequel	set in	trailer

2 Match these definitions to the words in Exercise 1.

1 a book or film that continues the story of a previous book or film
2 a film that not many people went to see at the cinema
3 describing where and when the story happens
4 a new version of an old film
5 an advertisement for a film, including short extracts from it
6 the most important person in the story
7 income
8 a short description of a book or film
9 a work of extremely high quality
10 a person who regularly goes to see films
11 one of the sections of a film or book that is broadcast or published in parts
12 a film or book that is a major success

3 Complete the sentences with a word or phrase from Exercise 1 in the correct form.

1 As a regular ____________, I enjoy watching the ____________ so that I can plan which film to watch next.
2 The 2015 film *Pan* was a ____________ of the 2003 film *Peter Pan*. Unfortunately, it was a ____________, generating less ____________ through ticket sales than was spent on making it.
3 I really enjoyed the latest ____________ of the *Maleficent* series. It wasn't exactly a ____________ but it was quite good fun. I do enjoy films where the ____________ is evil – and Maleficent certainly is!
4 *The Empire Strikes Back* is one of the best ____________ ever. The second movie was as much of a ____________ as the first.
5 According to the ____________, the book is ____________ the South of France.

4 Work with a partner. What are the pros and cons of reading books and watching films? Complete the table.

	Books	Films
Pros	*You use your imagination more.*	*Can be done with friends.*
Cons		

5 Quickly read the article and missing paragraphs on the opposite page. Which of your pros and cons from Exercise 4 are mentioned?

6 Read the sentences that come just before and after gap 1 and answer these questions.

1 Complete these sentences.
   a Before gap 1, Mia is saying why she likes ____________.
   b After the gap, the writer refers to someone who believes you can't ____________.
2 What do you think the missing paragraph will be about?
   a someone saying why they like films
   b someone else saying why they like books
3 Which paragraph A–G goes in gap 1? Which words helped you decide?

7 Answer the questions about gaps 2–6.

1 The paragraph before gap 2 ends by talking about things books and films have in common. What might follow this?
2 What does the phrase 'Films, on the other hand' in the paragraph after gap 2 suggest about the content of gap 2?
3 What view does Clara Perera express after gap 3? What view might she disagree with?
4 What view is expressed just before gap 4?
5 What does the word 'though' in the sentence after gap 4 suggest about the content of gap 4?
6 What does the word 'however' in the sentence after gap 5 suggest about the content of gap 5?
7 The paragraph before gap 6 gives an example of a series of films which were not as good as the books. What might come next?

8 Choose from the paragraphs A–G the one which fits each gap (2–6). There is one extra paragraph which you do not need to use.

The **film** or the **book**: which is better?

26

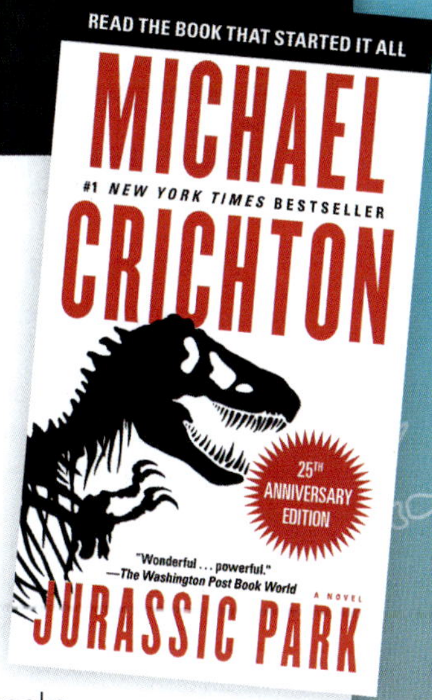

Which do you prefer, films or books? We asked people for their thoughts. For 19-year-old Mia, books win hands-down. 'I enjoy sitting curled up in an armchair on rainy afternoons, engrossed in a story and oblivious to everything around me. I refuse to do anything else until I've finished the chapter I'm on,' she confesses.

1

But, according to Stephen King, author of bestsellers such as *It* and *The Shining*, comparing films and books in that way is akin to comparing apples and oranges: they are both fruit, but taste completely different. However, while this may be true, it is certainly possible to find some broad similarities between books and films. To be successful, they both need to have main characters that readers or viewers can relate to – even if the characters are villains. They need a strong plot too.

2

Films, on the other hand, have music, visual effects, costumes and scenery to make them alluring to the audience – all features that books lack. Also, watching a film is a sociable activity, which can be done with family and friends.

3

Primary school teacher Clara Perera disagrees with that view. She claims that 'films ruin books for children': while reading fosters imagination, movies 'spoon-feed' youngsters and discourage them from imagining scenes and characters for themselves. She refers to psychologists who have warned that exposing children to lots of films can risk harming their creativity.

4

There is undoubtedly a problem with films, though. The need to generate revenue at the box office puts pressure on film-makers to do remakes of older films or sequels to successful movies, and these are often inferior in quality and less critically acclaimed than the originals. Some books also have sequels, which may or may not be as good as the originals, but there is less at stake financially. A box office flop, however, can cost film-makers millions of dollars.

5

Many films based on popular books have been regarded as somewhat underwhelming, however. *The Hunger Games* trilogy, set in a dystopian world in the future, is an example of this. Almost everyone we spoke to preferred the books to the films. Josh, a college student, said: '*The Hunger Games* films were faithful to the books – they got most of the details right. But they just didn't have the same feel; there was definitely something missing.'

6

Ultimately, there will probably never be agreement about whether books or films are better. We may be able to agree, nevertheless, that both are excellent ways to tell a story and an enjoyable way to spend our free time.

A There are exceptions, though, and, occasionally, interviewees name films they consider even more engaging than the books they were based on. *Jurassic Park* is often mentioned as an example of this. Presumably, an action-packed story featuring creatures as impressive as dinosaurs was always likely to work well in movie form.

B In other words, there seem to be good things about films, just as there are good things about books – they are just different. Given this, is there any value in debating whether one is any better than the other? Surely, it's down to personal choice; some people simply like books while others like films.

C In particular, it generally costs more to watch a film than to read a book, although this is changing with online streaming now becoming more competitively priced. Having said that, financial factors are not a significant consideration for most of the people we spoke to.

D Media studies lecturer Nathan Bush rejects such criticism. He argues that films often 'help young minds to grow by setting them free'. By showing things that audiences wouldn't necessarily experience in their everyday lives, films provide all sorts of opportunities for learning and development.

E For medical student Lucia, by contrast, reading is a chore rather than a pleasure. 'I couldn't stand it when I was little, and even now, if someone gives me a book, I rarely get past the blurb,' she laughs. A regular cinemagoer, she is always waiting for the latest blockbuster. 'I watch all the trailers and plan what I'm going to see. Films are definitely better than books!'

F Not all follow-ups fail, of course. The later instalments of the *Harry Potter* film series certainly didn't disappoint. In fact, those films, like the books, are generally considered masterpieces. The colourful stories of wizards and magical creatures lend themselves superbly to the silver screen. With perfect casting and amazing special effects, the film-makers did full justice to J.K. Rowling's brilliant narratives.

G However, there are also key differences. Those keen on reading say that books 'include' the reader, making them feel they are actually experiencing the joy or pain of characters in the story. They give a deeper insight than films can into what the characters are thinking and feeling, and they provide a more detailed context for the narrative.

TALKING POINTS

Do you think it's better to read the book or see the film first? Why?
Are there any books that wouldn't make good films or films that wouldn't make good books?

GRAMMAR
GERUNDS AND INFINITIVES

1 **Match extracts 1–6 from the article to rules a–f.**

1 I **enjoy sitting** curled up in an armchair on rainy afternoons.
2 Given this, is there any value **in debating** whether one is any better than the other?
3 While this may be true, it is certainly **possible to find** some broad similarities between books and films.
4 For medical student Lucia, by contrast, **reading** is a chore rather than a pleasure.
5 Those **keen on reading** say that books 'include' the reader, making them feel they are actually experiencing the joy or pain of characters in the story.
6 I **refuse to do** anything else until I've finished the chapter I'm on.

> **a** We use a gerund (*-ing* form) after a preposition.
> **b** Some verbs are followed by a gerund.
> **c** Some verbs are followed by *to* + infinitive.
> **d** A gerund can be the subject of a sentence or clause.
> **e** Some adjectives are followed by *to* + infinitive.
> **f** Some adjectives are followed by a preposition + gerund.

2 **Find other examples in the article on page 45 of**

1 verbs followed by a gerund
2 verbs followed by an infinitive
3 a gerund as the subject of a sentence or clause
4 a gerund following a preposition

» **GRAMMAR REFERENCE AND PRACTICE PAGE 149**

27 **3** **You will hear a boy called Joseph talking about a film he saw recently. Did he enjoy the film?**

27 **4** **Write the verbs in the correct column. Sometimes both may be possible. Then listen again and check. You will hear the verbs in the order in which they appear in the box.**

begin hate stop start consider carry on expect enjoy happen claim arrange agree continue deny want risk

Verbs followed by gerund	Verbs followed by *to* + infinitive

5 **Complete the sentences with the gerund or *to* + infinitive form of the verbs in brackets. Sometimes both may be possible.**

1 The man was accused of ________ (spy) but he claimed ________ (be) innocent.
2 I'm keen on ________ (study) film at university but I'm worried about ________ (pass) all my exams.
3 Have you tried ________ (watch) movies with subtitles to improve your listening skills?
4 Olivia had arranged ________ (meet) Jacob outside the cinema, but they happened ________ (bump into) each other on the way there.
5 Michaela was anxious not ________ (be) late for the movie as she expected the cinema ________ (be) full.
6 Emma Watson is famous for ________ (play) the part of Hermione in the *Harry Potter* film series, but after the last instalment, she was ready ________ (move on) to other projects.

6 **Read the pairs of sentences (a1 and a2, b1 and b2) and answer questions 1–3.**

a1 I **tried** to read *War and Peace* but it's just too long and difficult.
a2 I **tried** playing Quidditch last week and it was great fun!
b1 I **prefer** to read the book before I see the film.
b2 I **prefer** reading to watching films.

1 Which verb forms follow the words in bold?
2 Which verb has a different meaning depending on whether it is followed by a gerund or *to* + infinitive?
3 Which sentence means 'I tried but didn't succeed'?

7 **Do the pairs of sentences have similar or different meanings? Explain the differences to your partner.**

1 **a** I can't stand sitting close to the screen.
b I can't stand to sit close to the screen.

2 **a** Harvey forgot to read the chapter about global warming.
b Harvey forgot reading the chapter about global warming.

3 **a** Ivan stopped watching the TV programme.
b Ivan stopped to watch the TV programme.

4 **a** Lizzy continued to read historical novels.
b Lizzy continued reading historical novels.

5 **a** I tried to open the window.
b I tried opening the window.

8 **Correct any mistakes in these sentences. Some are correct.**

1 Jason refused playing the part of an ugly sister in Cinderella.
2 I recommend reading this book when you have plenty of time.
3 I stopped talking to Mrs Parsons when I met her in the supermarket.
4 Read is more educational than watch movies.
5 In addition to act, he is a successful film director.
6 Oh no! I've forgotten giving the book to Hannah.
7 People shouldn't risk getting injured for the sake of a film.
8 The students enjoy watch films in class.
9 There is a need of reaching a wider audience.
10 More people should have the opportunity attend the film festival.

9 » **WORK IN PAIRS. TURN TO PAGE 130.**

VOCABULARY

ENTERTAINMENT: ADVERB AND ADJECTIVE COLLOCATIONS

1 Work in pairs. Look at the six films below. Can you match any of them to the descriptions?

1 *The Irishman*
2 *The Revenant*
3 *James Bond* series
4 *Star Wars* series
5 *The Devil Wears Prada*
6 *Lost in Translation*

a This is set in space, focusing on a battle between the Jedi Knights and the Dark Lords of the Sith.
b This features the adventures of a British secret service agent, also known as 007.
c This is about a lorry driver who gets involved in organised crime in Philadelphia.
d This is about a developing friendship between two people from the USA who find themselves in Tokyo.
e This film is about a young woman who wants to be a journalist but ends up working in the world of fashion.
f Set in 1823, this tells the story of Hugh Glass's struggle for survival through the harsh winter wilderness of North America.

2 Have you seen any of the films in Exercise 1? If so, tell your partner what you thought of them.

28 **3 You will hear Rahul and Alicia discussing films. If they like the film, put (✓). If not, put (✗). If they haven't seen it or don't give an opinion, put (?).**

	Rahul	Alicia
The Irishman		
The Revenant		
James Bond series		
Star Wars series		
The Devil Wears Prada		
Lost in Translation		

EP 28 **4 Listen again and match the adverbs to the adjectives to make collocations.**

Adverbs	Adjectives
critically	funny
painfully	successful
highly	unknown
internationally	acclaimed
hysterically	slow
largely	anticipated

5 Complete the sentences with a collocation from Exercise 4.

1 I didn't enjoy the book. There was too much description and not enough action: in fact, it was ....
2 When we were kids we used to laugh so much at Mr Bean. We found it ....
3 Daniel Radcliffe was .... until he rose to fame in the title role of the *Harry Potter* movies.
4 The next movie in the *Tomb Raider* series is one of the .... films of the year. Lots of people are really looking forward to it.
5 *Joker* was one of the most .... films of 2019 – almost all the reviews were positive.
6 *Titanic* was one of the most .... films of all time. It was enjoyed by people all over the world.

ENTERTAINMENT: COMPOUND ADJECTIVES

29 **6 You will hear Alicia talking about her favourite actress. Who is she and why does Alicia like her?**

EP 29 **7 Listen again and complete the extracts with the compound adjectives you hear.**

action-packed award-winning best-known highest-paid low-budget Oscar-nominated record-breaking thought-provoking world-famous

1 Needless to say, she's ....
2 She's had a .... number of Golden Globe nominations.
3 She's played 21 .... roles …
4 Although she did a few .... films, such as *The River Wild* back in the 1990s …
5 … she's .... for her .... roles.
6 My absolute favourite of her films has to be the Academy .... *Sophie's Choice* …
7 … Meryl once said she prefers .... films.
8 … she's one of the .... actresses in the industry!

8 Complete the sentences with a compound adjective from Exercise 7.

1 *The Matrix* is probably one of the most .... movies of all time. It really makes you question what life is all about.
2 *Harry Potter and the Philosopher's Stone* is a .... book. Over 120 million copies have been sold – more than any other novel.
3 The *Die Hard* films are some of the most .... ever made: they are full of activity and excitement.
4 Although Orlando Bloom is an .... actor, he has never been shortlisted for an Academy Award.
5 The original Rocky film was very .... – they only had about $1 million to work with, which was not much even back in the 1970s.
6 Some of the .... actors and actresses have earned well over $50 million in their careers.

9 » **WORK IN PAIRS. TURN TO PAGE 130.**

WRITING
A REVIEW

1 **Discuss the questions with a partner.**

1 Do you ever read reviews of books, films or plays to help you decide what to read and see? Do you find them helpful?
2 What kind of information do you usually find in reviews?
3 Have you ever read a film or book review you disagreed with? What was it?

2 **Read the task. What aspects of the play or film do you need to focus on?**

> You see the following announcement on a website, *Musical Theatre*:
>
> **Reviews wanted**
> Send us a review of a musical you have seen – either a stage play or a film. How well did the musical tell the story? How effective was the use of costumes and special effects? Was there anything that particularly impressed you?
>
> Write your **review**.

3 **Read the reviews of the stage and film versions of the musical *Cats*.**

1 How many stars do you think the reviewers would give the musical?

★★★★★ Excellent
★★★★ Very good
★★★ OK
★★ Not great
★ Terrible

2 Did the reviewers address all three parts of the question?

4 **Read the reviews again. How does each describe the aspects of the film or play which were asked about in the task? Complete the table.**

	The film	The play
Plot/Story		
Costumes		
Special effects		
Anything impressive		

REVIEW OF THE FILM *CATS*

The film version of the musical *Cats* was highly anticipated by fans of the stage version. *Cats* doesn't have much of a plot, and **my impression is that** the director, Tom Hooper, added a few subplots of his own. However, his main intention was to use computer-generated imagery (CGI) to make the humans seem more feline, a potentially brilliant idea which sadly backfired. **Personally, I feel that** the film-makers should have taken more time to get it right, even if it meant missing the planned release date.

To be fair, the costumes were stunning; however, **on the whole**, the technology which was supposed to put the actors' faces on cats' bodies did not really work. What was intended to be a visual feast ended up just being too much for the viewer to take in. The cats appeared quite sinister, making it, **in my opinion**, unsuitable for children. There were times when the special effects knocked me sideways – but not in a good way.

Jennifer Hudson

For me, the highlight of the whole film was Jennifer Hudson as Grizabella singing the world-famous song *Memory*. However, a special mention should be given to award-winning actress Dame Judi Dench for her portrayal of the patriarch Deuteronomy. Casting a mature and critically acclaimed actress in this key role was a stroke of genius; it is unfortunate that the film was such a box-office flop. **To sum up**, although audiences were massively disappointed with the screen adaptation of this classic musical, there were a few bright moments, thanks to the wonderful cast.

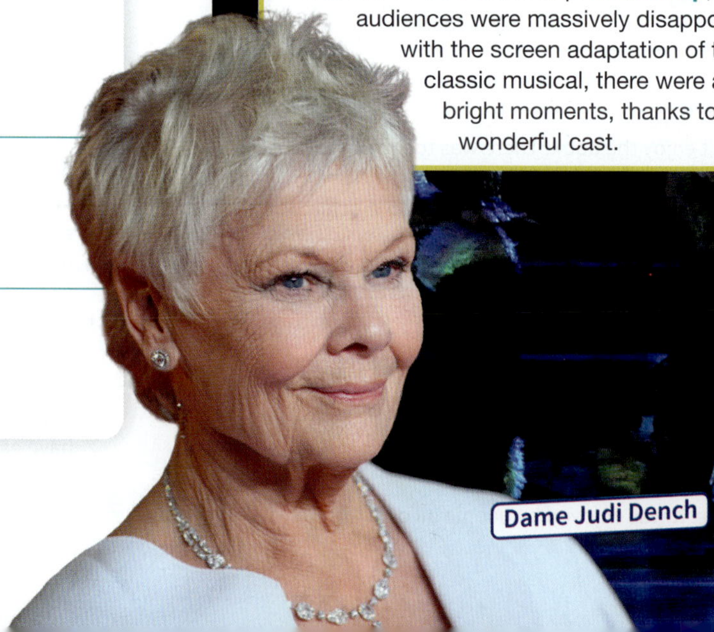

Dame Judi Dench

REVIEW OF THE WEST END MUSICAL *CATS*

Fulfilling a lifelong dream, I finally got to see the legendary musical *Cats* on stage in London's West End. *Cats* is well-known as a musical phenomenon but, like many others, I didn't know the story behind the show. **In short**, the bizarre and puzzling plot is that the cats all want to go to a place called the Heaviside Layer, where a better life exists, but only one can go. Their leader, Old Deuteronomy, has to make the decision. The play takes place during a special event called the Jellicle Ball, where all the cats make their case for why they should be chosen.

The set was, **in my personal view**, impressive, largely thanks to the amazing lighting, which totally blew me away. The shining eyes of the cats right at the start were quite frightening and signalled the introduction of some evil characters. Tyler John Logan gave an exceptional performance as the mysterious and shady cat Macavity. **To my mind**, the costumes were a triumph. They varied from the simple to the flamboyant, depending on the character. The make-up, too, made everyone look like cats, while reflecting the personality of the individual.

What impressed me most was the music: the songs were nothing short of brilliant. It was a real treat to experience the entire cast singing the classic number *Mister Mistoffelees*, with the audience roaring the chorus alongside them. **The only downside** was the plot, which could definitely have been a bit more interesting. **Overall** though, the performance was simply outstanding and I was honoured to witness one of the most iconic shows in the West End.

5 Complete the *Prepare to write* box with phrases from the reviews. Some are already included.

PREPARE TO WRITE

Giving opinions

1 ....
2 ....
In my opinion
The best/worst aspect is
What I (dis)like is
To be fair
3 ....
For me
In my personal view
4 ....
5 ....
The only downside was

Summarising

In brief
All things considered
6 ....
Overall
To sum up
7 ....
Taking everything into consideration
In summary

6 Which option is more suitable for a written review?

1 *If you ask me / I'm confident that* the film will be nominated for several awards.
2 *It seems to me (that) / The way I see it* the sequel was even better than the original.
3 *It's generally acknowledged that / Most people agree that* action-packed films are most popular among young people.
4 *From my perspective, / I definitely thought that* the music was too loud at times.
5 *As I see it / I've no doubt that* this film will be a box-office flop.
6 *At the end of the day / In conclusion*, I can highly recommend this film to anyone.

7 Read this task. How many things do you have to write about? Write a plan for your review.

You see the following announcement in an arts magazine:

> **Reviews wanted**
> Have you recently seen a movie or read a book based on historical events? You should tell us briefly about the event the film or book was based on, explain which aspects of the event it focused on and say how life today differs from the period in the film or book.

Write your **review**.

8 Write your review in 220–260 words. Try to use words and phrases from the *Prepare to write* box.

BRAINSTORMING

LIFE SKILLS

Brainstorming ideas

There will be many times during your studies and your career when you are part of a team that has to come up with ideas for projects or find creative solutions to various problems. Brainstorming is a group activity that lets people think freely and generate lots of ideas together without fear of criticism.

1 **Read the *Life skills* box and answer the questions with a partner.**

1 What team projects have you been part of?
2 Did you brainstorm ideas for these projects? If so, how did you do it? If not, how did you come up with ideas?
3 Can you think of other reasons why brainstorming is a good way of getting ideas?

2 **Read the article and match headings 1–6 to sections A–F.**

1 Use storytelling questions
2 Take notes
3 Aim for quantity over quality
4 Praise, don't criticise
5 Welcome all ideas
6 Set a time limit

3 **Read the article again and answer the questions.**

1 Why can the job of writing TV series be stressful?
2 Why does the writer talk about a rock band?
3 Why should group members avoid responding negatively to others?
4 The writer recommends special roles for two members of the group. What are they?
5 Which of the writer's ideas do you think is the most useful?
6 Which of the ideas do you think is the most difficult to do well?

30 **4** **Listen to Claire, Adam and Hannah brainstorming ideas for a short film for a competition. Which of these ideas do they *not* mention?**

a artificial intelligence and education
b artificial intelligence and war
c artificial intelligence and space exploration
d artificial intelligence and crime.

30 **5** **Listen again and tick the correct boxes. There may be more than one answer for some questions. Who**

	Claire	Adam	Hannah	no one
1 thinks the group doesn't need a time limit?				
2 asks another student to say more about an idea?				
3 criticises an idea?				
4 praises an idea?				
5 ignores an idea?				
6 has kept a record of the brainstorming?				

6 **Discuss the questions with a partner.**

1 How well did Claire, Adam and Hannah brainstorm?
2 How could they improve next time?

Have you ever been watching an episode of a TV series and suddenly thought, 'How did they come up with such a great story?' Most series these days, from *The Walking Dead* to *Stranger Things*, are written by a team of writers who work together in a 'writers' room' to develop characters, story lines and dialogues. Given that viewers are hungry for episode after episode and season after season, these writers are often under enormous pressure to work quickly and to a very high standard. But how does a team of writers go from a blank page to a finished script? Without a doubt, one of the keys to their success is brainstorming. Let's look at how that works.

A ....

Don't start the session thinking, 'We must come up with good ideas.' Tell yourselves, 'We must come up with *many* ideas.' You won't end up using every idea that occurs to you, but the more you generate in total, the greater the number of good ones you'll eventually have to choose from.

B ....

Brainstorming is about the free generation of ideas, but you still need to concentrate. Knowing you only have a certain amount of time helps to focus everybody's mind. What's more, you'll be less likely to consider individual ideas carefully if you don't have time to do so, which means you'll have time for more ideas. I suggest nominating a member of the group to be the time-keeper and keep everyone on track.

Welcome to the writers' room!

31

C

As well as concentration, brainstorming also needs focus. Asking questions can help you to achieve this. For instance, if you're trying to come up with ideas for a brand new series, I recommend asking yourselves the following:

- Where and when is the story set?
- Who is/are the main character(s)?
- What is interesting or unusual about them?
- What are they trying to achieve?
- What or who is preventing them from achieving this?

D

Some ideas will not sound very good, but that's OK; ideas generate more ideas. Imagine a rock band trying to write their next song. If the musicians just sit around looking at their instruments, waiting for the perfect song to pop into their heads, they'll be sitting there forever. But if they start to experiment with melodies, playing different combinations of notes, then even if the first few combinations sound awful, a song will eventually start to take shape. Something that seems ridiculous at first might lead to a brilliant idea later on. Asking one another to expand on ideas will help this process. This brings me to the next point.

E

Brainstorming lets you share your creativity and come up with ideas and solutions together, so it's important to respond to one another. However, avoid saying things like, 'That won't work' or 'That's no good'. Criticism at this stage will make people feel uncomfortable and reduce the flow of creativity. Phrases such as 'I like it' and 'That's a good idea' or 'That has possibilities' are simple but effective.

F

Finally, it's essential to write everything down so that you don't forget it later. Decide at the beginning who is going to be the note-taker. You don't have to use a notebook. Post-it notes work even better because you can stick them on a whiteboard and move them around. Seeing different combinations of ideas next to one another can often generate even more ideas.

Project

Creating a TV series

A large streaming company wants to fund the production of a major new TV series. In groups, you're going to brainstorm ideas for a series called *The Secret Life of the Willis Twins*. You will then pitch your story to your classmates. Finally, everyone will decide which series should get the funding.

1 DECIDE

In groups, choose a genre for your series (comedy, drama, science-fiction, horror etc.).

2 THINK

Brainstorm ideas for the series using the advice from the article.

3 PRESENT

Present your ideas to your classmates.

4 CHOOSE

As a class, choose the best idea. This one gets the funding!

5 DISCUSS

Follow-up: Discuss these questions in your group.

- How much of the advice in the article did you follow during your brainstorming?
- What brainstorming skills do you need to work on in the future?

7 AGAINST ALL ODDS

ABOUT YOU

▶ 07 **Watch the video and then answer the questions.**
What goals would you like to achieve in life?
What obstacles might you have to overcome to achieve them?
What strategies do you think you could use to overcome them?

VOCABULARY AND READING
CHALLENGES AND ACHIEVEMENTS

EP **1 Check the meaning of the words and phrases in the box. Does each one have a positive or negative meaning?**

adversity	against all odds	break down barriers	
endurance	overcome	self-belief	self-discipline
setback	suffer defeat	thrive	

2 Complete the first paragraph of an article with the words and phrases in Exercise 1.

BEATING THE ODDS

There are many athletes who have [1] .... adversity to achieve success. Early failure is a common [2] .... and only those with enough [3] .... – those who know they can do it – will go on to [4] .... in their chosen sport. Unless you have high levels of [5] .... – that is the ability to keep going no matter what life throws at you – you could easily let problems hold you back. The sporting community has tried hard to [6] .... to allow those from disadvantaged backgrounds or with disabilities to participate and reach their goals. Every sportsman or woman will [7] .... at some time in their career, but with hard work and [8] ...., it is possible to succeed [9] .... The four athletes featured in our article have stared [10] .... in the face but overcome it. If you read on, you will definitely be inspired.

3 Look at the photos of the four athletes on the opposite page and read the quotes 1–4. Who do you think said each quote?

1 'I hope I would inspire kids everywhere to know that you can do anything you put your mind to.'
2 'We only live once, so make it worth it.'
3 'Be fearless in the pursuit of what sets your soul on fire.'
4 'I know that fear is an obstacle for some people, but for me, it's just an illusion.'

4 Which quote do you like best? Why?

5 Read the rest of the article on the opposite page quickly. What obstacles has each athlete overcome to achieve success?

6 Read the article again. Write BH (Bethany Hamilton), MJ (Michael Jordan), SB (Simone Biles) or YM (Yusra Mardini) for each question.

Who

1 represented a newly formed team?
2 was not initially recognised as having sporting ability?
3 had an unexpected reaction to a trauma?
4 discovered their talent by chance?
5 helps others with a similar disadvantage?
6 used their talent to save others?
7 has gained huge wealth through sport?
8 has won more awards than anyone else in their sport in their country?

7 Discuss the questions with a partner.

1 What do you admire about each athlete?
2 What else would you like to know about them?
3 Do you have a favourite? Why?

BETHANY HAMILTON

If you grow up in Hawaii, you learn to surf at an early age. Bethany Hamilton was out on the waves by the age of seven and was showing exceptional promise, receiving her first sponsorship at the tender age of nine. Everything was going well when, at the age of 13, her life changed forever. Lying on her surf board in the ocean one morning, she suddenly felt severe pressure on her left arm. Strangely, she felt no pain as she noticed the water around her turning red and realised she had lost her arm. It later became apparent that a four-metre tiger shark had attacked her, and her life would never be the same again. Hamilton was determined to overcome this setback. Her self-belief was so strong, she was back in the water just a month after the accident and is currently ranked among the top 50 female surfers in the world. The striking thing is that if she weren't an amputee, she probably wouldn't have helped as many people as she has done through her charity, *Friends of Bethany,* which supports other young amputees – people who have lost an arm or a leg.

MICHAEL JORDAN

Some might be surprised to see basketball legend Michael Jordan featured in an article about those who have beaten adversity, but at school he was not considered talented. He suffered a huge number of defeats, losing over 300 games and missing the winning shot 26 times, according to the man himself. You might think it's strange that he kept count of his failures, but Jordan believes he wouldn't be where he is if he hadn't been defeated so many times. It takes self-discipline to keep going when you get knocked back so many times, but the former Chicago Bulls player has plenty of that. Despite his early defeats, he won the NBA's Most Valuable Player award six times and won gold at the Olympics twice. In recent years, this remarkable sportsman became the first NBA player to become a billionaire. Not bad for someone who was told he was no good.

SIMONE BILES

Born into a troubled family, gymnast Simone Biles was taken into the care of the state aged five when her mother was unable to look after her. She was later adopted by her maternal grandparents. In her new home, Biles began to thrive. On a school trip when she was six, she was introduced to the sport of gymnastics. Observing her natural ability, the instructor said she had the potential to be an excellent gymnast. Biles has been criticised for her body shape, but she considers this just another minor obstacle to overcome. She says she wouldn't be such a good gymnast if she didn't have a stocky build. Biles went on to win four gold medals at the Olympics in Rio De Janeiro in 2016 and holds the most medals of any US gymnast. She later took a break from gymnastics to write her book *Courage to Soar: A body in motion, a life in balance* in which she calls for endurance in difficult times and urges people never to give up on their dreams.

YUSRA MARDINI

Life is hard if you're a female athlete in war-torn Syria, as swimmer Yusra Mardini discovered. When both her pool and home in Damascus were bombed, she knew she had to get out. Along with her sister, Sara, she fled through Lebanon to Turkey. Then, while they were sailing across the sea to Greece, their dinghy broke down. Against all odds, no lives were lost. If Yusra and Sara hadn't been such expert swimmers, the outcome would have been tragic. They and two other swimmers pulled the dinghy through the water, finally reaching the shore three hours later.

Mardini went on to become the face of the first ever team of refugees to take part in the Olympics. Now based in Berlin, her work continues to break down barriers and challenge people's perceptions of refugees. She is a goodwill ambassador for the United Nations High Commissioner for Refugees and has met world leaders including Pope Francis and the President of the United States. Her message to the world is that those who flee their countries to escape war and other hardships can still achieve great things.

TALKING POINTS

What kind of obstacles do people often have to overcome?
Do you know any other sportspeople or celebrities who have faced adversity in their lives?
Is there anyone who has been an inspiration to you because of obstacles they have overcome?

GRAMMAR
CONDITIONALS

1 Read the extracts and answer the questions in *italics*.

1 **If you grow up** in Hawaii, **you learn** to surf at an early age.
Is that a true statement?
2 **If Yusra and Sara hadn't been** such expert swimmers, the outcome **would have been** tragic.
Were they good swimmers? Was the outcome tragic?
3 **If you read on, you will** definitely be inspired.
Do you think most people will read on? Will people be inspired?
4 She says **she wouldn't be** such a good gymnast **if she didn't have** a stocky build.
Is she a good gymnast? Does she have a stocky build?

2 Match examples 1–4 from Exercise 1 to rules a–d.

We use the
a zero conditional to describe situations that are generally true.
b first conditional to describe likely events in the future and their results.
c second conditional to describe unreal or unlikely situations in the present or future and their results.
d third conditional for imaginary situations and their imaginary results.

» **GRAMMAR REFERENCE AND PRACTICE PAGE 150**

3 Match clauses 1–6 to a–f to form conditional sentences.

1 If you try hard enough,
2 Bethany wouldn't change her life
3 Unless you're very careful,
4 If I got the chance,
5 Simone wouldn't have won so many medals
6 They will qualify for the team

a if she hadn't trained so hard.
b you can do anything.
c I'd definitely go to watch the Olympics.
d you will lose the competition.
e even if it were possible.
f if they keep up the same standards.

4 Answer the questions about the sentences in Exercise 3.

1 Are the sentences zero, first, second or third conditional?
2 What do you notice about the sentences that begin with the conditional (*if*) clause?

5 Look at the two mixed conditional sentences from the article and answer the questions.

A Michael Jordan wouldn't be where he is today if he hadn't been defeated so many times.
Where is he today? Has he been been defeated often?
B If Bethany Hamilton weren't an amputee, she probably wouldn't have helped as many people as she has done.
Is she an amputee? Has she helped many people?

Which sentence, A or B, talks about:

1 an imaginary possibility in the present which is affected by the past?
2 an imaginary possibility in the past which is affected by the present or by a permanent situation?

6 Complete the description of the two mixed conditional forms.

1 Imagined present result of a past condition:
If + past perfect, ______ + infinitive
2 Imagined past result of a present condition:
If + past tense, ______ + past participle

7 Make mixed conditional sentences from the prompts.

1 Dan is not happy because he wasn't selected for the team.
2 You didn't win the race because you aren't fit enough.
3 Zain is stubborn and didn't listen to the advice I gave him.
4 The pool is full of leaves because the attendant forgot to put the cover on.
5 Ana made it to the Olympics as she is incredibly talented.

8 Choose the correct verb form.

1 If children *start* / *will start* training young, they are more likely to reach Olympic level.
2 It would be better if governments *spend* / *spent* more on sports facilities.
3 If the players *listened* / *had listened* to the coach, they would have triumphed.
4 I'd be playing in the match today if I *hadn't broken* / *didn't break* my ankle.
5 What *will* / *would* the tennis club do if the funding is not available?
6 Would you take the job if it *were* / *is* offered to you?

9 Complete the text with the correct form of the verb in brackets. Put any other words in brackets in the correct position.

If the average person had been asked about the Paralympics 30 or 40 years ago, they probably [1] ______ (not, know) what they were. If you asked people today, they [2] ______ (all, know) exactly what they are and probably enjoy watching them. Disabled athlete Darren said, 'If the Paralympics didn't exist, I [3] ______ (not, even, try) to take up sport. When you [4] ______ (think) of a sportsman or woman, you don't usually picture someone in a wheelchair.' Like many others, he goes on to say that he [5] ______ (not, live) such a happy, healthy life if he hadn't joined his local wheelchair basketball club. Even for those who are not sporty, the Paralympians are an inspiration. According to hearing-impaired office worker, Matt, 'Nowadays if someone sees my hearing aid, they [6] ______ (not, make) assumptions about my skills and abilities. The Paralympics have gone a long way towards changing attitudes in a positive way.'

10 » **WORK IN PAIRS. TURN TO PAGE 130.**

VOCABULARY
NOUN SUFFIXES

33 **1 You will hear a psychologist giving advice on helping people overcome negative emotions. What advice does he give about helping a friend?**

33 **2 Listen again. Write down the nouns you hear which are formed from the following verbs and adjectives.**

0 negative	*negativity*	**5** replace	....
1 unfair	....	**6** disapprove	....
2 accept	....	**7** interfere	....
3 courteous	....	**8** motivate	....
4 inaccurate	....		

EP **3 Form nouns from the words in the box and add them to the correct part of the table. Some words may take more than one suffix.**

adverse agent aggressive conscious employ endure exaggerate extend jealous prosper refer rich survive

-(s)ion	-ity	-ness	-ance	-y
	adversity			
-cy	**-ment**	**-al**	**-ence**	**-(t)ion**

4 Complete the words with a suffix from the table above.

1 When we played against Roma, we were overwhelmed by their hospital....... .
2 While I was training in the gym, I heard a disturb....... outside.
3 There was an explo....... as the tyre hit something on the race track.
4 I've just had to pay £500 for the renew....... of my gym membership.
5 The athletes are now training hard in readi....... for the competition.
6 Harass....... of players in the opposing team will result in a fine.
7 Both teams getting the same score is a rare occurr....... in cricket.
8 Do we have any indica....... of when the postponed race might take place?

EP **5 Match each set of sentences to a suffix.**

-dom -hood -ship

1 I wonder if I could get an apprentice....... in the field of sport.
Taking part in sports can help develop leader....... skills.
Some kind of censor....... of news is needed.
2 Nobody in my neighbour....... goes jogging.
I spent much of my boy....... playing chess.
I used to run 10km a day but mother....... changed that.
3 Every child should have the free....... to choose the sport they like.
Many people in the United King....... go horseriding.

6 Complete the sentences with a noun ending in *-ship*, *-hood* or *-dom*. Make the noun plural where necessary.

1 Some sportspeople manage to balance .... with their sport. (parent)
2 Absolutely nothing happened in that match. I almost died of ....(bore)
3 Most celebrities achieve .... only after a lot of hard work. (star)
4 One thing that often helps athletes is to get ...., especially from a well-known brand. (sponsor)
5 Many top footballers come from poor ...., where they learned their skills on the streets. (neighbour)
6 If you can get a ...., you will get your university tuition fees paid. (scholar)
7 Some athletes who show a lot of promise as youngsters do not fulfil their potential as they reach .... (adult)

7 » WORK IN PAIRS. **TURN TO PAGE 130.**

8 Use the word given in capitals at the end of some of the lines to form a word that fits in the gap in the same line.

BILLIE JEAN KING: A TENNIS LEGEND

Billie Jean King is one of the all-time greats of the tennis world. Born in 1943, she had a sporty **(0)** *childhood*, excelling in baseball (CHILD) from an early age. In 1965, she came close to winning the US tennis championships. Her **(1)** .... to do so didn't deter her, but (ABLE) instead fuelled her **(2)** .... to do better. It was this attitude (DETERMINE) that made her into a tennis superstar.

King was not afraid to challenge **(3)** .... In 1973, former (DISCRIMINATE) men's tennis champion Bobby Riggs claimed he could beat any woman and invited King to a match. She refused his **(4)** ...., which (PROPOSE) was accepted instead by King's main rival, Margaret Court. To King's great **(5)** ...., Riggs defeated Court, just as he had said he would, (ANNOY) so King decided to play him herself.

King badly wanted an **(6)** .... from the tennis world that (ADMIT) female players could play as well as the men, but she doubted the **(7)** .... of taking on the player who had beaten Court, the (WISE) women's number 1 at the time. However, King beat Riggs. This incident helped raise **(8)** .... of the issues facing women both in sport (AWARE) and in society.

LISTENING

1 **You are shortly going to listen to people talking about their achievements and ambitions in different sports. Look at the phrases from the extracts. Which sports do you think the people will talk about?**

Europe's highest peak	the dry slopes
the junior belts	the Tour de France
Bend it like Beckham	

2 **Study Tasks One and Two below and answer these questions.**

1 How many different speakers will you hear?
2 How many different tasks do you complete for each speaker?
3 Are the speakers talking about the same or different topics?
4 For each task, how many options do you have to choose from?
5 Do you think you should attempt both tasks on the first listening?

You will hear five short extracts in which people are talking about their sporting achievements and ambitions.

TASK ONE

For questions 1–5, choose from the list (A–H) the difficulty each speaker had to overcome.

A barriers related to culture
B their own mental state
C the attitude of their peers
D a lack of family support
E the cost of equipment
F serious physical injury
G the opinions of professionals
H geographical conditions

1 Speaker 1 ......
2 Speaker 2 ......
3 Speaker 3 ......
4 Speaker 4 ......
5 Speaker 5 ......

TASK TWO

For questions 6–10, choose from the list (A–H) what each speaker hopes to accomplish in the future.

A become the best in their age group
B compete regionally
C succeed in the sport's greatest challenge
D participate in a world-famous event
E achieve a personal record
F be awarded the sport's top title
G become professional in the sport
H empower a group under-represented in the sport

6 Speaker 1 ......
7 Speaker 2 ......
8 Speaker 3 ......
9 Speaker 4 ......
10 Speaker 5 ......

34 **3** **Listen to Speaker 1, focusing only on Task One. Choose from the list the difficulty that applies to Speaker 1.**

34 **4** **Listen to Speaker 1 again, focusing only on Task Two. Choose from the list what the speaker hopes to accomplish.**

35 **5** **Listen to Speaker 2. Try to answer both Task One and Task Two while listening. Then listen again and check your answers.**

6 **Which approach do you think was better?**

A Focus on Task One only during the first listening and Task Two during the second listening.
B Focus on both tasks during the first listening. Use the second listening to check your answers.

36 **7** **Decide whether you are going to use approach A or approach B. Listen to Speakers 3, 4 and 5 and do both tasks. Listen to the recording twice.**

8 **Discuss the questions with a partner.**

1 Which speaker's story did you find most interesting? Why?
2 Who are your sporting heroes?
3 If you could create a new sport, what would it involve?

SPEAKING
REACTING TO WHAT PEOPLE SAY

37 **1 You will hear three short conversations. Match them to the photos.**

Conversation 1 ☐ Conversation 2 ☐
Conversation 3 ☐

A

B

C

37 **2 Listen again. In which conversation does one of the speakers express**

a surprise? **b** sympathy? **c** lack of interest?

38 **3 You will hear three conversations in which people react to short extracts from the Listening section on the previous page. For each one, decide if they react with *surprise*, *sympathy* or *lack of interest*. Think about both the words the speakers use and their tone of voice.**

38 **4 Listen again and complete the *Prepare to speak* box with phrases you hear.**

PREPARE TO SPEAK

Reacting to what people say

Expressing sympathy

1 ....

2 ....

That's such a shame.
Oh dear!
I'm sorry to hear that

Expressing surprise

Really? How amazing!

3 ....

Never! What a fantastic achievement!
Wow! Are you serious?

Expressing indifference

4 ....

Uh huh.
Mmm.

5 Work with a partner. Take it in turns to read out the statements. Respond using a suitable expression from the *Prepare to speak* box. Make sure your response sounds surprised, sympathetic or lacking in interest.

1 There's a student in my class who can run 100 metres in 10.5 seconds.
2 I worked as a sports nutritionist, but I've just been made redundant.
3 My brother has just started a temporary job at a big chain of outdoor shops.
4 The Olympic torch is passing through my town next week.
5 My sports club membership is about to run out.
6 I twisted my ankle while doing the high jump yesterday.

6 Complete the exclamations with words from the box. There is more than one answer for each.

appalled behaviour dismayed ending horrific news result sad shocking story stunned surprise unbelievable

1 How ....!
2 What terrible ....!
3 What a great ....!
4 That's ....!
5 That's a wonderful ....!
6 I'm ....!

39 **7 Read the information about echo questions, then listen to a short conversation. How many echo questions do you hear?**

An echo question is a question spoken by a listener which repeats part of what the speaker has just said. It is used if the listener hasn't fully understood what was said, or to express surprise, sympathy or disbelief.

39 **8 Listen again. What does the girl say after each echo question?**

1 In 2011? ....
2 Only a few months before? ....
3 The United States? ....

9 Work with a partner. Read out the statements in turn and respond with a suitable echo question, followed by a reaction.

0 **A:** The longest recorded point in tennis took 29 minutes.
B: *29 minutes? That can't be right.*
1 Apparently, in that 29 minute point, the ball crossed the net 643 times.
2 There have been three Olympic Games held in countries that no longer exist.
3 Did you know that England didn't take part in the first three football World Cups?
4 Michael Jordan and the Chicago Bulls didn't have a three-game losing streak for eight years.
5 Simone Biles got to be the US's flag-bearer at the closing ceremony of the Olympics.
6 I read that 2% of cases at Accident and Emergency departments in the UK are from sports injuries.

10 Write five items of real or fake 'news' about yourself, your school, or your town.

11 Work with a partner. Take it in turns to read your items and respond to your partner's using expressions from this section.

8 MAKING ENDS MEET

ABOUT YOU

▶ 08 **Watch the video and then answer the questions.**
Are you more of a spender or a saver?
At what age should children first be given money?
Do you think that teenagers should be paid by their parents for helping with household tasks?

VOCABULARY AND READING
MONEY AND WEALTH

1 Which of the following sayings do you agree most/least with, and why?

1 Money makes the world go round.
2 There's no such thing as easy money.
3 A fool and his money are soon parted.
4 Save money, and money will save you.

EP **2 Match the words to their definitions a–i.**

1 Justin wants to go travelling for a year after school, but I've no idea how he thinks he's going to **fund** it.
2 To most people, a super-yacht is an **unaffordable** luxury. Except, of course, if you're exceptionally **well-off**.
3 The cash dispenser on my street only lets you **withdraw** £50 at a time.
4 Marina's parents are going to let her have a monthly **allowance** while she's at college to pay for transport, books and so on. Without their **support**, she wouldn't be able to study at all.
5 Having spent all her money, Roser was completely **broke**, and had to move back in with her parents.
6 When he finishes school, Iñigo plans to **take out a loan** in order to set up his own laptop repair business.
7 I'm looking for my first car to buy, but the cars in the big showrooms in town are a complete **rip-off**. The ones in our local garage are much better value for money.

a wealthy
b financial help
c having no money left
d too expensive to buy
e borrow money from a bank
f get the money to pay for something
g something that is not worth the money you pay for it
h get (an amount of money) from a machine or bank
i an amount of money given regularly for a particular purpose

3 Choose which sentence the word can be used in: a or b, or both a and b.

1 **broke**
a I'm absolutely .... until I get my allowance at the end of the month.
b The north side of the town is reasonably affluent, but some neighbourhoods in the south are quite ....

2 **take out a loan**
a Before I could pay the deposit on my apartment, I had to .... from the bank.
b I needed a couple more euros to pay for my cinema ticket, so I had to .... from my sister.

3 **allowance**
a The job has a starting .... of €23,500.
b My brother drives a lot for his job, and he gets a monthly .... of up to €250 to spend on fuel.

4 **fund**
a I'm taking a holiday job this summer in order to .... my gap year.
b The council plans to .... the new buses with money raised from car parking charges.

5 **unaffordable**
a I heard of someone who left his .... Stradivarius violin on the metro, but he got it back eventually.
b We were hoping to go on a big holiday this year, but I'm afraid it's just .... at the moment and will have to wait.

6 **well-off**
a My grandparents live in a rather .... area right beside the river.
b Tom's uncle is extremely .... – they go to the Caribbean every year.

4 Suggest an alternative in the sentences in Exercise 3 where the given word can't be used.

5 Quickly read the article about money on the opposite page and discuss which sections (A–D) the following comments might be a response to.

1 'I guess it's true that the more someone has, the more they want!'
2 'Maybe being well-off isn't so wonderful after all.'
3 'Perhaps they just thought their time was more important than other people's.'
4 'That's an interesting result – perhaps they found the low pay insulting!'

MONEY **MATTERS**

40 Does how much money we have really affect who we are, and how we behave?

A What do most of us do once we become reasonably well-off? Well, essentially, we isolate ourselves away from other people. We buy a car so we needn't take the bus, even if it means taking out a loan to do so. We stay in expensive, quiet hotels rather than the guest houses we used to frequent when we were broke. And after years of wishing the people in the next-door flat would make less noise, we finally move out into a house behind a nice big wall. We use money to shield ourselves from risk, noise and inconvenience. But this comes at a cost. We become isolated, cutting ourselves off from chance encounters, unfamiliar laughter, fresh air, and random interaction with strangers. Researchers have concluded again and again that the single most reliable predictor of wellbeing is a sense of belonging in a community. Yet people use their riches to achieve exactly the opposite.

B Two psychologists in California monitored traffic intersections where drivers have to give way and found that people in expensive cars (hence assumed to be wealthy) were four times more likely to cut in front of other drivers, compared to folks in more modest vehicles. When the researchers posed as pedestrians waiting to cross a street, all the drivers in cheap cars respected their right of way, while those in expensive cars drove right on by 46.2 percent of the time. This was a significant finding, given that stopping for pedestrians is a legal requirement. In another study, one of the psychologists got 100 pairs of strangers to play the board game Monopoly, randomly assigning one of each pair the role of 'rich player', who would roll two dice instead of one, and received twice as much financial support in the game as the other player. Inevitably the 'rich player' would accumulate more wealth and win. While discussing the game afterwards, they often put their win down to their game strategy, even though their victory should have been seen as inevitable.

C Let's imagine a prosperous banker, living in a multi-million-euro home. His net worth is about €3.5 million, but he wishes he didn't have to work 70 hours a week, so that he could enjoy the fruits of his success … Well, perhaps he could. Assuming a reasonable return of 5%, he could easily sell off his home, invest the proceeds and take early retirement. He could then sail through the rest of his life giving himself an annual allowance of around €175,000, more than enough to fund a lifestyle of luxury. And he'd still have enough to withdraw thousands from his savings whenever he wanted. So why doesn't he? Well, many such high-fliers don't actually see themselves as being particularly affluent, as others have accumulated much vaster fortunes. After all, what's a €2 million apartment, when your neighbour's is worth €4 million, and they have a private jet, which for you is unaffordable?

D Researchers James Heyman and Dan Ariely proved that money alters how you value your time and effort. They created an experiment to measure how motivated a person was to complete a task based upon money. Subjects were asked to drag circles across a computer screen. One group was asked to do this as a 'favour', another group for $0.50, and the last group for $5. The subjects were timed, and it was actually the group asked to 'do a favour' that did it the fastest. Next was the $5 group, and last was the $0.50 group. Heyman and Ariely suggested that there are two predominant reasons for completing a task. The first is social. By recognising a task's social value, we see it as part of our social duty, and are usually willing to lend a hand. When money is offered as the incentive, however, we start thinking more about the business value, and measure our time against the financial reward, which may be why the $0.50 group was the slowest. They possibly thought $0.50 was a rip-off and wished their efforts were being more generously rewarded, or they were wishing they hadn't agreed to participate, and this may have adversely affected the effort they were willing to put in.

TALKING POINTS

Do you think people would work harder if they were paid more?
If there was a time in your life when you could afford not to work, would you work anyway?
Would you rather have an interesting job that didn't pay a lot, or a dull job with high pay? Why?

6 You are going to read an article about how money may affect our behaviour. In which section (A–D) is the following mentioned?

1. Some rich people work harder than they need to.
2. People are generally happy to give their help for free.
3. Less well-off people are more likely to comply with the law.
4. Wealthy people sometimes don't consider themselves very well-off.
5. People may be unrealistic about the reasons for their financial success.
6. Increased wealth doesn't create the conditions for being happy.
7. Rich people often show a lack of consideration for others.
8. A person who wants to be paid more might not do their job so well.
9. Different reasons for doing something can affect the way activities are carried out.
10. People distance themselves from others when they become wealthier.

GRAMMAR
WISH AND IF ONLY

1 Read the examples and answer the questions.

A We wish the people in the next-door flat would make less noise.
1 Are the people next door noisy?
2 Is the speaker happy about this?
3 Is it possible for the people next door to make less noise?

B He wishes he didn't have to work 70 hours a week.
1 Does he have to work 70 hours a week?
2 Is he happy about this?
3 Can he work fewer hours?

C They wished they were being paid more.
1 Are they happy with their pay?
2 Do they think the situation could change?

D They were wishing they hadn't agreed to participate.
1 Did they previously agree to participate in the experiment?
2 Are they happy about this?
3 Is it possible for them to change this earlier decision?

2 Complete the rules with the words in the box.

past continuous | past perfect | past simple | *would*

We use:
a *wish (that)* + ______ or ______ to talk about something we would like to be different in the present or future.
b *wish (that)* + ______ to express regret about the past.
c *wish (that)* + ______ + infinitive if we are annoyed about something and want it to change.

» **GRAMMAR REFERENCE AND PRACTICE PAGE 151**

3 Complete the sentences with the correct form of the verb in brackets.

1 I wish I ______ all that money to my brother. (not lend)
2 Alejandro wishes he ______ better Italian. (able / speak)
3 Don't you wish we ______ an exam tomorrow? (not have)
4 I wish my internet provider ______ putting up its prices. It's outrageous. (not keep)
5 We all wish the leisure centre ______ by the council last year. (not close down)
6 Emma wishes her boss ______ sending her emails when she's on holiday. (stop)

4 Look at the pairs of sentences, and then complete the rules in the box (top right) by selecting the correct option.

1 I wish our teacher wouldn't give us so much homework.
If only we didn't get economics homework every night!
2 I wish my parents had given me money for my birthday.
If only I hadn't spent all my money on that jacket!
3 Don't you wish new phones were cheaper?
If only new phones were cheaper.

We can use *if only* instead of *I wish (that)* to talk about things we would like to be different.
1 *If only* means the same as *I wish* but expresses a *stronger / weaker* wish.
2 We use *if only* to express *our own / other people's* wishes.
3 We *can / can't* use *if only* in questions.

41 **5 Listen to Greg and Emily talking. How do they both feel about their jobs?**

41 **6 Choose the correct option. Then listen again and check.**

1 If only I *wouldn't apply / hadn't applied* for an office job.
2 If only it *wasn't / wouldn't be* so boring!
3 If only *he'd give me / he gave me* something different to do.
4 If only *you'd be / you wouldn't be* a bit more understanding.
5 If only I *would earn / earned* half as much as the boss!
6 If only they *wouldn't / couldn't* ask questions all the time.

7 Correct any mistakes in these sentences. Some are correct.

1 I'd have got a better mark in the exam if only I'll finish all the questions.
2 My family all wish we wouldn't live in such a cramped apartment.
3 The holiday was fun, but if only the weather had been better!
4 If only money really did grow on trees – life would be so much easier!
5 Dad said he'd give me £10, but if only I helped him tidy the kitchen first.
6 I wish my boss won't keep asking me to work weekends.

8 Think of a suitable comment to conclude the contributions to an online forum, using *I wish* or *If only*. Try to use a variety of tenses.

Moneytalk.com

Come on, own up! We all make mistakes with money, and we'd like you to share yours with us! (Your mistakes, not your money …)

Jed99 I'm a keen musician, and I splashed out on a guitar that, to be honest, was out of my price range. And I spent so much that I had to miss out on a camping holiday I'd been planning with my mates. I [0] *really wish I'd bought a cheaper one!*

Laura Mattock When I got a phone call supposedly from my phone company saying I still owed them 64 euros from an unpaid bill, I panicked, and paid there and then over the phone. It was only later that I realised I'd been a victim of a scam. [1] ______

WesleyLovesPresley The other day I left my jacket on the bus, with a wallet full of cash in the pocket. I got the jacket back, but guess what – not the wallet!
[2] ______

Janine2004 I can never resist a bargain, and the other day, there was a half-price offer on shoes. I think I overdid it – I bought three pairs! [3] ______

9 » **WORK IN PAIRS. TURN TO PAGE 131.**

VOCABULARY
MONEY: IDIOMS AND PHRASAL VERBS

1 **What advice have you been given about money? Do you follow the advice?**

42 **2** **Listen to the podcast about how teenagers can manage their money. Which three pieces of advice does the woman talk about, and in what order?**

A Try to become financially independent.
B Don't become a victim of online fraud.
C Only buy what you really need.
D Don't believe everything you see.

EP 42 **3** **Listen again. What do you think these expressions might mean?**

1 a false economy
2 pour money down the drain
3 daylight robbery
4 go from rags to riches
5 make ends meet
6 break the bank

4 **Complete the sentences with an expression from Exercise 3.**

1 My cousin has to do two jobs just to ________ – to feed himself and have a roof over his head.
2 Buying a cheap scooter turned out to be a ________ because it's so fuel-inefficient, so I'm probably spending more in the long run.
3 I wish I hadn't ________ by paying for a course of guitar lessons, because I've spent a fortune, but I'm not improving.
4 Don't go to the café at the airport. It's £5 for a cup of coffee – that's ________!
5 *Slumdog Millionaire* tells the story of how a young man ________ by winning a TV quiz show.
6 Getting a bike needn't ________, as you can get a second-hand one.

5 **Read the beginnings of the true stories on the right and discuss how you think each ended.**

43 **6** **Now listen to how the stories actually ended.**

EP **7** **Look at the phrasal verbs in the stories. Which phrasal verb means the following?**

1 distribute
2 become cheaper
3 save money for later
4 spend a lot of money
5 look for the best price in different places
6 inherit money from someone who has died
7 cheat someone by making them pay too much for something
8 manage to live (with a small amount of money)

8 **Complete the questions with a phrasal verb from the stories, taking care to use the correct form and word order. Then ask and answer with a partner.**

1 If someone in your class ________ a substantial amount of money, what would you advise them to do with it?
2 How easy do you find it to ________ (money) for your future?
3 Have you ever waited for the price of something to ________ before buying it? And if so, what was it and why did you wait?
4 When you buy clothes, do you ________ for bargains, or do you prefer to ________ something expensive?
5 Are there any shops or restaurants which you avoid because you feel they ________ (you)?

1 Child star Jackie Coogan, who appeared alongside Charlie Chaplin in *The Kid*, accumulated some $4 million in earnings by the age of 21. As a minor in the eyes of the law, the money was paid to his mother and stepfather, his legal guardians. But rather than **putting** it **aside** for him, they lived a life of luxury, **splashing out on** fur coats and diamonds. 'Every dollar a kid earns before he's 21 belongs to his parents,' said his stepfather. On learning that his fortune of $4 million had been squandered, Coogan sued them. In court, Coogan was ...

2 In 1919, oilman J.D. McMahon conned investors after he talked them into investing in a 480-foot (146-metre) skyscraper for the booming Texas oil town of Wichita Falls. But the architectural drawings had the scale in inches, not feet, and so a rather more modest 480-inch (12-metre), four-storey building without a lift or stairs was constructed. McMahon took the money and went on the run. Investors accused McMahon of **ripping** them **off** and sued. The judge ruled that ...

3 When eccentric millionaire Wellington Burt died in 1919, his will contained a rather unusual clause. It prevented his immediate family from **coming into** the money. Instead, his fortune was to be put into a trust fund until 21 years after the death of his youngest grandchild, and then **shared out** between 12 of his future, as yet unborn, descendants, leaving them more than enough to **get by on** for the rest of their lives. When the grandchild finally died in 1989, ...

4 An anonymous individual from England was **shopping around**, looking for a bargain in charity shops. Noticing that a yellow vase had **come down** in price to just one pound, he bought it. Not knowing about Chinese pottery, he offered it for sale on an online auction site, where it ...

WRITING

A FORMAL LETTER OR EMAIL

1 **Look at the photos. If you needed money, which of these jobs would you apply for? Why? How useful is it for students to have part-time jobs?**

2 **Match 1–7 to a–g to form phrases referring to skills and experience which employers look for. Then for each skill name a job in which that skill is particularly important.**

1 being able to perform well under	**a** sales
2 a sense of	**b** skills
3 experience of working in	**c** player
4 the ability to meet	**d** attitude
5 being a strong team	**e** humour
6 excellent communication	**f** deadlines
7 a can-do	**g** pressure

3 **Complete the tips from a careers advice website for young people by matching the headings to sections A–D.**

Educational background	Personal information
Personal statement	Work experience

Writing a successful

job application

Whether you're writing a CV of your own or completing an online application form, the sections tend to be quite similar. Here's an overview.

A .... If applicable, list your employment history, describing your main duties and responsibilities, emphasising any that are most closely related to the job you're applying for.

B .... Just include the basics, such as your name, email address and other contact details.

C .... This is a well-structured, carefully argued case that you're the right person for the job, referring to the job specification set out in the advert.

D .... Provide information on your academic achievements, including the institutions you've attended, courses taken and any qualifications gained.

4 **Complete the tips by writing *You should, There's no need to* or *Don't* or *Never* in each gap. Then add a reason.**

0 ..*You should*.. take a look at the company's social media page before you apply, because … *it will help you find out about the company.*

1 .... exaggerate or say things which aren't true in your application, because …

2 .... know what your strengths are, and write about these in your application, because …

3 .... use formal verbs, such as *demonstrated, completed, achieved* and *inspired*, because …

4 .... express yourself in a way which suggests you have an extremely high opinion of yourself, e.g. *I demonstrated my genius at an early age; my English is perfect* because …

5 .... use vague language, e.g. *I did some work in a café for a while*, because …

6 .... select appropriate examples of your achievements and skills from your past experience, because …

7 .... finish the whole application in one sitting, because …

5 **Improve these extracts from job applications by replacing the verb in *italics* with one of the formal verbs with a similar meaning from the box in the correct form.**

assist	complete	construct	demonstrate
enhance	establish	gain	inspire	launch
provide	supervise		

1 I *got* project management experience when a friend and I *started* a school newspaper.

2 When I was *looking after* a group of younger teenagers, I *did* judo coaching.

3 I *showed* strong interpersonal skills by *having* excellent relations with the elderly people I was *helping*.

4 Last year, I *did* a pool lifeguard training course, which greatly *improved* my understanding of pool safety procedures.

5 While working at a youth camp, I *got* the children to *make* their own shelters out of branches.

6 **Look at the task and discuss how you would organise your answer.**

Kids' Summer Camp – Helpers Wanted

We provide week-long Summer Outdoor Sports Camps for children aged 8–12 and need temporary staff to help with the coaching and activities. Accommodation and competitive rates of pay are provided. Experience of similar work is desirable but not essential. To apply, explain why you would like to do the job and outline how your skills and experience make you a suitable candidate.

Write your **email**.

7 **Quickly read Simon's answer through to the end. Has he fully addressed the task?**

Dear Sir or Madam,

I am writing to apply for the post of helper looking after youngsters on your summer camps. There are several aspects of the work which **(1)** *sound good / particularly appeal to me*: the outdoor activities and the opportunity for interaction with children, as I **(2)** *am considering a career in teaching / might become a teacher*. The camp would **(3)** *enable me to develop my skills in / help me get better at* managing groups of children.

I **(4)** *gained / got* relevant experience at my school tennis club **(5)** *in my role as / when I was* an assistant coach. This involved helping the head coach in organising the children into groups, watching them play and **(6)** *telling them what to do / providing instruction* in order to enable them to play **(7)** *to the best of their ability / really well*. What I learned from this was how to **(8)** *focus on the positives / talk about the good things*. For example, instead of explaining why a boy's previous shot went into the net, I would explain to him what he needed to do in order to hit it over the net next time.

In addition, for the past two years, I have worked as a childminder for some of the families in the apartment building where I live. **(9)** *Stuff I do includes / My duties include* collecting the children from pre-school and keeping them entertained until their parents arrive home from work. **(10)** *I have demonstrated that I am consistently punctual / I am always punctual* and reliable, qualities that I would bring to this role as well.

I would be delighted to have the opportunity to join your summer camp and look forward to hearing from you.

Yours faithfully,

Simon Bogart

8 **Select the *options* which would enable Simon to produce a sophisticated answer and demonstrate a wide range of grammar and vocabulary.**

9 **Complete the phrases in the *Prepare to write* box.**

PREPARE TO WRITE

A letter of application

Applying for the job

I would like to apply for the [1] ………… which was advertised …

The post would [2] ………… me to develop my skills …

I feel I would be well-suited to …

Describing skills

I am a strong [3] ………… player with a can-do [4] ………… .

I am able to work effectively [5] ………… pressure and meet [6] ………… .

I have first-hand experience of …

Signing off

I would be [7] ………… to have the opportunity to discuss my application further at an interview.

Formal verbs

assist, construct, demonstrate, enhance, inspire, provide, supervise

10 **Now write your answer to the task below in 220–260 words.**

Look at this email to students at your school from the Director of your local Tourist Information Centre.

Work experience opportunity

As part of this year's Youth Employment Week, your local tourist office is offering students a week's paid work experience. Roles are available in either our café or our visitor reception area. Apply by email to the tourist office, stating which role you are interested in and why, and describing any relevant skills and experience you have. You should also explain how the work experience would contribute to your future career plans.

Write your **email**.

LIFE SKILLS WORK SKILLS

JOB INTERVIEWS

LIFE SKILLS

Preparing for and carrying out a job interview

At some point in the next few years, you'll probably start to have interviews, either for university or for work. It's important to know how to prepare for and perform well in an interview in order to give yourself the best chance of success.

1 **Answer the questions with a partner.**

1 In some countries, teenagers have part-time jobs. What are the pros and cons of this?
2 Some universities interview students as well as looking at exam results. Why do you think they do this?
3 What is it important to do and not do before and during an interview?

2 **Read the *Top tips* for interviewers and interviewees. What two kinds of interview do they talk about?**

44

Top tips for interviewers

▶ Explain the format of the interview

The interviewee will be nervous, so try to make them feel comfortable. One way to do this is by explaining what's going to happen. For example, a typical interview starts with a short introduction to the company and job or to the university and the degree, followed by a series of questions for the interviewee and then finally some time for the interviewee to ask any questions he or she might have. If that's the format you choose, let the interviewee know before you start.

▶ Ask open-ended questions

Questions that start with 'Do you …?' or 'Have you …? and so on can be answered with a simple 'yes' or 'no'. In some cases, that's enough. However, you'll learn much more if you ask some questions that start with 'what', 'how' or 'why'. For example, if you're interviewing somebody for a history degree, then instead of asking, 'Do you like 20th century history?' ask them why they like it or how they think it should be taught in schools. If it's for a job that involves coaching a children's sports team, then after asking 'Do you have experience of working with children?' make sure you ask the interviewee *what* experience they have or *why* they like such work.

▶ Ask 'What would you do if …?' questions

When it comes to job interviews, you want to know how well the interviewee would do the job they're applying for. Therefore, think of problems they might actually encounter and ask them what they would do in such situations. For instance, returning to the example of coaching the children's sports team, you might ask, 'What would you do if two children started to fight in front of you?' or 'Imagine a child has a serious accident during a game. What would you do first?'

Top tips for interviewees

▶ Do your research

Before the day of the interview, research the company or the university you're applying for. The interviewers will expect you to know about them before you walk in the room and will be unimpressed if it becomes clear you don't know anything at all. What's more, you should also think of what kind of questions you might be asked and practise your answers beforehand, with a friend or family member if possible.

▶ Answer interview questions with examples

The interview is your chance to sell yourself. This means not just talking about your experience and abilities but also giving examples of them. For instance, if it's for a job in a primary school, don't just say, 'I've worked with children before.' Let the interviewer know when and where you worked and what the experience involved. If there's something you'd like the interviewer to know – maybe you've done first aid training, for example – but the interviewer doesn't ask you about it directly, find a way to include it in one of your answers.

▶ Have some questions of your own

Interviewers can tell who really wants a job or a place on a course and who doesn't. After they've finished asking you their questions, they'll probably say, 'Is there anything you'd like to ask us?' Make sure you have at least one or two questions that show your interest. For instance, in a job interview, 'What training will I get?' will show you're serious about doing your work well. However, don't ask questions that suggest you're lazy or don't really care, such as 'How long is the lunch break?' or 'When can I take my first holiday?'

Remember: You shouldn't take it personally if you aren't chosen for a job. Instead of thinking, 'If only I'd done this!' or 'I wish I had said that!', think of each interview as a learning experience to help you do better next time.

3 Read the *Top tips* again and say whether these statements are true (T) or false (F).

1 In a typical interview, the interviewee only answers questions.
2 Questions about hypothetical situations can help you learn about an interviewee.
3 Preparation for an interview is better done alone.
4 Examples can show why an interviewee is good for a job.
5 You shouldn't mention something about yourself unless the interviewer asks you about it.
6 Some questions can give a bad impression of the interviewee.

45 4 Listen to Jackie and Ben being interviewed for a job in a clothes shop. They've both read the *Top tips* for interviewees. Who follows most of the advice?

45 5 Listen again and answer the questions.

1 What did Jackie do in her uncle and aunt's bookshop?
2 What experience does she mention that the interviewer doesn't ask about?
3 What situation does the interviewer describe?
4 Thinking about the *Top tips*, what does Jackie's question at the end tell us?
5 What details does Ben tell the interviewer about his work in the hospital shop?
6 How is Ben's response to the situation with the angry customer different to Jackie's?
7 What does Ben fail to do?

6 With a partner, decide who should get the job and why.

7 What skills and experiences could you talk about in an interview for a job in a shop?

Project

Role play: a job interview

You are going to role-play an interview for the following job:

Funtastic SPORTS CAMPS Needs You!

We organise exciting summer camps for children and we are now hiring activity leaders for this July.

Responsibilities include:

- looking after groups of twenty to thirty children for two weeks
- leading sports and arts and craft activities
- helping with cooking and cleaning

Do you like children? Are you energetic and motivated to be part of a great team? If so, then apply today!

1 ASSIGN ROLES

In groups of four, divide into two pairs: pair A and pair B.

2 PREPARE

With your partner, prepare a list of six interviewer's questions, using the *Top tips* advice.

3 THINK

Individually, imagine you're preparing for the interview. Use the *Top tips* advice. You can invent skills and experience if necessary.

4 INTERVIEW

Pair A interviews the students from Pair B, one at a time.
Pair B interviews the students from Pair A, one at a time.
While your partner is being interviewed, listen and take notes. How well do they follow the advice?

5 DECIDE

With your partner, decide which student from the other pair gets the job.

6 FEEDBACK

Give each interviewee feedback on how well they did and how they can improve next time.

REVIEW 2 UNITS 5–8

VOCABULARY

1 Complete the article with words from the box.

advances breakthrough cutting-edge drawback prototype radical triggered

Technological [1] .... have led to virtual reality being put to a wide range of uses. However, one [2] .... when we compare VR with actual reality is that the senses of touch, taste and smell are missing. Now a major scientific [3] .... might mean that users can experience one more sense, namely touch, virtually. Researchers from Northwestern University have created a [4] .... of a device which adds touch to what VR can do. Imagine being on a video call with a loved one and being able to hold hands. This [5] .... technology makes that a reality. When you touch your screen, a response will be [6] .... on the patch worn on the other person's skin. The system, known as epidermal VR, could lead to [7] .... improvements in the lives of people who have lost arms or legs.

2 Match the sentence halves.

1 Online streaming is a new but important
2 Set in one of the most beautiful places on earth,
3 After watching the trailer,
4 Cinemas are not as full as they used to be,
5 The film-makers must have been so disappointed
6 I bought the book after reading the blurb,

a that the movie was a box-office flop.
b I decided that it wasn't my kind of film.
c except when the occasional blockbuster is showing.
d the film was an absolute masterpiece.
e source of revenue for Hollywood film-makers.
f but I was quite disappointed with the story.

3 Add a word from the box to the correct place in each sentence.

by down (x2) into out (x2)

1 Gemma splashed on several new outfits for her holiday.
2 Phones and laptops often come in price a few months after they are released.
3 I never buy bottled water. In my opinion, it's like pouring money the drain.
4 Aaron hasn't always been wealthy – he came money when his great aunt died.
5 Melinda had to take a loan to pay her university fees.
6 Ava has to get on what she earns as a delivery driver.

4 The words in blue are in the wrong sentence. Move them to the correct place.

1 Santi gets a small **support** from his grandparents to help with his university expenses.
2 Since losing her job, Pilar is really **well-off**.
3 The government gives a lot of financial **allowance** for people to start their own businesses.
4 Designer shops are **unaffordable**; the clothes aren't worth the money.
5 House prices are becoming **a rip-off**; it's impossible for young people to get on the housing ladder.
6 Sofi and Dan always eat at expensive restaurants. They must be **broke**.
7 The government is going to **withdraw** a new arts centre for the town.
8 Hold on a minute. I need to **fund** some money from the ATM.

5 Complete the article with words and phrases from the box.

adversity against all odds apparent appropriate conscious inferior overcome self-discipline thriving vulnerable

LILY RICE, WHEELCHAIR MOTOCROSS CHAMPION

Lily Rice, from Wales, is an example of someone who has succeeded [1] .... Born with a rare genetic condition, Lily is no stranger to [2] .... She has had to undergo many operations, but she has [3] .... every setback with cheerful determination. She has always been [4] .... of the need to work harder than others to achieve her goals, but has never let her disability make her feel [5] .... to others in the sporting world.

Lily started her sporting career as a Paralympic swimmer, but a few years later, she discovered the sport of Wheelchair Motocross (WCMX). It was immediately [6] .... to Lily that this was something she could be good at. However, she would need a wheelchair that was more [7] .... for the tricks involved in the sport. As luck would have it, the sport's founder, Aaron Fotheringham, had one to spare. Lily applied the same [8] .... she had always shown and started making history within a very short time. After just seven months, she became the first female in Europe to achieve a wheelchair back-flip. Lily's condition makes her more [9] .... to injury, but she tries not to spend too much time thinking about that. Lily is still [10] .... and at the very top of her sport.

GRAMMAR

1 **Choose the correct verb form. Sometimes both are correct.**

1 We *were going* / *will be going* to see the critically acclaimed film but the trailer put us off.
2 The company *will produce* / *will have produced* a prototype by the end of the year.
3 It is predicted that all vehicles *will be running* / *are running* on clean energy within about 30 years.
4 No one thought that Matt *would get* / *will get* a part in the play, but he was offered the main role.
5 What do you think you*'ll be doing* / *'re going to do* in five years' time?
6 I think people *will be stopping* / *will have stopped* using cash by the middle of the century.
7 If Victoria doesn't train harder, she *will suffer* / *will be suffering* a major defeat.
8 We*'re going to see* / *will see* the highly anticipated new Tarantino movie, which is out tomorrow.

2 **Complete the sentences with the verb in brackets in the correct form: *-ing* or *to* + infinitive.**

1 Matias claims .... well-off but I don't see how he can be. (be)
2 Camila denied .... unable to make ends meet. (be)
3 American swimmer Michael Phelps is famous for .... the most gold medals at the Olympics. (win)
4 Did you remember .... the money from the bank? We'll need it today. (withdraw)
5 Unfortunately, the council has stopped .... the annual film festival. (fund)
6 We were disappointed .... the film had been a box-office flop. (hear)
7 You really can't afford .... on unnecessary things. (splash out)
8 .... a new product takes a major effort from the entire team. (launch)

3 **Correct any mistakes in these sentences. Some are correct. The type of conditional is given in brackets.**

1 If there would be less negativity in the club, I might have become a member. (mixed)
2 If products were marketed properly, they tend to sell better. (zero)
3 The film would have been a blockbuster if Kate Winslet plays the main character. (third)
4 If I won a million euros, I would share it out among my friends and family. (second)
5 You might find that bag at a more reasonable price if you will shop around. (first)
6 James wouldn't be broke if he hadn't wasted all his money on that holiday. (mixed)
7 The product will be more successful if they had put more time and money into the prototype. (third)
8 If Monica weren't so hostile towards her rivals, she will probably enjoy the tournaments more. (second)

4 **Read the text below and think of the word which best fits each gap. Use only one word in each gap.**

A CASHLESS FUTURE?

The development of contactless payments has meant a steep decline in the number of payments made in cash. Many believed that security issues would prevent contactless from catching **(0)** *on*, but that wasn't the case. While it may seem as though a cashless future lies **(1)** ...., that is unlikely to happen for many years. 'If we abandoned cash completely, it **(2)** .... certainly put the most vulnerable at risk,' says economist Poppy Everett. Banker Amal Rodrigo agrees that rushing **(3)** .... a cashless world could be a disaster for the poorest members of society.

Many elderly people are afraid of **(4)** .... left behind by technology in a world moving faster than they could ever **(5)** .... imagined. In some rural areas, too, credit and debit cards are **(6)** .... upon with suspicion, especially by those who were brought up **(7)** .... believe that being in debt is somehow immoral.

The change will be gradual. It is predicted that technology-based companies will lead the way and **(8)** .... well have stopped accepting cash by the end of the decade.

5 **Complete the second sentence so that it has a similar meaning to the first sentence, using the word given. Do not change the word given. You must use between three and six words, including the word given.**

0 'I would love to be able to borrow some money from the bank,' Mark said. **TAKE**
'If only *I could take out a loan,*' Mark said.
1 Roland was unsure of his next steps. **GOING**
Roland didn't .... do next.
2 They will make the roads wider within the next ten years. **BEEN**
The roads .... end of the decade.
3 I only decided to buy an electric car because it's environmentally friendly. **TAKEN**
I .... to buy an electric car if it hadn't been environmentally friendly.
4 Do you think it is useful to ask the public for their opinion? **VALUE**
Is there .... the public for their opinion?
5 I regret buying a new phone so quickly. **RUSHED**
I wish .... a new phone.
6 We moved here a year ago next Friday. **LIVING**
Next Friday we .... exactly one year.

9 EDUCATING GENERATION Z

? ABOUT YOU

▶ 09 **Watch the video and then answer the questions.**
What other subjects or skills would you have liked to be taught in school, apart from the usual ones?
Do you know about any very unusual schools? Would you have liked to attend one?
What do you think about schools where the students themselves choose what to study?

VOCABULARY AND READING
EDUCATION

EP **1 Match the definitions to the words and phrases in the box.**

aspirations | career path | careers advice | critical thinking | internship | leadership | networking | scholarship | social skills | trainee

1 building up and maintaining contacts with people who may help you in your professional life
2 a person who is in the process of being trained for a specific job
3 the act of leading a group of people
4 hopes, dreams, goals and ambitions of an individual in his or her life
5 the ability to think independently and not accept everything you are told
6 work experience, often unpaid
7 the development of an employee in his or her profession
8 advice given to young people on careers which may be suited to their skills and interests and how to enter them
9 money given to a student to allow them to study at a particular school or university, often dependent on their ability
10 the ability to behave in a socially appropriate manner and interact with others in an acceptable way

2 Are the words in the box in Exercise 1 associated with school/university, with work or with both?

3 Complete the sentences with a word or phrase from Exercise 1.

1 Alistair was really happy to get a job as a ________ hairdresser in his local salon.
2 Whatever field of work you are in, ________ is vital, as the more people you know, the better.
3 Without ________, you won't get very far in life. Everyone needs to have positive relationships with others.
4 It is easier to get a ________ to an American university than a British one as they tend to have more money available to help less well-off students.
5 When I was at school, we didn't really get much ________. Most people just went out and got whatever job they could find.
6 Many young people now want to be YouTubers rather than following a more traditional ________.
7 The ability to make crucial decisions and communicate effectively are essential ________ skills in the modern workplace.
8 There is a lot of fake news on the internet these days, which is why it is so important for young people to develop ________ skills.
9 One way of building up your CV is to do an ________. You may not get paid, but it can give you an advantage later on.
10 Schools should help students to raise their ________ as that is the first step on the road to success.

4 Look at the title of the article on the opposite page. Would you answer the question Yes or No? Why? Compare your ideas with a student who answered differently.

5 Read the article quickly. Which of your points were mentioned?

6 Read the article more carefully and answer the questions.

1 What non-academic reasons does the YES! writer give for the importance of children going to school?
2 What changes does the writer mention in terms of
 a the school curriculum?
 b teaching methods?
3 What is the opinion of the YES! writer on the careers advice given in schools?
4 What systemic problems does the NO! writer blame for schools not preparing students for work?
5 What should schools be doing, according to the NO! writer?
6 According to the NO! writer, how could schools improve the careers advice they give to students?
7 Is there anything the writers of the two texts agree on?

7 Discuss the questions with a partner.

1 Who do you agree with more, the YES! or the NO! writer?
2 Does your school prepare you for the workplace?

DO SCHOOLS PREPARE YOU FOR WORK?

46

YES!

Going to school has always had a vital purpose outside of the subjects studied and exams passed, which is to impart social skills to young people, allowing them to play a positive role in society. Even back in the days of memorising facts, schools prepared you for work by teaching you basic language and maths skills and also things like punctuality, discipline and consideration of others. All of these are still relevant today – the workplace may be changing but there are still rules to follow. Schools still do an excellent job at instilling a good work ethic in students. While the family is their earliest influence, it is at school that they get to associate with different kinds of people and resolve any issues they may have.

Having said that, I do think schools have moved on. The curriculum today looks very different from when our parents were at school. My mum did cooking and needlework, while my dad did woodwork and metalwork. Nowadays, both genders do design and technology with options such as electronics, textiles and graphics. Schools focus on 21st century skills, such as critical thinking, media literacy and taking the initiative. Even with traditional subjects, students are likely to be asked to work as a group to research and give presentations. What this does is help them develop skills needed in the workplace, such as leadership and collaboration.

In many countries, it is now a legal requirement for students to be provided with independent career advice. Schools see it as their role to raise aspirations and help learners achieve their full potential. Many partnerships exist between schools and workplaces, and it is the students who benefit most as they get the opportunity to do internships in the holidays. In return, managers come into school to talk about career paths and how to develop the skills they are looking for. The days when schools only focused on academic pathways are long gone. Each student is viewed as an individual with their own unique set of talents.

NO!

Generation Z – those born in the last few years of the 20th century and first decade of the 21st – were born into a different world to those tasked with educating them. Schools don't prepare these young people for the complex working world they will enter. The blame doesn't lie with the schools themselves and certainly not with the teachers, for whom I have great admiration. It is the system which is responsible for this disconnect between schools and workplaces. What I mean is that governments have become obsessed with exam results, meaning that developing really useful skills has to take a back seat. Teachers are often under a lot of pressure to complete an over-long syllabus, resulting in a return to traditional 'lecture style' lessons rather than a more useful discovery-style methodology. This is the opposite of what students need to prepare them for working life.

Another issue is that the system forces students to make choices at a young age and labels them as 'academic' or 'practical' sometimes as young as 12. What schools should do is develop their students' flexibility; this is what employers need in our rapidly changing world. Similarly, schools are still organised along very traditional lines, with a series of bells dictating when to move on to the next timetabled lesson. This means that students don't learn to self-organise or prioritise – key workplace skills.

While governments have taken steps to ensure teenagers get career guidance, this is often done simply to fulfil government requirements. Schools simply don't have the time or resources to provide meaningful and individualised advice. They could, for example, make use of psychometric testing, which evaluates each individual's aptitude, preferences and potential. They could also use assessment centres, where students can spend a whole day taking part in a range of tasks to help them to identify where their skills lie. What actually happens is that the focus of the careers sessions is university applications and how to get scholarships. There needs to be more focus on getting students networking with potential employers, hopefully leading to a trainee position when they leave school.

TALKING POINTS

If you were designing a school curriculum for today, what would/wouldn't be on the curriculum?
How would the school day/week/year look different?
What kind of careers advice would be available?

GRAMMAR
CLEFT SENTENCES

1 Look at the two cleft sentences from the article and the non-cleft versions. What is the difference between them in terms of meaning and structure?

1 *Cleft:* What schools should do is develop their students' flexibility.
Non-cleft: Schools should develop their students' flexibility.

2 *Cleft:* It is at school that they get to associate with different kinds of people.
Non-cleft: At school they get to associate with different kinds of people.

2 Match example sentences 1–5 to rules a–e.

1 It's the students who suffer when the curriculum keeps changing.
2 What impresses me most is the students' work ethic.
3 What my brother decided to do was to apply for a scholarship.
4 It was for the sake of her career that she moved to Milan.
5 What students need to do is visit as many universities as possible.

We form cleft sentences with:
a *what* clause + verb + *is/was* + noun phrase
b *what* clause + verb + *is/was* + infinitive without *to*
c *what* clause + verb + *is/was* + *to* + infinitive
d *it* + *is/was* + noun phrase + relative clause
e *it* + *is/was* + adverbial phrase + relative clause

» **GRAMMAR REFERENCE AND PRACTICE PAGE 152**

3 Change these examples of cleft sentences into non-cleft sentences.

1 It is the system which is responsible for this disconnect between schools and workplaces.
2 What this does is help them develop skills needed in the workplace, such as leadership and collaboration.
3 It is the students who benefit most as they get the opportunity to do internships in the holidays.

4 Complete the sentences with *It* or *What*.

1 .... this school excels in is developing critical thinking.
2 .... upsets me most is that tuition fees are going up.
3 .... is Sarah I went to school with, not her sister, Rachel.
4 .... was his poor maths result that stopped him graduating.
5 .... I believe is that education matters, because without it, countries can't develop.
6 .... is the Minister of Education who is responsible for our increased workload.
7 .... the government needs to do is to give more support to schools.

5 Rewrite the sentences, emphasising the underlined information. Start each sentence with the word in brackets.

0 Tom got the highest mark in the class. (It)
It was Tom who got the highest mark in the class.
1 Lack of education is the leading cause of poverty in most countries. (It)
2 Toby desperately wanted to become a police officer. (What)
3 I loved singing in the choir most when I was at school. (What)
4 Businesses should pay for educating the workforce of the future. (It)
5 If you can read this, you should thank teachers. (It)
6 The lack of funding for special education annoys me most. (What)
7 Its excellent education system led to Singapore's success. (What)
8 In the UK, most polytechnic colleges became universities in 1992. (It)

6 Correct any mistakes in these sentences. Some are correct.

1 It was John what suggested running the course on Saturdays.
2 What Robbie said was he prefers this class to his last one.
3 What we should do arrange a meeting with the headteacher.
4 Is it parents who need to encourage their children.
5 What work best is allowing students to choose their own project.
6 It made me choose the school was its exam results.
7 It was Davide came late today, not Ariel.
8 It's by writing things down that I learn best.

7 Complete the cleft sentences so that they are true for you.

1 What I'd love to do most after high school is ....
2 It is .... that I find most difficult at school.
3 It is .... who helps me most with my studies.
4 What schools should do to help students is ....
5 What annoys me most in life is ....

8 Share your ideas from Exercise 7 with a partner. Ask him or her follow up questions. Try to expand your answers using cleft sentences where appropriate.

Example
A: *What would you love to do most after high school?*
B: *Well, what I'd love to do is to go to university in another country.*
A: *Which country?*
B: *Maybe the States, but what I'd really love to do first is to spend a year travelling around Asia.*

VOCABULARY

EDUCATION: PHRASAL VERBS

47 **1 Listen to a girl called Francesca talking about a term she spent at a boarding school in the UK. Answer the questions.**

1 What problems did she have?
2 How did she feel when she left the school?

EP 47 **2 Listen again and complete what Francesca says with the phrasal verbs you hear.**

When my parents decided to send me to school in the UK for a term, I had a really hard time. It was half way through the year and I didn't know how I would be able to [1] ________ with the other students. For one thing, the way of learning was quite different from my country. We would often be asked to [2] ________ a topic before the next lesson but back home we were always told exactly what to do. Then there were so many assignments to do that I was always forgetting to [3] ________ my work. And also teachers didn't spend much time [4] ________ the work in the next lesson, so we didn't really get a chance to learn from our mistakes. Added to all this, my English was not too good and I realised that I was [5] ________. To be honest, I didn't think I had any chance of [6] ________ the end of term exams and I was very tempted to [7] ________. But, to my amazement, I passed every subject and was actually sad when we finally [8] ________ for Christmas.

3 Match the phrasal verbs you wrote in Exercise 2 to the definitions in the box.

finish the term   leave before the end
not do well enough   reach the same point
pass   research   review   submit

Example
1 reach the same point

EDUCATION: VERB AND NOUN COLLOCATIONS

EP 48 **4 Listen to part of a headteacher's talk to students who are hoping to go to university and complete the summary with verbs which collocate with the nouns in bold.**

The headteacher is talking to the students about [1] ________ their **applications** to universities. She advises them to try and [2] ________ a **visit** to a few of them. Going to the universities will help students to [3] ________ an **understanding** of campus life. Some students may have [4] ________ themselves the **goal** of entering a high-ranking university, which [5] ________ very high **standards** for its students. Students should only apply if they are likely to [6] ________ the **requirements** of the course they want to do. The headteacher believes that if the students work hard, they can [7] ________ their **dreams**. She moves on to talk about ways in which students may [8] ________ their **fees**.

5 Choose the incorrect or least likely option.

1 University is a good opportunity to gain *understanding of* / *insight into* / *a goal of* / *experience of* different ways of life.
2 Students need to submit their *essays* / *requirements* / *homework* / *proposals* by the end of this week.
3 I have every confidence that I will be able to fulfil my *ambition* / *goal* / *dream* / *want* of becoming an engineer.
4 Unfortunately, Pete's parents were unable to pay *fees* / *understanding* / *attention* / *a visit*.
5 It is important for teachers to set *homework* / *standards* / *applications* / *goals* for their students.

6 Read the text below and decide which answer (A, B, C or D) best fits each gap.

DYSLEXIA

Dyslexia is a specific learning difficulty in which people find reading and writing challenging. All teachers need to **(0)** *B* attention to the children in their care in order to identify the condition. They should look out for students who are **(1)** ________ behind in class. Before being diagnosed, children might avoid **(2)** ________ in homework, in an attempt to hide their difficulties. In the past, a high percentage of dyslexic students would have **(3)** ________ out of school, but now we know that, with the right support, dyslexic students are just as likely as any other students to excel.

Teachers in mainstream schools have gained an **(4)** ________ of the condition over the past few decades and now the majority of students with dyslexia are able to **(5)** ________ through their exams and finish high school. Teachers who work with dyslexic students have over time gained **(6)** ________ of what works best for them. Also, governments have set **(7)** ________ for the amount of support they must be given, including extra time in exams. There is no reason why anyone with dyslexia can't achieve any **(8)** ________ they set themselves.

	A	B	C	D
0	gain	(B) pay	get	have
1	falling	going	coming	catching
2	doing	setting	submitting	handing
3	walked	dropped	left	broken
4	admission	acceptance	understanding	opinion
5	pass	make	get	go
6	insight	experience	intelligence	information
7	standards	marks	opinions	beliefs
8	proposal	dream	requirement	goal

7 >> WORK IN PAIRS. TURN TO PAGE 131.

LISTENING

1 **Read this introduction to an article about an alternative school in the USA. Do you have any schools like this in your country?**

Community High School of Arts and Academics in Roanoke, Virginia was founded by a group of parents who were frustrated by the limitations of the national curriculum. They wanted their children to become independent learners who could follow their own interests rather than studying a pre-defined course. The students' and teachers' passions have a great influence on what is studied, and students' work is not graded.

2 **Read questions 1 and 2. Identify the key words in the questions and options. Note down some synonyms for them.**

You hear two friends talking about the alternative school in Exercise 1.

1 How does the boy feel about students influencing the curriculum?
- **A** He is confident it would be popular with all the students.
- **B** He is sure that all students would choose the same subjects.
- **C** He is unconvinced that it would work in practice.

2 How would both speakers feel about having no grades?
- **A** It may put some students at a disadvantage.
- **B** It would be harder to enter higher education.
- **C** It would take the pressure off the students.

49 **3** **Listen once. For questions 1 and 2, choose the answer (A, B or C) which fits best according to what you hear. Discuss your answers with a partner.**

49 **4** **Listen again and check your answers.**

5 **Read the extract from the audioscript. Discuss why each of the incorrect answers for questions 1 and 2 is wrong.**

Girl: Did you read the article about the school in Virginia which doesn't teach the normal curriculum? Apparently, students can study whatever they're interested in.

Boy: But what happens if they're all interested in different things?

Girl: Well, I suppose it's by consensus – like what the majority want to study. It sounds quite democratic, doesn't it?

Boy: Yes. I like the sound of that. Though what I'd want would be to study music every lesson, but I don't expect that would appeal to everyone. What if the rest of the class liked history or something that wasn't relevant to your personal career goals?

Girl: Well, I think it would be good if all schools and students agreed with them about not giving grades. School would be a lot less stressful and more fun.

Boy: It's not about enjoying yourself, is it? I mean how do the students compete with those from other schools when it comes to jobs and college admissions?

Girl: They prepare them for the SATs – you know, the university admission tests – but I'm not so sure about those who want to do something else after high school.

50 **6** **You hear two friends discussing a geography assignment. Listen twice and answer questions 3 and 4. Discuss your answers with a partner. Explain why the other options are wrong.**

3 What is the girl's biggest problem with the assignment?
- **A** finding evidence from her own experience
- **B** learning the technical terms for parts of the river
- **C** getting the assignment finished by the deadline

4 Why does the boy mention the field trip?
- **A** to let the girl know what she had missed
- **B** to tell the girl he has enough information
- **C** to explain how it helped with the work on rivers

51 **7** **You hear two friends who have met after a long time. Listen twice and answer questions 5 and 6.**

5 What is the woman's attitude to her school days?
- **A** She remembers them with affection.
- **B** She regrets her bad behaviour.
- **C** She is very glad they are over.

6 What do they agree about their experience of school in general?
- **A** It was easy to play tricks on their teachers.
- **B** Some aspects of school were good fun.
- **C** Their teachers were extremely dull.

8 **Discuss the questions with a partner.**

1. Would you like to go to an 'alternative' school like the one in Roanoke? Why? / Why not?
2. Have you ever been on a field trip? Do you think they are a good way to learn?
3. How do you think you will look back on your schooldays?

SPEAKING
TALKING ABOUT YOURSELF

1 What do you think is happening in the photo?

2 What type of things might you talk about when you meet new people? Discuss with a partner.

52 **3** Listen to four people answering questions about themselves. Do they talk about any of the topics you mentioned?

4 Read Marisol's answer. Find examples of the following:

1 expressions to gain thinking time
2 linking words and expressions
3 complex sentence structures
4 advanced vocabulary and collocations
5 fluency markers, for example *in fact*, *on the whole*, *you see*
6 organising the response

> Well, there are lots of positive aspects to my home town, so it's quite hard to choose just one. But, if I had to, I'd say I like the main square best. Why I say that is that there are lots of cafés and restaurants where you can meet your friends and relax. Another thing is that, architecturally, the square is stunning, with a lovely fountain in the middle. Actually, people go there just to chill out and there's a great atmosphere. So that's the reason it's my favourite thing about my town.

5 Discuss with a partner which of the following can be a challenge when you are speaking English.

a understanding the other speaker's pronunciation
b understanding the other speaker's fast speech
c the other speaker's use of difficult or colloquial language
d not being able to think of the word I need on the spot
e not having the specific vocabulary to express exactly what I want to say
f not being able to think and speak fast enough
g my pronunciation or grammar
h thinking of relevant ideas
i other

6 Why do you think you have the difficulties you discussed in Exercise 5? What possible solutions can you think of?

53 **7** Listen to three students answering a question each. What questions do you think they were asked?

53 **8** Listen again. What difficulties did the students have? What solutions did they use?

53 **9** Look at the *Prepare to speak* box. Can you remember any phrases from the students' answers? Add them to the correct category. Then listen again and check.

PREPARE TO SPEAK

Overcoming problems

Asking for repetition
Sorry, I didn't catch that. Could you say it again?
Sorry, could you [1] .... ?
Would you mind repeating the question?
Sorry, what was that?

Trying to gain time
Mm, I haven't really thought about that before.
Mm, well that's an [2] ....
Hmm, let me think about that.
... there are a few other [3] .... about this.

Paraphrasing
What would [4] .... ?
... one of those things you use for ...ing
... things that ...
... the/a person who ...
It's when people/you ...
It's something like ... / something which ...
It's what you do when ...

10 With a partner, ask and answer these questions from Exercise 7.

1 Do you often use the internet for your studies?
2 How important do you think it is to speak another language?
3 Do you think school trips are a valuable way to learn?

11 » **WORK IN PAIRS.** **STUDENT A, TURN TO PAGE 131. STUDENT B, TURN TO PAGE 132.**

12 Work in pairs. Prepare answers to *your* questions only. How will you structure your answers? Note down the vocabulary and linkers you will use.

Student A
1 Do you prefer academic or practical subjects? Why?
2 What do you enjoy most about going to school?
3 What do you hope to be doing in five years' time?
4 Which extra-curricular activity would you like to introduce to your school? Why?

Student B
1 How do you use technology in your studies?
2 What extra-curricular activities do you do at school?
3 Who helps you most with your studies?
4 What subject would you add to your school's curriculum if you could? Why?

13 Ask and answer the questions with your partner. Try to use the phrases from the *Prepare to speak* box.

10 CRIME AND PUNISHMENT

? ABOUT YOU

▶ 10 **Watch the video and then answer the questions.**
Why do you think some people end up committing crimes?
Are there any 'crimes' which you think aren't serious enough to be classed as crimes at all?
Why are TV series about criminals so popular?

VOCABULARY AND READING
PUNISHMENT FOR CRIME

EP **1 Select the most suitable headline for each news story.**

Burglar found not guilty   Fake phantom fined
Suspect released and all charges dropped
World's stupidest criminal

1 27-year-old Nicholas Wig has been **charged with** burglary after he broke into an empty house in Minnesota and logged onto his Facebook page on the property owner's computer. He then stole a number of items and left the house, forgetting to log out of Facebook. He was **arrested on suspicion of** burglary following a phone call from the victim. If **found guilty of** the offence, he could be **sentenced to** up to ten years in prison and ordered to **pay damages** to his victim.

2 24-year-old Anthony Stallard from Portsmouth, UK was **reported to** the police when he was seen waving his arms around and shouting 'woooooo' in a cemetery. He **pleaded guilty to** behaviour which was likely to cause distress, and was **issued with** a £35 penalty. Mr Stallard is believed to be the first person to be **prosecuted for** pretending to be a ghost.

2 Check the meaning of the words and phrases in Exercise 1.

3 Complete the questions with a verb from Exercise 1 in the correct form.

1 If you saw someone you know breaking into a house, would you ______ them to the police?
2 Should police officers be allowed to use force when they are ______ someone for a violent offence?
3 For what offences can people be ______ with a fine in your country, and how common is this?
4 Should a fifty-year-old man be ______ for a crime that he committed as a 25-year-old, or should he be let off?
5 If a person ______ guilty in court to the crime that they've been ______ with, should their punishment be less severe?
6 Should criminals be allowed to ______ damages to their victim in order to avoid being ______ to a term in prison?

4 With a partner, ask and answer the questions in Exercise 3.

5 What is happening in the pictures? How serious are these issues? What can be done about them? Should they be considered crimes?

A

B

C

D

6 Quickly read the article on the opposite page about an approach to tackling crime. Which of the offences shown in pictures A–D is mentioned? What reason is given for handing out severe punishments for minor offences?

7 Read the article again. For questions 1–6, choose the answer (A, B, C or D) which you think fits best according to the text.

1 The writer suggests the subway incident described in the first paragraph shows
A how carefully supervised night-time transport is.
B how badly some people behave in public.
C how excessive police actions can sometimes seem.
D how little awareness there is of certain regulations.

2 What were the New York authorities said to have done to Mr Castillo?
A accused him of a crime he was innocent of
B put his health at risk without justification
C given him a long prison sentence
D fined him an unreasonable amount of money

3 What does 'go after' mean in paragraph 3?
A follow behind   **C** arrest
B try to catch   **D** charge

BROKEN WINDOWS

– a theory of crime

It was 4 am and the downtown subway was almost empty when the man in the blue coat reclined and nodded off to sleep. Little did he know at the time that this would land him in trouble with the law. As the train passed through Brooklyn, a tap on the shoulder woke him up. It was a police officer. The man had fallen asleep lying across two seats, and that, according to the police officer, was a crime, for which he was now being arrested. Not only was he detained for the next 12 hours, but he was also issued with a fine before being released. And all that for a petty violation, which would have merely been considered bad manners were it not for Rule 1050(7)(J) of the city's transit code – sitting improperly on a subway seat.

However, the law doesn't always side with the police. A diabetic called Juan Castillo filed a case against New York City when he found himself charged with the same offence while riding the subway to work in Manhattan. Mr Castillo had lifted his leg onto a seat to give himself the injection of insulin that his condition made necessary. Not for one moment did he imagine that this simple act would lead to a criminal charge. However, police officers arrested and imprisoned him, denying him access to the medication which he needed for his diabetes. The court ruled that under no circumstances should the police have withheld Mr Castillo's medication, and that in doing so, they had endangered his life. Mr Castillo was awarded $150,000 in damages. Other police prosecutions have done little to win over the hearts and minds of New York's population, such as the case of 55-year-old dentist Caroline Stern and her boyfriend, George Hess, 54, arrested on a subway platform in July. 'We were dancing,' said Stern. 'That's it.'

Observers may well wonder just what the New York Police are playing at, by pursuing such minor offences. Is it an attempt to massage the crime figures by making needless arrests to hit their targets? Don't they have any real criminals to go after? In actual fact, the zero-tolerance approach to policing New York's subway over recent decades has its basis in one of the most influential sociology theories of the twentieth century – the Broken Windows Theory, a concept put forward by the criminologists James Wilson and George Kelling. They argued that if, for example, a window is broken and left unrepaired, people walking by will conclude that no-one cares about the damage, and no-one is in charge. This in turn leads to more buildings being vandalised; a sense of lawlessness spreads from the building to the street onto which it faces, and gradually to the surrounding area. This effectively becomes an invitation to further anti-social or criminal behaviour. It is an epidemic theory of crime, arguing that criminality is infectious and can spread from a simple broken window to an entire community.

Wilson and Kelling's theory has been applied in many urban areas around the world. Only when you take care of the minor crimes can you hope to have success in dealing with the major ones, claimed a former New York City police chief. And he may be on to something. When 19-year-old Kyron Hornsey was reported to the police and subsequently arrested on suspicion of occupying a number of seats on the subway, he was taken to the police station. There, officers recognised his face from a wanted poster, and he was charged with a number of robberies. Not until he broke subway seating laws had officers finally been able to catch him. He was tried in court for robbery, found guilty of six offences, and sentenced to a year's imprisonment.

But by no means is everyone convinced that the scheme is working. Critics have alleged that in many cases, police officers who make arrests for these minor offences are driven by the prospect of overtime pay for dealing with the paperwork following the arrest. This was hardly the reason for which the police crackdown against the rule-breakers was introduced. Many of the arrests were made by the police's homeless outreach unit, although their focus is supposed to be on getting more homeless people off the streets and into shelters. Before law-makers around the world try to imitate New York's zero-tolerance approach, they ought to bear this in mind.

4 What point does the theory described at the end of the third paragraph make about broken windows?
- **A** They can lead to an atmosphere where crime flourishes.
- **B** Buildings which have them tend to be dangerous places.
- **C** As soon as they are mended, they are likely to be smashed again.
- **D** Many people may wish to move away from a neighbourhood which has them.

5 The arrest of Kyron Hornsey is mentioned to illustrate how
- **A** criminals often use the subway when going to commit a crime.
- **B** police activity on the subway is failing to reduce overall crime figures.
- **C** the police frequently recognise wanted suspects when they are riding the subway.
- **D** people detained over minor subway offences may well be responsible for more serious crimes.

6 Opponents of the zero-tolerance approach to subway policing say that
- **A** police officers find it hard to keep up with the documentation.
- **B** the result is likely to be an increase in homelessness.
- **C** the police officers are not paid for the extra work resulting from the arrests.
- **D** some arresting officers may have hidden motives.

TALKING POINTS

To what extent do you think arresting someone for putting their feet on a train seat is justified?
If there was no other litter in the street, would you drop the first piece? If the street was full of litter, might you add to it?
How convincing do you think the Broken Windows Theory is?

GRAMMAR
INVERSION

1 Match 1–6 to a–f to make sentences from the article.

1 **Little** did he know at the time that this
2 **Not only** was he detained for the next 12 hours,
3 **Not for one moment** did he imagine that
4 **Under no circumstances** should the police have withheld
5 **Not until** he broke subway seating laws
6 **Only when** you take care of the minor crimes

a Mr Castillo's medication.
b this simple act would lead to a criminal charge.
c but he was also issued with a fine.
d can you hope to have success in dealing with the major ones.
e had officers finally been able to catch him.
f would land him in trouble with the law.

2 Compare these versions of the sentences with those in Exercise 1. How are they different?

1 He didn't know that this would land him in trouble with the law.
2 He was detained for the next 12 hours and issued with a fine.
3 He never imagined that this simple act would lead to a criminal charge.
4 The police shouldn't have withheld Mr Castillo's medication.
5 Officers had only been able to catch him after he broke subway seating laws.
6 Authorities can only have success in dealing with major crimes when they take care of the minor ones.

3 Find and underline the subjects, the auxiliary verbs and the verbs in the sentences in Exercise 1. How are the sentences beginning *Not until* and *Only when* different from the others?

4 Complete the rules with one of the options in brackets.

1 Inversion can be used in order to ________ the point being made. (*emphasise / question*)
2 Inversion is often used after words and phrases with a ________ meaning: *No way; Under no circumstances; Never; Not only* and so on. (*negative / positive*)
3 Inversion can also be used after words with a ________ meaning e.g. *Little; Rarely*. (*limiting / positive*)
4 Inversion usually makes sentences more ________. (*informal / formal*)
5 When you use *Only when* and ________, the verb in the second clause is inverted. (*Not only / Not until*)

» GRAMMAR REFERENCE AND PRACTICE PAGE 153

5 Complete sentences 1–7 by adding phrases a–g. Then discuss whether or not you agree with the statements and say why.

1 Little ________ how much suffering their behaviour causes.
2 Only when a criminal has been punished ________ to stop breaking the law.
3 Under no circumstances ________ to adult prisons; they should go to a young offenders' institution instead.
4 Not only ________, but they are also ineffective, as they provide opportunities for criminals to network.
5 Only when they increase the length of prison sentences ________ reduce the rate of serious crime.
6 Rarely ________ their mindset while in prison; most will reoffend once they are released.
7 No way ________ in a prison; it's too dangerous.

a are they likely
b do criminals change
c should teenagers be sent
d will governments be able to
e do most criminals care about
f are prisons expensive to run
g would I want a job

6 Rewrite the sentences so that the meaning is the same.

0 I'm rarely so shocked when reading about a crime.
Rarely *am I so shocked when reading about a crime*.
1 There's no way I'd ever steal something from a shop.
No way ________
2 You won't mend your ways until you've spent time in prison.
Not until ________
3 The murderer should not be released from prison under any circumstances.
Under no circumstances ________
4 He had four convictions for shoplifting, and he'd spent time in prison for assault.
Not only ________
5 We didn't realise that one of our classmates would become a notorious criminal.
Little ________
6 The old lady will only feel truly safe when the robber is behind bars.
Only when ________

7 Correct any mistakes in these sentences. Some are correct.

1 No way can be she guilty.
2 Not until have you been a victim of a crime yourself do you know how horrible it can feel.
3 Little did anyone realise that the grandmother of eleven was an accomplished bank robber?
4 Never has it been easier for criminals to commit online fraud.
5 With no circumstances should you touch anything at the scene of a crime.
6 Not only Cañon City, Colorado, USA have 13 prisons, but it also has a prison museum.
7 Rarely do people get tried twice for the same crime.

8 » WORK IN PAIRS. TURN TO PAGE 131.

VOCABULARY

CRIME AND PUNISHMENT: COLLOCATIONS

55 **1 Listen to two friends talking about a judge. Are the following sentences true, false or not stated?**

1 Judge Cicconetti specialised in trying people for major offences.
2 Judge Cicconetti issued punishments that he felt fitted the crime a person had committed.
3 The man is in favour of Judge Cicconetti's approach.

EP **2 Which one or two of the words on the right can be used with the words on the left to make collocations?**

0 organised	*crime* / ~~*offender*~~ / ~~*service*~~
1 petty	*crime* / *service* / *theft*
2 jail	*punishment* / *sentence* / *theft*
3 minor	*crime* / *offence* / *service*
4 light	*punishment* / *sentence* / *theft*
5 repeat	*offence* / *offender*/ *service*
6 community	*crime* / *offender* / *service*

55 **3 Listen again. Tick the collocations in Exercise 2 that the speakers use.**

4 Complete the blog with suitable collocations from Exercise 2.

People found guilty of [1] .... shouldn't be sent to prison if it's their first conviction. For example, if someone has committed a [2] ...., such as stealing a snack from a supermarket, they should be made to do [3] .... This could be something like picking up litter in a public park. This form of justice makes financial sense for society at large since whenever a judge issues a criminal with a [4] ...., the cost of locking them up is so high that it's just not worth it. The money could more usefully be spent on putting more police officers on the streets.

However, I think that for gang members involved in [5] ...., such as human trafficking and the illegal drugs trade, authorities should adopt a zero-tolerance approach. It is absurd for gangsters to be given [6] .... such as a fine, or a suspended prison sentence, meaning that they don't go to prison at all. If the criminal justice system was tough on them, perhaps they would learn their lesson, and there wouldn't be so many [7] .... who commit the same crimes again and again.

5 In groups, discuss to what extent you agree with the opinions in Exercise 4, and why.

CRIME: SUFFIXES

6 Complete the sentences with the words in the box. Then match 1–4 to a–d to see what punishments Judge Cicconetti gave to these offenders.

burglary cruelty theft vandalism

1 High school students who let down tyres on school buses were ordered to
2 A teenager found guilty of the .... of a bicycle was instructed to
3 A woman convicted of .... to animals after abandoning 35 kittens in a snowy wood was made to
4 A man who broke into someone's home was forced to

a attend a therapy session for victims of domestic ....
b spend ten days cycling to raise money for a local charity.
c organise a picnic for youngsters whose outing had been cancelled due to their act of ....
d spend a night alone in a forest.

EP **7 Complete the table. Most of the words have been used in this unit.**

Noun (thing/ activity)	Noun (person)	Verb	Adjective
1	burglar	burgle	–
2	criminal, criminologist	(de)criminalise	3
4	–	–	cruel
5	6	offend	7
8	prisoner	9	–
10	shoplifter	11	–
12	thief	13	–
14	vandal	15	–

8 In pairs, invent details 1–7 about one of the offenders below. Then swap your details with another pair and design an appropriate Cicconetti-style punishment to fit their crime and complete line 8 of the form.

1 Name: ....
2 Age: ....
3 Reason for arrest: ....
4 Scene of alleged crime: ....
5 Previous criminal history: ....
6 Who their victim was: ....
7 How their victim has suffered: ....
8 Punishment: ....

WRITING
AN ESSAY

1 Discuss the questions.

1. Which places in your area, city or country do you think have the highest rates of crime?
2. How often do you see police officers on the street in your area, and do you think there are enough? Why? / Why not?
3. Do you know of any measures being taken in your area to reduce rates of crime?
4. Do you think it's better for the authorities to be tough on crime or more relaxed?

2 Look at the essay task and discuss these questions.

- What are the advantages and disadvantages of the three suggested approaches to reducing crime?
- To what extent do you agree with the three opinions expressed, and why?

Your class has been discussing a newspaper article about ways to reduce crime in cities. You have made the notes below.

Ways to reduce crime in cities:
- increase police numbers
- educate about consequences of crime
- better local facilities

Some opinions expressed in the discussion:
"There are not enough police officers on the streets."
"Life in prison is extremely hard."
"When people have something to do, they don't commit crimes."

Write an essay discussing **two** of the ways to reduce crime in cities. You should explain **which way you think is more likely to succeed, giving reasons** to support your answer.

You may, if you wish, make use of the opinions expressed in the discussion, but you should use your own words as far as possible.

3 Read this student's answer. Does it answer the question satisfactorily?

It's probably fair to say that my city has a lot of crime right now, with some areas becoming very dangerous places. Something has to be done – the question is what.

One way in which this rise in crime could be tackled is for local authorities to spend more on policing. With such a small number of officers policing a whole city, it's not surprising that most crime goes undetected and most criminals unpunished. It is obvious that in order to catch a large number of criminals, there has got to be a sufficient number of police officers. But merely putting more police on the streets isn't enough to reduce crime rates. Crime figures won't come down until the law gets tougher on criminals. The authorities have to adopt a zero-tolerance approach and imprison those found guilty of even minor offences.

The real challenge though, is to change people's opinions and behaviour. Young people need to realise that crime does not pay under any circumstances. For this there is one measure which I am in favour of above all else. If someone who has finished their prison sentence manages to have a normal and successful life again, then they should be asked to go into schools and tell youngsters about their own experience. If kids could hear from an ex-criminal that a life of crime isn't worth it, that could be a very powerful deterrent.

Everyone is harmed by high levels of crime in their neighbourhoods. But it is my belief that our streets will only be safer places when the whole of society is involved in the fight against crime.

4 Consider the following comments about the sample answer. Which ones are true? Write *Yes* or *No*.

1. The opening paragraph is a relevant and appropriate introduction.
2. The writer's use of informal language in one sentence is inappropriate for an essay.
3. The writer hasn't demonstrated a good range of English, as they have failed to use enough different verb forms, e.g. continuous and perfect tenses.
4. The use of paragraphs is effective, with each one having a clear focus.
5. The writer explains in the third paragraph which measure they are more in favour of.
6. The writer's references to their own city are irrelevant, as the question does not ask for this.
7. The writer has used their own words when expressing an opinion from the discussion.
8. The final paragraph provides a suitable conclusion.
9. The writer uses an excellent range of natural idiomatic language.
10. Complex sentence structures in the essay include successful examples of inversion.

5 The answer in Exercise 3 is good, but the student could demonstrate their language ability further by using idiomatic expressions such as these. Replace the phrases in orange in the essay with these idiomatic phrases.

adversely affected	get their life back on track
it goes without saying	hearts and minds
invest more heavily in	is experiencing a crime wave
it's no wonder	no-go zones

6 Find three sentences that can be rewritten with inversion using the following structures:

1 Not until … (in paragraph 2)
2 Under no circumstances … (in paragraph 3)
3 … only when … (in paragraph 4)

7 Complete the phrases in the *Prepare to write* box with a word from the essay.

PREPARE TO WRITE

Opening paragraphs

Start with a common opinion or observation

It's probably [1] .... to say that …
It's widely believed/accepted that …
Many people hold the opinion that …
It's no [2] .... that …
According to …, …

Mention a question or controversy

… the [3] .... is what.
There are many different views on …
There's no real consensus on whether …

Closing paragraphs

Make recommendations

There is one [4] .... which I am in favour of above all else.

Restate your position

Having looked at / considered / explored … I've come to the conclusion that …
It is my opinion / [5] .... that …
Personally, I …

Discuss what could happen in the future

If … were to …, they/it could …
Perhaps one day, … will …
It is my hope that …

8 Put the following offences in order from the most serious to the least, giving reasons. Then decide what could be done to deter offenders from doing them again.

- playing loud music late at night
- having a barbecue in a park in which it's not allowed
- parking in a space reserved for disabled drivers
- stealing a packet of biscuits from a large shop

9 Read the writing task and write a plan for your essay.

- Decide which two antisocial behaviours you will discuss, and which you will argue is a priority.
- Plan three to five paragraphs. For each one, think of the central topic and the points that you want to make.
- Consider using some inversion structures in your essay. (But don't overdo it – two or three will be plenty!)
- Pay attention to your opening and closing paragraphs. Select an approach and some suitable phrases from the *Prepare to write* box.

Your class has been discussing the seriousness for society of antisocial behaviour. You have made the notes below.

Antisocial behaviour among young people:
- dropping litter
- acts of vandalism
- petty theft

Some opinions expressed in the discussion:
"Dirty streets are unpleasant for people to walk in."
"Graffiti can sometimes be a real work of art."
"All crimes are serious – there's no such thing as petty crime."

Write an essay discussing **two** of the antisocial behaviours among young people. You should explain **which is the more serious problem, giving reasons** to support your answer.

You may, if you wish, make use of the opinions expressed in the discussion, but you should use your own words as far as possible.

10 Write your essay in 220–260 words.

LIFE SKILLS LEARNING TO LEARN

ACADEMIC NOTE-TAKING

LIFE SKILLS

Taking notes

Taking notes methodically is an essential skill that is useful not only at school but in further education and work as well. It helps you consolidate what you learn, do homework, prepare presentations and revise for exams.

1 Do the questionnaire and calculate your score (see page 135). Do you agree with what it says about you?

NOTE-TAKING QUIZ

1 Tick the sentence that best describes you.

a ◯ I don't take notes very often.
b ◯ I take notes often but hardly ever review them.
c ◯ I take notes often and review them often.

2 Tick the thing(s) you do when taking notes.

◯ use different colours
◯ underline key information
◯ use bullet points

3 What do these abbreviations mean? Tick the one(s) you use in your notes.

◯ b/c ◯ s/b
◯ e.g. ◯ s/t
◯ prob ◯ w/o

2 Read the *How to* guide about note-taking opposite. Match headings 1–4 to paragraphs A–D.

1 Techniques for better note-taking
2 Brain activation: why notes are necessary
3 A skill to use beyond the classroom
4 Notes, cues and summaries

3 Read the *How to* guide again and answer these questions.

1 How does taking notes help you learn?
2 How do the following help when taking notes?
  a abbreviations b bullet points
  c symbols, pictures and diagrams
3 What are 'cues' and when do you write them?
4 What are the two ways you can use your cues?

56 **4** Read Ben's notes as you listen to part of a lecture about the police. What information has he missed? Ignore letters a–f for now.

April 29	History of the police in the UK
Before 1829?	Before 1829 – no police, only army and volunteers wanting rewards
(d)	(a)
1829	1829 – Robert Peel (politician) set up world's 1st prof. police force in London
Name?	(b)
Initial public reaction?	At first public suspicious – thought they were 2nd army
Why did public trust grow?	Public trust grew b/c ... • police followed code of conduct • wore blue uniforms (so diff from army – red) • X guns
(e)	(c)
(f)	

56 **5** Listen again, adding the missing notes in (a), (b) and (c). Then in (d) and (e) write cues for the notes you have added.

6 Study the notes for five minutes. Then cover them and use the cues to test your memory.

7 Write a summary of what you've learned in (f).

57 **8** Listen to part of an introduction to a university course in forensic science. Are these statements true or false?

Forensic scientists

1 work directly with suspects.
2 work mainly inside.
3 only try to find out who committed the crime.
4 only work with biological evidence.

57 **9** Use the Cornell Method to divide a page of your notebook. Then listen to the lecture once or twice again and take notes. Don't forget to use

- abbreviations
- different colours/underlining
- bullet points.

10 Write cues for your notes. In another lesson, use the cues to test what you remember and then write a summary of what you've learned.

How to: Take notes like a pro!

A ....

There have probably been times in class when taking notes has seemed like too much effort. However, it's that effort itself that helps you learn. When you're listening to your teacher in class (or reading a textbook), you may well be following everything, but understanding is not the same as learning. To really learn and remember something, you have to process the information yourself. Taking notes helps you to do this. After all, you can't take good notes without thinking about how to put the information you hear or read into your own words.

B ....

Firstly, research shows that the more notes you take, the more you learn. More than likely, you already use a range of abbreviations to help you take down what the teacher is saying, but don't be afraid to invent your own. Secondly, you should be using different colours or underlining to indicate key information, as well as bullet points for writing lists. Thirdly, using symbols, pictures and diagrams can make your notes both more visual and more memorable. However, if you want your notes to be really efficient, it's just as important to have a general system for taking them and to make sure you review them properly.

C ....

The Cornell Method is one of the best known systems for taking notes. It is easy to use in class and ideal for exam revision. All you do is divide the page of your notebook into three sections.

- The largest of these is for the notes themselves – this is where you write **during** class.
- The next is for 'cues' which you write **after** class. Cues are either key information, such as names and dates, or questions that you write for yourself to help you remember the content of the lesson. When it's time to revise, you cover the notes with a piece of paper and use the cues to test what you remember. Alternatively, if you're studying with a friend, you can take turns to test each other with each other's cues.
- Finally, there's a section at the bottom of the page where you write a summary of what you've learned. It's not easy to write a summary of something unless you have understood it well, so this will also help you to process what you've learned.

D ....

Learning to take good notes requires practice, but like any skill, the more you do it, the easier it will become and the better you will be at it. What's more, it's a skill that will benefit you throughout your life, in higher education and in work. Notes are a valuable learning resource. Taking them really is worth the effort.

Project
Presenting and taking notes

In groups of three, you are going to prepare a presentation and take notes on your classmates' presentations.

1 DECIDE

Decide which member of the group is going to research each of these programmes.

- Erasmus
- The JET Programme
- Peace Corps

2 RESEARCH

Research the programme and prepare a presentation. Include information about

- the objective of the programme
- the length and location of the programme
- the criteria for joining
- the skills that participants gain.

3 PRESENT

Take turns to give your presentations.

4 NOTE

Take notes on the other presentations. Use the Cornell Method.

5 REVIEW

Write cues for the notes and use them to remember and summarise what you learned.

11 WORKING UP AN APPETITE

? ABOUT YOU

▶ 11 **Watch the video and then answer the questions.**

How important to you is eating healthily?

Is there any particular food or drink that you'd struggle to live without?

Do you think schools should teach students about nutrition? Why?

VOCABULARY AND READING
DESCRIBING FOOD

EP **1 Discuss the meaning of the words and phrases.**

1 This chocolate mousse is so **rich** that it definitely doesn't need any cream with it.
2 Strawberries are extremely cheap for the couple of months when they're **in season**, but for the rest of the year they're imported and twice the price.
3 When my dad finishes work late and he can't be bothered to cook, he just gets a **ready meal** from the supermarket and microwaves it when he gets home.
4 I have a weakness for all **fatty** foods, whether it's cheese, chocolate or anything deep-fried. That's why I eat **junk food**, even though it's not good for me.
5 We always add salt when we cook vegetables, otherwise they taste **bland**.
6 Not all **preservatives** are artificial – natural substances like salt and sugar can also make foods last longer.
7 **Produce** can only be described as **organic** if it is farmed without any industrial fertilisers or pesticides.
8 I don't eat many potatoes because they're **high in** carbohydrates, but **low in** protein.

2 Complete the questions with a suitable word or phrase from Exercise 1.

1 How much of the ______ in your family's fridge at the moment do you think is locally grown?
2 Do you and your family ever microwave a ______, or do you always cook everything yourselves?
3 Do you reckon ______ food tastes better than other produce, or is it just clever marketing to get people to pay more for their food?
4 Do you believe that so-called 'energy drinks' (which are ______ caffeine) really help you keep going for longer when you do sport?
5 What foods are now ______ in your country, and are you eating them more often than at other times?
6 Would you rather buy organic produce or food containing ______ that would enable it to last longer?
7 If you're at home eating something that tastes a bit ______, what would you add to enhance the flavour?
8 When you eat meat, do you cut off the ______ parts or do you think they add flavour?
9 Should all fast food be considered as ______, or is some of it healthier than that?
10 Do you enjoy eating ______ food that contains lots of butter or cream?

3 With a partner, ask and answer the questions in Exercise 2.

4 Quickly read the introduction to the article on the opposite page. What are the writer's concerns, and what is the writer optimistic about?

✓ **5 Read the introduction to the article again and decide which answer (A, B, C or D) best fits each gap.**

	A	B	C	D
0	A gathered	(B) raised	C arisen	D grown
1	A backs	B builds	C makes	D stores
2	A influx	B input	C income	D intake
3	A cancelling	B limiting	C shortening	D withdrawing
4	A argued	B reported	C discovered	D accused
5	A amounts	B courses	C ingredients	D portions
6	A deeply	B highly	C much	D well
7	A reaching	B gaining	C getting	D finding
8	A attempt	B ideal	C measure	D viewpoint

6 Work in two groups. Group A read Cassia's argument. Group B read Lewis's argument. Does the writer

1 explain why junk food is so popular?
2 accept that poor diets can lead to health problems?
3 discuss the financial consequences of having a sugar tax?
4 give an example of a product that should be taxed but isn't?
5 explain how they personally would be affected by a sugar tax?
6 suggest that their behaviour might not be consistent with their opinion?
7 mention a country where a sugar tax might not have been as effective as people say?

7 Speak to someone who read the other argument and summarise to each other what you read. Then decide if you agree more with Cassia or Lewis.

THE SUGAR TAX DEBATE

59

A study which was recently published has **(0)** ___B___ concerns over the poor diet of many teenagers in the UK. Figures released show that sugar **(1)** ________ up no less than 14.1% of an average 11 to 18-year-old's **(2)** ________ of calories, three times the recommended amount. Experts advise **(3)** ________ the amount of sugar they eat to about 30 grams per day. However, there is some cause for optimism, as teenagers are **(4)** ________ to be consuming two-thirds of the quantity of sugary drinks they did just eight years ago.

Along with other age groups, teenagers are still eating too much saturated fat, and not enough so-called superfoods, such as oily fish like mackerel, which is high in omega-3. Adults eat an average of 4.2 **(5)** ________ of fruit a day, whereas for teenagers, daily consumption is only 2.7. This is **(6)** ________ short of the recommended 'five-a-day', with only 8% of teens **(7)** ________ this target.

Clearly, improving young people's diets is a priority if we are to avoid a diet-based health crisis in the years to come. One **(8)** ________ that has gained popularity in recent years is the so-called 'sugar tax', which has increased the price of junk food, ready meals and other goods high in sugar. However, it's a divisive issue, so let's take a look at the cases for and against.

Why a sugar tax is necessary

Cassia Follings, 17

I think we all accept that we're in the midst of a health crisis, and that poor diet is largely to blame for this. When my friends and I go out and then decide to get a bite to eat, we tend to go for junk food: burgers and fries with a soft drink, then maybe a dessert if I've still got room. I'm perfectly aware that my burger is high in salt, the fries are fatty, and that the dessert is so rich that I probably won't even be able to eat the whole thing!

So, am I part of the problem? Well, you could argue that I am, but let's face it – a meal in a fast food restaurant is as much as you can afford when you're seventeen, unless your parents are loaded! The thing is that almost all fast food is high in fat, sugar or salt – or sometimes even all three. And there's a simple reason – these are the cheapest ingredients out there, so fast food is cheap to make. Manufacturers sell food that's absolutely full of fat, sugar and salt, and people easily get hooked on the stuff.

You could argue that fast food chains should get their act together, do the decent thing and just reduce levels of salt, sugar, artificial preservatives and all the other stuff they use. But they won't. Because if they did, the food would be so bland and tasteless that no-one would buy it. We all love the salt, fat and sugar, and if you took these out, there'd be nothing left, and they'd have no customers.

The solution, as I see it, is for junk food to be made much more expensive. If they can tax tobacco because it's unhealthy, why not do the same for junk food? If a tax – and I mean a massive one, not just 5 or 10% – was introduced on products that are really high in fat or sugar, junk food would be much more expensive. And then if a burger and donuts in a takeaway cost the same as a fresh organic salad in a restaurant, well my friends and I would go for the lighter option, and I'm sure we'd eat more healthily as a result, though we would have to eat out much less often. So until that happens, I'll be enjoying more bargain junk food every weekend with my friends!

Making junk food more expensive would be unfair on young people

Lewis Jackson, 18

I'm not a fan of fast food myself. But I accept that other people are, and I don't think governments should have the right to dictate to others what they should or shouldn't eat. First of all, adding a sugar tax could raise the price of a soft drink from say £1 to £2. Who pays the extra £1? The kid buying the drink, that's who – and the whole idea is to tax companies not consumers, isn't it? It's the young and the poor who will be hit hardest by a sugar tax, and that's not fair.

Sugar taxes are being introduced in a number of countries, but none of them work. The UK introduced a tax on fizzy drinks, but not milky ones, so when a well-known hot drinks chain sold their extra-large hot chocolate containing fifteen teaspoons of sugar, it was exempt from the tax. Where's the sense in that?

Supporters of the idea of a sugar tax point to the example of Mexico, where consumption of sugary drinks fell after it was introduced. But it hasn't been proved that the tax led to the fall; there could have been other causes. Besides, countries with high taxes on tobacco products still have high numbers of smokers, so why would a sugar tax be any different? Are people really going to be persuaded to improve their diet just because some things cost a bit more? Personally, I doubt it.

While I accept the need for people to eat healthily, I feel sugar has been singled out unfairly. It's not the only ingredient with health implications. What about factory-made ready meals, which contain so many preservatives to prolong their shelf life? Those can't be good for you, surely? And even fresh, healthy produce gets imported from the other side of the world. So why not introduce a food carbon tax to offset the massive amounts of pollution caused by inconsiderate people who want to eat organic avocadoes all year round, even when they're out of season? Will anything ever be done about that?

TALKING POINTS

Some people say that eating healthily is more difficult for poorer people. Why do you think that is?

Besides a sugar tax, what other measures could encourage people to have healthier diets?

Should someone whose diet has endangered their own life be allowed to continue eating unhealthily, or should they be forced to improve their diet?

GRAMMAR
THE PASSIVE

1 Complete the sentences with a phrase from the box.

are being introduced	are reported	was introduced
gets imported	going to be persuaded	had been introduced
hasn't been proved	weren't being taken	will be hit

1 Teenagers .... to be consuming fewer sugary drinks.
2 If a tax .... on products that are high in fat or sugar, junk food would be much more expensive.
3 But it .... that the sugar tax in Mexico led to the fall in sales of sugary drinks.
4 It's the young and the poor who .... hardest by a sugar tax.
5 Sugar taxes .... in a number of countries.
6 Are people really .... to improve their diet just because some things cost a bit more?
7 Until recently, many commentators felt that their concerns about the growing obesity crisis .... seriously.
8 If a sugar tax .... years ago, the population today would be much healthier.
9 Even fresh, healthy produce .... from the other side of the world.

2 Match each of these tenses to a sentence in Exercise 1.

a future passive (with *will*)
b the *get* passive
c future passive (with *going to*)
d present continuous passive
e past continuous passive
f present perfect passive
g past perfect passive
h present simple passive
i past simple passive

3 Complete the rules with a word or phrase from the box.

past participle	someone or something
transitive	who or what

1 We use the passive when we want to show how .... is affected by an action.
2 We can use *by* to show .... does the action or we can omit the agent if it is unknown or unimportant.
3 Most .... verbs can be used in the passive.
4 The passive is formed with *be* or *get* and the .... of the verb.

» GRAMMAR REFERENCE AND PRACTICE PAGE 154

4 Join phrases in A, B and C to make sentences in the passive. Then identify which two sentences are false.

A	B	C
1 Weekly pizza deliveries	(use)	as currency by the early civilisations of South America.
2 Approximately 100 billion burgers	(allow)	to contain traces of insect.
3 Chocolate	(consume)	to astronauts on the International Space Station from 2025.
4 Apples, pears and cherries	(consider)	to be members of the rose family.
5 The year 2008	(call)	worldwide so far this century.
6 The food you buy	(make)	the International Year of the Potato.

5 Change these sentences into the passive. Choose whether it is appropriate to include or omit the agent.

1 Brazil produces 15% of the world's coffee.
2 Someone in the kitchen had put peppercorns on our ice cream instead of chocolate sprinkles!
3 I hope that by the end of the month, app users will have downloaded my healthy eating app 10,000 times.
4 Compared to fifty years ago, fewer people these days gather foods which grow wild.
5 One online review has described Tony's Bistro as 'possibly the worst restaurant in the world'.

6 Look at the sentences below. Choose from a–c the reason why they are incorrect. Rewrite the sentences in the active voice.

1 The road surface has been being repaired for the last four months.
2 The house is lived in by five people.
3 Roughly 11,000 branches worldwide are had by South African fast food chain Nando's.

We don't use the passive with:
a a number of state verbs (e.g. *have*, *belong*, *lack*, *resemble*, *suit*)
b intransitive verbs (verbs which don't take an object)
c some continuous tenses (e.g. present perfect continuous)

7 Rewrite any sentences that are incorrect, using the active voice if necessary.

1 Make sure the meat is chopped up into thin strips before frying it.
2 That cookery podcast has been being listened to by loads of people.
3 A very special talent is had by the chef.
4 A fantastic bakery is lived next to by my cousin.
5 Our family meal out was postponed because my mum was sick.
6 This time tomorrow, a meal out will be being had by my friends and me to celebrate my birthday.

8 Correct any mistakes in these sentences. One is correct.

1 The restaurant wasn't opened yet, so let's go back in five minutes.
2 Please ensure that guests are made aware that we've run out of fish.
3 Most restaurant kitchen staff paid by the hour.
4 A new book of stir-fry recipes have just been published.
5 In a few years, potatoes will have been being eaten in Europe for 500 years.
6 I've never understood why aubergines are also being called eggplants – they don't taste anything like egg!

9 » WORK IN PAIRS. TURN TO PAGE 131.

VOCABULARY
DESCRIBING FOOD: COLLOCATIONS

1 **Look at the marketing ideas that cafés and restaurants use to tempt customers to spend money. Would they make you more likely or less likely to go there?**

- serve food in novel ways, e.g. on a wooden chopping board or on a garden spade
- give dishes foreign names
- run all-you-can-eat offers
- name dishes after their inventor, e.g. 'Aunty Daisy's banana cake'
- offer discounts for social media followers
- include details on the menu about how a dish is prepared, e.g. 'sun-dried tomatoes, finely chopped and sprinkled over a bed of pan-fried mushrooms'

EP **2** **Look at the two menus. What is the difference between them? Would you rather go to the Golden Valley Bistro or Bev's Café? Why?**

Golden Valley Bistro

1. Shoulder of veal, with **locally sourced** greens and **pan-fried** potatoes
2. Ocean-caught haddock with triple-cooked potato wedges
3. Casserole of **slow-roasted** aubergine, torched peppers and **sun-dried** tomatoes topped with a Parmesan crust
4. **Gluten-free** pizza with a range of premium toppings created just for you
5. **Free-range** chicken in a rich creamy sauce, enveloped in **homemade** pastry

All dishes served with a **freshly baked** roll

BEV'S CAFÉ – BEST GRUB IN TOWN!!!!

a. Chicken pie
b. Fish 'n' chips
c. Beef with veg
d. Mixed veg stew with a cheese topping
e. Build-your-own pizza

ALL DISHES COME WITH BREAD

3 **Match up the meals from the Golden Valley Bistro and Bev's Café that mean a similar thing.**

4 **Complete the names of the dishes 1–8 with collocations from Exercise 2. What is the writer's main point? Do you agree?**

THE MOODY COOK'S BLOG

Dear restaurant owners everywhere,
The names you use for food on your menus – they're driving me crazy. Isn't it time to just tell it like it is?

- 1 ______ **eggs**
  Don't expect me to believe your chickens are roaming around at liberty. I know they're crammed into a barn.
- 2 ______ **fish**
  Really? How else are you going to cook a fillet of sole?
- 3 ______ **tomatoes**
  Is that really how you get them to lose their moisture?
- 4 ______ **vegetables**
  Just because a guy delivers produce with mud on, that doesn't mean you're saving the planet.
- 5 ______ **desserts**
  No they're not, unless you live in your restaurant kitchen.
- 6 ______ **food**
  It's only people who are allergic to gluten who actually need this. The rest of us don't.
- 7 ______ **bread**
  Are you trying to say you actually made it yourself?
- 8 ______ **meat and vegetables**
  Just because something was cooked in an oven and not in a microwave, that doesn't make it slow.

FOOD AND DRINK: EXPRESSIONS

EP **5** **Complete the expressions used when talking about food. Then listen to three conversations to see if you were right.** 60

easy (on something) halves horse house in stomach sweet tooth when

1 I have a ______.
2 Go ______ on the cream!
3 Say ______!
4 Tuck ______!
5 I could eat a ______!
6 Your eyes are bigger than your ______!
7 Let's go ______.
8 It's on the ______.

6 **Which phrase can you use if**

1 you are absolutely starving?
2 you like sugary foods?
3 you want to split the bill equally with someone else?
4 someone thinks they can eat more than they really need?
5 you only want a small portion of something?
6 you want somebody to tell you when the food or drink you're giving them is enough?
7 food or drink is being offered free by a restaurant?
8 you are inviting someone to start eating their food?

7 **Write a dialogue including as many of the phrases in Exercise 5 as you can.**

LISTENING

1 In groups, ask and answer the following questions.

1 Do you ever post photos of food online? Why? / Why not?
2 Have you ever commented on someone else's pictures of food? What did you say?
3 Why do you think so many images of food and drink are shared on social media?

2 In Exercise 5 you will hear a vlogger called Norma giving some hints about food photography. Which of the following do you think would be good subject matter to take a photo of? What changes might you make before taking the photos?

- a ready meal that's just been microwaved, still in its plastic packaging but with the lid off
- a homemade cake in its baking tin before it is taken out of the oven
- a jar of sundried tomatoes with the lid off
- an organic avocado sliced in half, with the stone still on one of the halves
- uncooked green vegetables on a green plate, viewed from above

3 What advice would you give someone who wants to upload photos of food to their social media pages?

4 Look at gaps 1–8 in Norma's Nutrition Vlog. What type of information do you think is needed for each gap?

5 Listen to Norma and complete the sentences with a word or short phrase. Listen again for any answers you missed.

LOG IN | REGISTER

Norma's NUTRITION VLOG

61

TIPS FOR PHOTOGRAPHING FOOD

Norma says that a lot can be learned from the **(1)** .... on websites.

Food photography has become an essential **(2)** .... for business owners.

Norma uses the word **(3)** '....................' to describe what food photography can be like as a career.

Because of photography **(4)** .... is much less popular for breakfast than it used to be.

For an effective food photo Norma recommends including **(5)** .... alongside the food.

Norma suggests the trick of using **(6)** .... to create marks on meat.

Norma believes **(7)** .... can create the conditions for excellent photos.

Norma recommends taking photos from **(8)** .... and then choosing the best shots.

6 Look at the tricks that professional food photographers use in food advertising. Which do you think are genuine tips?

TRICKS OF FOOD PHOTOGRAPHY

1 Photograph small portions, leaving empty space on the plate around the food.

2 To make vegetables look appetising, undercook them slightly, as overcooked veg lose colour and look bland.

3 Spray a little oil onto hot food before photographing it, as this gives it an attractive shine.

4 Instead of photographing milk, use builders' glue instead.

5 A roast chicken looks plumper and more appealing if it is stuffed with paper napkins.

Turn to page 132 to check your answers.

7 Discuss the extent to which you agree with the following statements.

1 'I can't think of anything duller than having to scroll through all my friends' food photos on Instagram. Do they really think other people care what they had for lunch?'
2 'Food, and in particular fruit and vegetables, are so varied in colour, shape and texture that they make fantastic subject matter for photographers.'

SPEAKING

GIVING OPINIONS TACTFULLY

1 **Look at the definition of 'tact' from the *Cambridge Advanced Learner's Dictionary*. How do you say 'tact' in your language?**

tact *noun* [U]

the ability to say or do the right thing without making anyone unhappy or angry:

He's never had much tact and people don't like his blunt manner.

2 **Match 1–3 to a–c to make sentences. Discuss whether you agree with each and why.**

1 Tact is basically lying to others
2 Tact is the art of making a point
3 Being tactful means saying the right thing at the right time,

a without making an enemy.
b in the way you'd like them to lie to you.
c as well as not saying the wrong thing at the wrong time.

3 **Read the following posts and discuss with a partner which ones describe a person being tactless. How would you feel, and how would you react, in those situations?**

My friend texted to invite me for lunch at her parents' flat on Saturday. I just texted back in a hurry, 'Can't. Busy then.' But now she's avoiding me. Have I offended her?

I was arranging to meet some friends in town today. I suggested we meet at Joe's Café, and one friend said no, because it's for snobs. Everyone laughed and I felt stupid.

We got told our results in the science test today. The teacher said in front of everybody that mine was 'the lowest score in the whole class'. It was, well … humiliating.

4 **Put the headings in the right place to complete the article.**

Avoid blaming someone | Change statements into questions | Choose your words carefully | Express uncertainty | Mention the positive

Teen talk

HOME | ARTICLES | FORUM | LOG IN

Your best mate's just posted a selfie showing off their new hairstyle. They're obviously hoping for a compliment, but their new look is a disaster. Do you tell them, or keep quiet?

It can be all too easy to say something that hurts someone's feelings, so here are some tips about being tactful.

1 ....

Think of something complimentary to say, like 'Well, it's certainly very eye-catching.' A complimentary remark can also prepare the listener for the criticism that follows: 'The dessert was tasty, but perhaps a bit too rich for my liking.'

2 ....

Strong language like 'disgusting' or 'hideous' can upset people. A really useful phrase for this is 'not very'; rather than pointing out that your classmate's food choices are 'unhealthy', you could say they're 'not very healthy'.

3 ....

Instead of telling someone 'That won't work', you could ask 'Do you think that will work?' Making them negative is another way to express ideas and suggestions tactfully: 'Wouldn't it be better to go somewhere quieter?'

4 ....

You could introduce your ideas by saying 'I was wondering whether …' or 'Perhaps …'. Use adverbs like *quite*, *slightly*, *a bit* or *a little* to make any criticisms 'softer': 'That's a little inconvenient, I'm afraid.' Modal verbs (*might*, *may* or *could*) are useful here: 'That might not be the best idea.'

5 ....

Put yourself in your teacher's shoes for a moment. If a pupil says: 'You haven't explained question 2 to us' it contains a suggestion that the teacher is somehow at fault. The passive is useful for being tactful without accusing anyone, because it enables you to avoid saying who did something, as in 'Mistakes were made, but now we can try to put them right.'

62 **5** **Listen to three friends planning an activity for their classmates. How tactful is each person? Find examples of them following (or not following) the advice in Exercise 4.**

62 **6** **Listen again and tick the expressions in the *Prepare to speak* box which the friends use.**

PREPARE TO SPEAK

Ways of being tactful

Being indirect
I was thinking it'd be great to …
I don't seem to have …

Making suggestions
Wouldn't … be worth considering?
Might it be an idea for us to …?

Pointing out a problem
The thing is …
To be honest, …
Sorry, but …
There seems to be a problem …

Saying that you don't want to offend someone
I hope you don't mind me saying, but …
No offence, but …

Disagreeing with what's just been said
Well, it's not so much that … ,
But then again, …

Softening negative opinions
I'm not sure if …
That might be a bit / slightly / a little …

7 » **WORK IN PAIRS.** **TURN TO PAGE 132.**

12 GREEN TRAVEL

ABOUT YOU

▶ 12 **Watch the video and then answer the questions.**
How often do you travel within your country or abroad?
What kind of holidays do you like best?
What factors do you and your family consider when choosing a holiday destination?

VOCABULARY AND READING

TRAVEL

EP **1 Read the questions. What do you think the words and phrases mean?**

1 Do you prefer to go abroad or do you enjoy a staycation?
2 Would you rather follow a tour operator's itinerary or plan your own?
3 Would you be happy to pay a tourism tax to help clean up popular sites?
4 Would you pay more for a carbon neutral holiday?
5 How important is it for your holidays to be sustainable?
6 If you're bound for a far-away destination, do you usually offset your carbon footprint?
7 Do you like self-catering holidays or do you prefer to have your meals in restaurants while on holiday?
8 Do you prefer popular destinations or those that are off the beaten track?

2 Choose a definition for each of the words and phrases in Exercise 1.

a going to
b a place where few people go
c cooking meals for yourself
d a holiday spent at home going on day trips to local attractions or a holiday in your own country
e a list of places you plan to visit
f money paid to the government when you stay in holiday accommodation
g compensating for or not producing carbon emissions
h remove rubbish and make tidy
i compensate for emissions by funding CO_2 savings elsewhere
j not causing environmental damage, so able to continue for a long time

3 Ask and answer the questions in Exercise 1 with a partner.

4 Complete the sentences with a word or phrase from Exercise 1.

1 Many countries now charge a ________, which they use to protect their tourist sites.
2 Flight UL502, ________ Colombo, is delayed until 14.35.
3 I'm bored of visiting the major tourist destinations. I want to go somewhere ________ this year.
4 Some countries hope to be ________ by 2050 – we will all feel the benefits of breathing fresher air.
5 Ramona and Thierry are going to help ________ a local river at the weekend.
6 I don't really see the attraction of ________ holidays; I prefer going out to eat.
7 We are going to have a ________ this year as there are so many fascinating places to visit right here in Spain.
8 We've just received the ________ for our cruise: day 3 looks the most interesting as we're stopping off in Barbados.
9 Most large companies are not doing enough to ________ their ________, which means they pollute the environment more than they help it.
10 The government needs to do more to support ________ food production so as to avoid food shortages in the future.

5 Discuss the questions with a partner.

1 What other issues are associated with travel and holidays?
2 What more can be done to make travel greener?

6 Quickly read the four extracts opposite, from an article in which experts give their opinions on eco-travel. Does each expert have a generally positive or negative attitude towards eco-travel?

7 Look at the phrases from the article that each writer uses. Do they suggest a positive or negative attitude?

1 a positive impact a truly unforgettable experience beneficial has to be a plus
2 want to be considered remain to be persuaded unlikely to there is no guarantee
3 We're all to blame Some people feel guilty about avoid be suspicious of
4 it is important to dig deeper may seem like can make it appear … when in fact research … is flawed

8 Read the questions about the extracts. For each question, choose from the experts A–D. To help you, the highlighted sections show the parts of the extracts which enable you to answer question 1.

Which expert
1 has a different view from the others about how eco-tourism affects local communities?
2 has a similar view to A on the type of accommodation tourists should choose?
3 has a different view from C on offsetting your carbon footprint?
4 expresses a different view from B on whether it's realistic to expect a reduction in the number of long-haul flights?

GREEN TRAVEL? IS IT REALLY POSSIBLE?

63

Four travel experts give their opinion

A

No-one is happy to be told they are causing pollution, but it's true that we're all to blame when it comes to environmental damage. Some people feel guilty about flying, particularly flying long distances, and feel that their carbon footprint needs to be offset by donating to a sustainable project such as forest conservation. Personally, I'd encourage people to limit long-haul flights, though I'm aware this is a bit idealistic, and do something to offset the pollution caused if they do decide to travel a long way. Where possible, avoid major hotel chains in favour of greener options such as renting a holiday home. We do need to be suspicious of some of the operators that define themselves as 'green' because there can actually be even more exploitation of local people and environments.

B

There are a lot of travel companies that want to be considered 'eco-friendly'. I think they have good intentions, but a flight bound for the other side of the world is, by definition, not environmentally friendly. As regards offsetting your carbon footprint, I remain to be persuaded of the effectiveness of that. As a child I remember being told 'the world is your oyster'. Now 'stay local' is a better message, and one which is beginning to catch on, promising a decline in the number of long-haul trips. If you must go abroad, use local buses or trains and stay in a hostel or some other self-catering option which contributes to the local economy. You pay a tourism tax to the government when you stay at a hotel, but that is unlikely to help the local community and there is no guarantee that your money will be spent on environmentally friendly projects.

C

Green travel tends to focus on destinations which are off-the-beaten-track. These tours tend to have interesting accommodation options such as tree-houses or yurts. Green operators make a positive impact on the local environment or population, for example, through organising clean ups of beaches or rivers as part of the tour. A lot of eco-tours are based on traditional cultural activities. Being whirled around the dance floor on a salsa dancing holiday in Cuba, for example, is a truly unforgettable experience. Although for many it is a long-haul trip, the impact tourists have when there is beneficial. Eco-tour companies promote products created locally for tourists who wish to take home a souvenir. In addition, many automatically offset your carbon footprint as part of the package, which has to be a plus, though you should insist on being informed about how the money will be used.

D

It is important to dig deeper when a holiday is labelled 'eco' or 'green'. Many tours may well be less destructive for the environment but if they are located thousands of miles away, they will not be as green as they appear. Clever marketing can make it appear that locals are benefitting from tourism when in fact it is multi-national corporations who once again profit. We all want to take a souvenir home from a trip and buying ones made from local materials by local people may seem like an ethical choice. However, some materials are not sustainable and the people making them are not actually getting much for their labour. Research which found that home-sharing is better for the environment is flawed as there are too many variables. The best way to come close to a carbon neutral holiday is to choose a staycation. But, those who can afford it will continue to want to see the other side of the world. In my view, they should be forced to offset their carbon footprint by donating to a conservation project.

TALKING POINTS

Do you think individuals can really make a difference to the environment through changing the way they travel?

Should governments force companies and individuals to offset their carbon footprints?

Would you be in favour of policies which limit people's flights to, say, one long-haul (return) and two short hauls per year?

GRAMMAR
PASSIVE GERUND AND INFINITIVE

1 Look at the extracts from the article. Complete the corresponding rules below with *be, to be* or *being.*

1 There are a lot of travel companies that **want to be considered** 'eco-friendly'.
2 I **remember being told** 'the world is your oyster'.
3 No-one is **happy to be told** they are causing pollution.
4 You should **insist on being informed** about how the money will be used.
5 They **should be forced** to offset their carbon footprint by donating to a conservation project.
6 **Being whirled** around the dance floor on a salsa dancing holiday in Cuba is a truly unforgettable experience.

> 1 .... + pp (past participle) after certain verbs (e.g. *want, need, is/are supposed*)
> 2 .... + pp after certain verbs (e.g. *consider, enjoy, risk*)
> 3 .... + pp after adjectives (e.g. *likely, happy, surprised*)
> 4 .... + pp after prepositions (e.g. *congratulate on, concerned about, insist on*)
> 5 .... + pp after modals (e.g. *can, could, might, must, should*)
> 6 .... + pp as a noun phrase (e.g. *Being vaccinated before your trip is important …*)

» **GRAMMAR REFERENCE AND PRACTICE PAGE 155**

2 Choose the correct form of the verb.

1 Leo expected *being* / *to be* picked for the team.
2 The group had a great time *being* / *to be* shown the most important landmarks.
3 Colin denied *having been* / *to have been* told about the changes to the itinerary.
4 The students were disappointed *being* / *to be* told their trip had been cancelled.
5 The passenger was too important *being* / *to be* removed from the flight.
6 Jack was really angry about *being* / *to be* lied to.
7 We arrived at the guest house only *being* / *to be* told they didn't have our reservation.
8 Andrew absolutely detests *being* / *to be* told what to do.

PASSIVE STRUCTURES WITH TWO OBJECTS

3 Look at this sentence from the text. Identify the direct object (DO) and the indirect object (IO).

You pay a **tourism tax** to **the government** when you stay at a hotel.

4 Sentences A and B are passive versions of the example in Exercise 3. In each sentence, decide whether the bold words are the subject (S), a direct object (DO) or an indirect object (IO).

A **A tourism tax** is paid to **the government** when you stay at a hotel.
B **The government** is paid **a tourism tax** when you stay at a hotel.

5 Complete the rules by choosing the correct option.

> When a sentence in the active voice has a direct object and an indirect object (e.g. *Locals sell souvenirs to tourists.*) the sentence can be transformed into the passive voice in two ways:
> **a** with the *direct* / *indirect* object of the active sentence as the subject of the passive sentence
> **Tourists** are sold souvenirs (by locals).
> **b** with the *direct* / *indirect* object of the active sentence as the subject of the passive sentence
> **Souvenirs** are sold to tourists (by locals).
> The two passive sentences *share the same meaning* / *have different meanings*.

6 Read examples 1 and 2 and answer questions a–d.

> 1 The area receives thousands of visitors every day. Tourists are sold souvenirs and shown around the main sights by locals.

a In the highlighted sentence, is *tourists* known information (i.e. something that has been mentioned previously) or new information?
b Is *souvenirs* known information or new information?

> 2 Locals produce many different types of souvenirs by hand. These souvenirs are sold to tourists who visit the area in their thousands …

c In the highlighted sentence, is *tourists* known information or new information?
d Is *souvenirs* known information or new information?

7 Complete the rules by choosing the correct word.

> When active sentences with two objects are transformed into passive sentences, we usually:
> **a** make the *new* / *known* information the subject of the passive sentence.
> **b** leave the *new* / *known* information as the object of the sentence.

» **GRAMMAR REFERENCE AND PRACTICE PAGE 155**

8 Make the sentences passive in two different ways.

1 The airline offered Ana a free flight to compensate for her bad experience.
2 Kate's guitar teacher taught her a few words of Spanish.
3 Chloe sent an email to the hotel manager, thanking him for his generosity.
4 The hotel promised Carl an upgrade.

9 » **WORK IN PAIRS. TURN TO PAGE 132.**

VOCABULARY
FORMAL AND INFORMAL LANGUAGE

64 **1 You will hear two speakers talking in different contexts. Answer the questions.**

1 Who is speaking?
2 Who are they speaking to?
3 What are they talking about?
4 Where do you think the speakers are?

EP 64 **2 Listen again to Speaker 1 and fill in the gaps.**

Speaker 1

1 If you look out of the window now, you will see the Sigiriya rock, which rises to a ________ of almost 200 metres.
2 The site was ________ by King Kashyapa for his new capital in the 5th century.
3 The main palace was ________ on top of the rock.
4 The numerous colourful frescoes, which decorate the sides of the palace ________ up to 500 beautiful maidens.
5 There is evidence that the surrounding area may have been ________ since prehistoric times.
6 Taking photographs of the frescoes is strictly ________; however, postcards may be purchased from the kiosk.

64 **3 Listen again to Speaker 2. What phrases does she use to express the same information that Speaker 1 gives in Exercise 2? Which speaker's language is more formal?**

4 Decide if the word in Column B is more formal or more informal than the neutral word in Column A.

A	B
child	1 kid
say	2 express
wrong	3 incorrect
start	4 commence
friend	5 mate
dishonest	6 dodgy
virus	7 bug
buy	8 purchase

5 Complete each sentence in the pair with one of the words given. Which is the more formal sentence?

1 a Please ________ books to the library after use.
b When are you going to ________ that book you borrowed off me, mate?
return give back

2 a I can't believe you ________ your job just because the boss was rude to you!
b I'm writing to ________ my post as Editor.
quit resign from

3 a Smith & Co. ________ the issue of CO_2 emissions from cruise ships.
b The cops ________ the robbery but they didn't find out much.
investigated looked into

4 a They don't ________ you smoke in cafés.
b Smoking is not ________ inside the cinema.
permitted let

5 a My mum ________ me a new pair of trainers.
b Unfortunately, the coffee maker I ________ from you is faulty.
bought purchased

6 a I remember ________ badly sunburned once.
b Due to the recession, the number of people who risk ________ unemployed has increased.
becoming getting

7 a 80% of our students have ________ in getting a place at university.
b Well done, Reuben. I heard you ________ to get into a good uni.
succeeded managed

FORMAL AND INFORMAL WAYS OF EXPRESSING QUANTITY

65 **6 You will hear a news item about a strike. What causes and effects of the strike are mentioned?**

EP 65 **7 Listen again and complete the phrases.**

1 ________ passengers are stranded this evening
2 Over the last five years ________ employees have been affected by redundancies …
3 Rates of pay for casual staff have fallen ________ ________.
4 The partial closure of five airports has caused ________ confusion …
5 It was ________ inconvenient …
6 … they had ________ sympathy with the strikers.
7 The reality is that ________ strikes in recent history …

66 **8 You will hear a boy called Kai telling his mother about the strike. What detail of the story did Kai get wrong?**

66 **9 Which of the options do you hear? Which is more informal?**

1 Apparently, *loads of* / *a lot of* people are stuck in different places …
2 *Tons of* / *Many* workers have lost their jobs …
3 … the rest are not paid very *well* / *much*.
4 It's supposed to be *really* / *pretty* bad in some places.
5 Some people are *a bit* / *a little* confused …
6 *Lots of* / *A lot of* flights have been cancelled …

10 » WORK IN PAIRS. **TURN TO PAGE 132.**

WRITING
A LETTER

1 Discuss the questions with a partner.

1 What do you think a 'geography field trip to an eco-resort' might include?
2 What might students enjoy about this kind of field trip?
3 What kind of things could go wrong or be disappointing on such a trip?

2 Read the task and answer the questions.

> You are a student at an international college. Your class recently went on a geography trip to an eco-resort. You travelled there by train, stayed in shared accommodation and went on excursions to local areas of interest. Write a letter to the college principal explaining which aspects of the trip you and your classmates were happy with, which aspects were considered disappointing, and suggesting how the trip could be improved for students in the future.
>
> Write your **letter**.

1 Which of your ideas from Exercise 1 could you include in your letter?
2 What kind of language would be appropriate?
3 How would you start and finish your letter?

3 Read the opening paragraph of the sample answer.

1 What information does it contain?
2 Highlight some examples of formal language.

Dear Mrs Harwood,

I am writing on behalf of the students who attended the geography field trip to Woodlands Lodge to let you know our thoughts on the visit.

4 Decide how many paragraphs you would divide the main body of the letter into. What would each paragraph focus on?

5 Put sentences a–k into the appropriate paragraph. Then order the sentences within each paragraph.

Body paragraph 1	*b,*
Body paragraph 2	
Body paragraph 3	

(a) *For instance, get students to interview the staff and make blog posts, and maybe hold a quiz on the last night.*
(b) *First of all, I would like to inform you that the students were, overall, satisfied with the field trip.*
(c) *We have since learned of a wind farm, as well as producers of organic fruit and vegetables in the area, so we are rather confused as to why they were not on the programme.*
(d) *Firstly, include some activities to raise awareness of the ways in which Woodlands Lodge is sustainable.*
(e) *We also appreciated that we travelled by train to minimise the harm done by our journey.*
(f) *What was disappointing about the field trip was that most of the excursions were unrelated to the purpose of the trip.*
(g) *We would like to propose a few changes for next year's trip.*
(h) *For example, we went to see historical and architectural sites, which, while interesting, didn't teach us much about ecological issues.*
(i) *One aspect that was particularly useful was learning how the lodge functioned in an environmentally friendly way, with zero waste and clean energy.*
(j) *Secondly, make sure all outings are to locations which teach students about environmental issues, such as those mentioned in the previous paragraph.*
(k) *The friendly staff there gave us a good insight into how tourist accommodation can be managed in a sustainable way.*

6 Read the end of the letter and choose the most appropriate options.

Thank you / Thanks for giving us this great / valuable opportunity to visit an eco-lodge. I hope / Hoping this feedback will be helpful.

Yours faithfully / sincerely

Paloma Hernández

7 Complete the *Prepare to write* box with phrases from the letter.

PREPARE TO WRITE

A letter giving feedback

Beginning

Dear Sir or Madam
Dear Mr/Ms/Miss/[1] ______ + surname
I am writing to …
The purpose of this letter is to …

Ending

I hope this [2] ______ / evaluation will be / has been helpful.
I hope you will find these comments useful.
I would appreciate a prompt reply / an explanation from you.
I look forward to hearing from you.
Yours faithfully
Yours [3] ______

Other expressions

We would like to propose a few changes.
One [4] ______ that was particularly useful was …
What was disappointing was …
We also appreciated that …

8 Match the sentence halves.

1 We would like to suggest that
2 I am writing on
3 I hope that you find
4 You should consider
5 I look forward to
6 The purpose of this letter is to
7 We were pleased
8 We were disappointed

a behalf of the students who participated in the exchange programme.
b let you know our thoughts on the recent trip.
c you upgrade the standard of the shared accommodation.
d hearing from you at your earliest convenience.
e to discover that the swimming pool was closed.
f this information useful in improving the facilities.
g with the resort overall but have some minor feedback.
h increasing the number of excursions on offer.

9 Match sentences 1–8 to the sentence a–h which has a similar meaning. Which two of the sentences a–h are too informal for this kind of letter?

1 The hotel was very poor value for money.
2 It was an extremely disappointing experience.
3 One pleasing feature was the stunning sea views.
4 The vast majority of people had a similar experience.
5 It caused a considerable amount of inconvenience.
6 Overall, we had a satisfactory experience on holiday.
7 I would be grateful for a full refund.
8 I wouldn't encourage other people to join your tours.

a We have heard that this was a common occurrence.
b I want my money back.
c Unfortunately, the trip did not meet our expectations.
d The holiday was OK but not brilliant.
e This made the situation rather difficult for us.
f I will let others know that I do not recommend this trip.
g I feel the accommodation was somewhat overpriced.
h We were absolutely delighted with the sights we could see from our balcony.

10 Read the task and plan your reply.

You recently watched a documentary about how holidays could be made greener. The suggestions included choosing staycations, travelling by bus and train instead of plane, and avoiding long-haul trips altogether. Write a letter to the TV channel, saying what you agreed with in the programme and pointing out which suggestions you feel are unrealistic. Explain how these ideas could be made more workable in practice.

Write your **letter**.

how you will start and finish the letter

how many points you will make

how many paragraphs your letter will have

which expressions from this section you will include

11 Write your letter in 220–260 words.

LIFE SKILLS SOCIAL RESPONSIBILITIES

EATING RESPONSIBLY

LIFE SKILLS

How to eat responsibly

Food production can have an enormous environmental impact. It is therefore important to be aware of where our food comes from and what its production involves. This way we can make informed choices about what we buy and what we eat, which in turn can help us to help the planet.

1 Do the quiz. Then find out your score on page 135.

How green are you with food?

1 How often do you think about where your food comes from?
- a Every time I eat.
- b Occasionally.
- c Virtually never.

2 If you eat meat, would you consider having 100% meat-free days?
- a Yes, I'd have them more than twice a week.
- b Yes, from time to time.
- c Definitely not.

3 How often does your family throw away food?
- a Hardly ever. / Never.
- b After some meals. / When things go off.
- c After most meals.

2 What is the connection between the orangutan and the food we eat?

3 Read the article. Sentences a–e are the final sentences of the paragraphs. Match them to gaps 1–5.

- **a** We need to relearn the value of food.
- **b** It's not only fresher and healthier but also better for the environment and your local economy.
- **c** Eating fresh food instead of processed food can reduce our impact on the planet.
- **d** By eating less meat and fewer dairy products, we can help sustain the planet.
- **e** This helps us to make better choices about what we put on our plate.

4 Read the article again. What do these numbers refer to? Which ones surprise you?

- **a** 222 million
- **b** around half
- **c** 14.5%
- **d** thousands
- **e** 1.66 million

67 **5** Listen to three people talk about responsible food choices. Which of the issues 1–5 in the article is each person trying to deal with?

Lee ……… Lola ……… Sherwin ………

6 Which of the ways to eat more responsibly would you try? Why?

67 **7** Listen again and answer the questions.

Which speaker

1. has recently developed a new routine?
2. took the advice of a relative?
3. suggests making a certain choice is easy?
4. enjoys the regular changes their new behaviour brings?
5. sympathises with the people who produce their food?
6. expresses surprise at a particular fact?

(IR) RESPONSIBLE FOOD 68

When you're enjoying a meal or a snack, you're unlikely to be thinking about climate change, biodiversity or global poverty. However, our food choices have consequences not only for the environment but also for the people who produce the food. Let's look at five reasons why.

1 MORE MEAT, MORE DAIRY, MORE DAMAGE

All around the world, more and more people are eating meat and dairy products on a daily basis. However, raising cattle uses up a lot of resources, including the water needed to grow their food and the fuel required for farm equipment. In fact, meat production creates around 14.5% of climate change gases. Growing crops to feed the animals also takes up enormous areas of land, which leads to deforestation. The fertilisers used for them also create a lot of environmental damage. Your burger or steak might be delicious, but by the time it gets to your plate, a lot of environmental damage has been done.

1 ………

2 THE DANGEROUS GAP BETWEEN FARMER AND CONSUMER

Who grew the fruit and vegetables you eat? Where were the animals raised? Most of us know very little about where our food comes from and we usually have no idea if the farmers are working in safe conditions or receiving adequate payment for their work. The reality is that many live in hunger and poverty, selling their produce extremely cheaply to companies that then sell it to us at vastly increased prices. However, fair trade organisations work with over 1.66 million farmers and workers around the world, helping them to improve their conditions and receive a fairer price for the food they produce. Fair trade products have a special label.

2 ………

3 THE DAMAGING CONVENIENCE OF 'ALL YEAR ROUND'

Enter any supermarket and it's hard to tell from the products on sale what season it is. Tomatoes and apples, for example, are always on sale. However, like most fruit and vegetables, they are seasonal, so when you see them on the shelves out of season, it means they've either been grown in industrial greenhouses or have been transported thousands of kilometres from other countries, all of which uses lots of energy. In fact, the more 'food miles' between the place where the food is grown and the place where it is sold, the worse the impact on the environment. What's more, transported food loses its freshness and is therefore less nutritious. We should buy food instead that is both in season and grown locally. [3] ....

4 THE PROBLEM WITH PROCESSED FOOD

A lot of the food we consume these days, from cookies to pizza, has been made in factories and contains large amounts of fat and sugar, making the global obesity crisis worse. What's more, it is estimated that around half of all packaged processed food contains palm oil. Not only is this vegetable oil easy to produce, it is also odourless and colourless, can keep products edible for a long time, and makes fried products crispy. However, its cultivation requires large scale deforestation which is destroying the habitats of many endangered animals, including orangutans, elephants and rhinos.

[4] ....

5 EMPTY STOMACHS AND BINS FULL OF FOOD

At one time or another, we've all thrown food away. It might not seem much at the time, but it all adds up. In industrialised countries, people waste around 222 million tons of food every year. In fact, around a third of all the food produced is wasted. At the same time, for millions of people around the world, finding enough to eat is a daily struggle. For those of us who don't have to produce our own food and can simply go to the supermarket whenever our kitchens are empty, the answer is simple. [5] ....

Project
Researching and presenting

You're going to give a presentation about how to eat responsibly.

1 THINK

With your classmates, brainstorm ways to eat responsibly not mentioned in the text and choose one you'd like to learn more about.

2 RESEARCH

Research the idea you chose. Using the advice on pages 80–81, take notes about:

- how it works
- how it helps the environment
- how easy/challenging it is to do
- any famous people/celebrities who do or have done it.

3 PLAN

Plan and rehearse your presentation.

4 PRESENT

Give your presentation and listen to your classmates' presentations.

5 CHOOSE

Choose one of the ideas to try for at least a week.

6 FEEDBACK

Report back to the class on how you're doing.

REVIEW 3 UNITS 9–12

VOCABULARY

1 Read the information about the people and answer the questions.

Who

1 is a trainee?
2 has followed a clear career path?
3 has received careers advice?
4 is networking?
5 is doing an internship?
6 has aspirations for the future?
7 needs a scholarship?
8 seems to have good social skills?

Alicia hopes to get good grades in order to get some financial support so she can study at university.

Felipe's teachers told him that since he was good at both maths and art, he should train to be an architect.

Shivani has a paid job but she is still learning how to do it and is not fully qualified.

Lena is spending the summer working for an insurance company. She is not being paid but is learning useful skills.

Daniel is at a conference, hoping to meet people who will be able to help him in his career.

Max started as an accounts assistant. He then got a supervisor role and later became head of department.

Rosalie has started a new job. She has introduced herself to everyone and listened to their advice.

César is still at school but he wants to be a rich and successful business owner one day.

2 Complete the blog post with words from the box.

behind fulfilled in out over
pay set submit through up

I was very sick during the school year that I turned 17. This meant that I fell [1] ______ in all my subjects. When I went back to school, I found it exhausting and was just not managing to hand [2] ______ my work on time because I'd fall asleep as soon as I got home. I considered dropping [3] ______ of school altogether. The reason I didn't is down to one inspirational teacher, Mr Briggs. He was concerned enough to [4] ______ my family a visit and offered to help me catch [5] ______ with my classmates. We worked together every day after school, going [6] ______ all the work I'd missed. He helped me [7] ______ realistic goals, like reading one page of the textbook every evening. Nothing too strenuous. He also encouraged me to [8] ______ applications to universities, which I'd more or less decided to give up on. Anyway, thanks to his support, I got [9] ______ all my exams and [10] ______ the entry requirements to my first choice of university.

3 Complete the extract from a travel agent's website. The beginnings of the words are given.

TRAVEL Home | About | Log in

Would you prefer to go abroad this year instead of having another [1]st______? If you are environmentally conscious and want your holiday to be [2]sus______, we can help! Here at Evergreen Travels we specialise in holidays that are [3]car______ ne______. All our destinations are [4]o______ the be______ tr______, so you will enjoy an unspoiled area in a remote part of the world. We undertake to [5]off______ your car______ fo______ so you don't have to worry about it. We support a wide range of initiatives which undo damage done by tourism, for example by [6]cl______ ______ beaches. We will tailor your [7]it______ to your group's interests and you can choose to have all your meals included or go for the [8]se______-ca______ option.

4 Put the events into the most logical order.

a The judge said although he was guilty of a minor offence, he was a repeat offender.
b The man was arrested on suspicion of shoplifting.
c He appeared in court and pleaded guilty.
d He decided never to commit another crime.
e He was sentenced to a short time in jail.
f The security guard reported him to the police.
g He was charged with theft.
h A security guard in a department store saw a man put some items into his bag without paying.

5 Match words from Column A with words from Column B. Which pairs are joined by a hyphen? Which words in Column C do the pairs collocate with?

A	B	C
gluten	roasted	bread
free	dried	eggs
sun	free	tomatoes
slow	fried	fish
freshly	sourced	produce
locally	baked	pizza
pan	range	chicken

6 Correct the mistakes in these sentences.

1 I'm so hungry I could eat an elephant.
2 I prefer not to eat rich or fat foods.
3 Could you tell me which vegetables are on season?
4 I'd forgotten that you had such sweet teeth.
5 I'm so full. My eyes were bigger than my head.
6 The bill's very expensive. Shall we go half?

GRAMMAR

1 **Change the sentences into the passive voice. Where possible, do so in two ways.**

1 The judge gave the offender 100 hours of community service.
2 You have to pay your tourism tax to the hotel you're staying at.
3 I think we should encourage children to learn to cook from an early age.
4 I remember my teacher telling us to think critically.
5 The waiter brought us a delicious bowl of hot and spicy soup.
6 It's always nice to see children developing their social skills.
7 The government says it doesn't want to leave any child behind.
8 Judges tend to give lighter punishments to first-time offenders.

2 **Make the sentences more emphatic. Begin with the word(s) at the end of each sentence.**

1 We should be developing leadership skills in our young people. (What)
2 Violent offenders should not be given community service. (Under no circumstances)
3 Hidden sugars in convenience foods cause the majority of health problems. (It)
4 The country won't be carbon neutral by 2050. (No way)
5 We need harsher penalties for those guilty of cruelty to animals. (What)

3 **Correct any mistakes in these sentences. Some are correct.**

1 Not only it is an exceptionally easy recipe to follow, it is an absolutely delicious dish.
2 On no circumstances can organised crime be allowed to continue.
3 Caleb was very upset about to be issued with a fine.
4 It is tourism that has contributed most to the country's development.
5 Parking offences have being decriminalised in all areas of the UK.
6 After much discussion, that we opted for this year was a staycation.
7 It is healthy fast food is most in demand these days.
8 Alexa hopes to offer a scholarship by a top university.
9 What I believe is that networking is the best way to help your career.
10 Adam's career aspirations include making him head of department by the age of 25.

4 **Read the text below and decide which answer (A, B, C or D) best fits each gap.**

Cruise ships, pollution and the law

In recent decades, the environment has **(0)** *C* greatly from the introduction of anti-pollution laws designed to protect it. These have **(1)** ______ more responsible behaviour in many industries, including tourism. Several cruise lines have been **(2)** ______ with large fines for dumping waste at sea. One US based cruise line **(3)** ______ guilty to charges of illegal dumping of hazardous waste and was fined $40 million.

On average, a cruise ship passenger's carbon **(4)** ______ is three times higher than it would be on land. This makes cruises one of the least **(5)** ______ holiday options. This is partly due to the low standards that have been **(6)** ______ by the authorities, which only require very basic treatment of waste. While fines are high, it is only when **(7)** ______ offenders are given more severe punishments that the situation will improve. Some suggest that lengthy jail **(8)** ______ should be given to the worst polluters.

	A	B	C	D
0	**A** aided	**B** improved	(**C**) benefited	**D** assisted
1	**A** resulted in	**B** carried through	**C** come about	**D** brought up
2	**A** given	**B** imposed	**C** applied	**D** issued
3	**A** admitted	**B** declared	**C** pleaded	**D** stated
4	**A** footstep	**B** footprint	**C** imprint	**D** trail
5	**A** sustainable	**B** renewable	**C** passable	**D** tolerable
6	**A** put	**B** placed	**C** set	**D** kept
7	**A** late	**B** primary	**C** second	**D** repeat
8	**A** punishments	**B** sentences	**C** times	**D** periods

5 **Read the text below and think of the word which best fits each gap. Use only one word in each gap.**

Le Cordon Bleu

When it **(0)** *comes* to cooking, *Le Cordon Bleu* is a name everyone associates with top quality. Founded in 1895, *Le Cordon Bleu* is **(1)** ______ a doubt the world's most famous cookery school. It has attracted chefs with a passion **(2)** ______ French cuisine from all over the world.

(3) ______ many people may not be aware of is that *Le Cordon Bleu*, while still the guardian of French culinary technique, has moved **(4)** ______ the times. It now has an international network of educational institutions, **(5)** ______ to mention restaurants, publications and consultancy services. The schools **(6)** ______ pride in providing students with hands-on learning which combines innovation with tradition.

It goes without saying that *Le Cordon Bleu's* philosophy of excellence remains the same. The popularity of televised cooking contests means that interest in the culinary arts is **(7)** ______ the increase and this iconic institution is still a place to **(8)** ______ many up-and-coming chefs are attracted.

13 LEARNING THE LINGO

? ABOUT YOU

▶ 13 **Watch the video and then answer the questions.**
What do you think is the best way to learn a language?
Do you consider yourself to be a natural language learner?
What would you say is your preferred means of communication?

VOCABULARY AND READING
COMMUNICATION: PHRASAL VERBS

EP **1 Match the sentence halves.**

1 I'd like José more
2 I know just enough Italian
3 I'm planning to brush up on my French
4 My friend talked me into throwing a party,
5 It was great to see my old friend Chris again
6 Stan came home from work so angry that he wanted to quit his job,
7 A girl came up to me the other day and said she recognised me,
8 Something weird happened today in our Chemistry lesson – Polina
9 When we heard today that the school was closing for the rest of term,
10 I'm not sure what the teacher was getting at when she said my accent was 'interesting' –

a and catch up on all his news.
b I just couldn't take it in at first.
c but his wife talked him out of it.
d in time for our holiday on Corsica.
e was she trying to say it's not very good?
f although I'm sure I'd never met her before.
g but now I think I've invited too many people.
h to get by when I'm visiting my cousins in Milan.
i suddenly burst out laughing, but I had no idea why!
j if he didn't go on about how clever he is all the time.

2 Check the meaning of the phrasal verbs.

3 Complete the sentences with a phrasal verb from Exercise 1 in the correct form.

1 For end-of-term exams, it's good to .... everything you've learned at least one day before the exam.
2 Translation apps work so well that we can easily .... without spending time learning foreign languages.
3 If someone I don't know .... me in the street, my natural instinct is to avoid them.
4 The best way to .... what's going on in the world is to see what's on your social media feeds.
5 If people in the media keep .... the climate crisis, ordinary people might get bored of hearing about it.

4 Discuss with a partner. Do you agree with the statements in Exercise 3?

5 Look at the title of the article on the opposite page. What do you think are the pros and cons of this type of technology? Then quickly read the article to see if any of your ideas are mentioned.

6 Do Carla and Jason have a mostly positive or negative opinion of translation apps?

7 Read the article again and look at the statements below. Are these opinions expressed by Carla, Jason, or both of them?

1 The accuracy of translation apps needs refining.
2 Apps will never be sophisticated enough to replace language learning.
3 The reason for learning languages in the future will change.
4 Certain professions will become unnecessary.
5 We should be wary of technology making us lazy.
6 Language learning has other benefits apart from being able to communicate.

SPEAKING THE SAME LANGUAGE

69

Translation apps – are they the future? Here are some of your views.

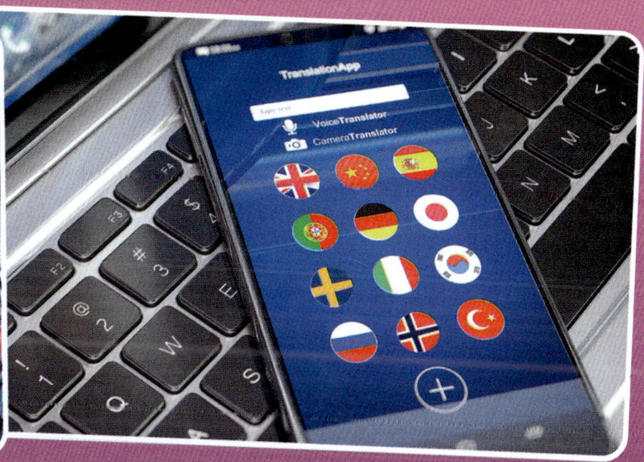

CARLA, 23, DUBLIN

A few months ago, I was passing through Frankfurt Airport when an old lady came up to me and started saying something repeatedly in a language I couldn't identify. I had absolutely no idea what she was going on about. Having just brushed up on my German before my trip, I tried speaking that with her, but it was no use. Then I remembered my translation app, so I took out my phone and got her to speak into it. The app recognised her language as Bulgarian, and translated it into English, poorly translated English admittedly, but adequate to get her message across. She'd had her flight cancelled and the airline had sent her to a fully booked hotel. The receptionist then had made her go back to the airport, although she had no idea why. With the aid of the translation app, the airline staff were able to get her booked into another hotel. So technology saved the day.

The thing is, I can get by in several languages, but that only works if the person I'm talking to knows one of them. I realised that people like me, who have spent hundreds of hours learning to speak languages, may soon be redundant. And it made me grateful that my parents had talked me out of becoming an interpreter – that's one profession that we won't be needing in the future.

So, does this signal the end of language learning? Well, they say that language learning sharpens your mind and broadens your horizons, and an app can't do that for you. In the past we often learned languages because we had to; in the future it'll be because we want to. It'll become purely a hobby, like taking up golf.

What at I'm getting at is this though: the future belongs not to people who speak the most languages, but the IT experts who develop the most user-friendly translation apps. Because as they improve, the day is not far off, I'm sure, when that's all we'll really need.

JASON, 22, LOS ANGELES

It seems that translation apps are revolutionising the way we get round language barriers. Language teachers everywhere must be terrified of the idea of language learning and teaching becoming obsolete. But could that ever happen?

There's a lot of buzz at the moment about how amazing translation apps are, but the fact is that they're still very hit-and-miss. They don't cope well with background noise, and the collection of poorly translated texts you can find all over the internet brings new meaning to the phrase 'lost in translation'. A friend of mine recently talked me into downloading one when we went overseas on vacation, and we would often burst out laughing when we heard the translations. One night we even ate in a restaurant which had had its spicy chicken wings mistranslated as 'angry flying chicks'. No doubt they had used a translation app too!

If we were to give up learning languages and just rely on apps, it would be a disaster. Language is not an exact science. Statements can be ambiguous; words have different meanings. Communication isn't just about words but body language, intonation and numerous other things that convey meaning. And without language learning we would miss valuable opportunities to enhance our social skills and experience new cultures.

Don't get me wrong. I'm not anti-technology. In fact, I think it's the future of language learning. The latest trend in this area is Virtual Reality (VR) learning, where you can you engage in virtual conversations and actively participate in lessons. Streaming services such as Netflix now have tools that let you catch up on all your favourite TV shows in their original versions with subtitles, and which pause automatically so you have time to take in what you just heard. It's fun and you can do it from the comfort of your home.

The point is this. Technology should help us to learn, rather than do all the hard work for us. It may be tempting to have a machine do everything for us, but where does that end?

TALKING POINTS

Do you have a translation app on your phone and have you used it? Did it work well?
Do you think that technology is making us lazier? In what way?
Do you think that translation apps will make learning languages redundant in the near future?

GRAMMAR
CAUSATIVES

1 **Read the extracts from the article and choose the correct answer.**

1 I took out my phone and **got her to speak** into it.
Whose idea was it for the old lady to speak into the writer's phone?
a the writer's **b** the old lady's

2 She**'d had her flight cancelled** …
Who had cancelled the flight?
a the old lady **b** someone else
Do you think the old lady was happy about what happened?

3 The airline staff were able to **get her booked** into another hotel.
Who organised the booking?
a the airline staff **b** the old lady

4 Streaming services now **let you catch up** on all your favourite TV shows.
Who or what allows TV viewers to watch their favourite shows?
a TV viewers **b** streaming services

5 The receptionist then had **made her go** back to the airport, although she had no idea why.
Whose idea was it for the lady to go back to the airport?
a the old lady's **b** the receptionist's
Do you think the old lady returned to the airport willingly or unwillingly?

6 It may be tempting to **have a machine do** everything for us …
Who or what would arrange for the machine to do all the work?
a the machine **b** the speaker
Does *have a machine do everything for us* mean the same as *get a machine to do everything for us*?
Which sounds more formal: the structure with *have*, or the structure with *get*?

2 **Match the causative structures a–f below to extracts 1–6 in Exercise 1.**

a *have* + object + past participle ____
- when somebody intentionally causes or arranges the action (e.g. *have your bike mended*)
- when something is done to someone with a bad result (e.g. *have your bike stolen*)

b *get* + object + past participle ____
- a more informal version of *have* + object + past participle

c *get* + *someone* + *to* infinitive ____
- similar in meaning to *ask* or *persuade*

d *have* + *someone* + infinitive without *to* ____
- the same meaning as *get someone to do something* but more formal

e *make* + *someone* + infinitive without *to* ____
- force someone to do something

f *let* + *someone* + infinitive without *to* ____
- allow someone to do something

» **GRAMMAR REFERENCE AND PRACTICE PAGE 156**

3 **Correct any mistakes in these sentences. One sentence is correct.**

1 My mum got me install a language learning app on her phone, and she uses it all the time now.
2 Some universities have all their student essays checked by special plagiarism-detecting software.
3 When I'm practising my Spanish, I find that having the other person to speak more slowly makes it easier to understand.
4 My dad likes to have cleaned his car by the guys in the garage, because he can't be bothered to do it himself!
5 They got rewritten the instructions in language that was easier for non-native speakers to understand.
6 It's better to let people to learn languages at their own pace.

4 **For questions 1–6, complete the second sentence so that it has a similar meaning to the first sentence, using the word given. Do not change the word given. You must use between three and six words, including the word given.**

1 It's easier to get someone to paint your room for you than to do it yourself. **PAINTED**
Having ______________ hard as doing it yourself.

2 The invigilators got the candidates to sit at least two metres apart for the exam. **NO**
The invigilators had the ______________ than two metres apart for the exam.

3 My friend talked me into joining her jazz band. **GOT**
My friend ______________ her jazz band.

4 Thieves illegally entered Mr Smith's shop last week. **HAD**
Mr Smith ______________ into by thieves last week.

5 The teacher insists on us submitting our homework before the lesson. **MAKES**
The teacher ______________ in before class.

6 Roser and Manuel have arranged for a professional photographer to take photos of them tomorrow. **HAVING**
Roser and Manuel ______________ professionally tomorrow.

5 » **WORK IN PAIRS. TURN TO PAGE 133.**

VOCABULARY
ADVERBS

1 Discuss the questions with a partner.

1 Are you into online gaming? If so, do you ever use English when you play?
2 Do you know anyone who takes part in gaming competitions?

70 **2 Listen to two classmates talking about twin brothers, Miguel and Javier, who took part in a gaming competition at the weekend. Are these statements true or false?**

1 Miguel and Javier weren't interested in computer games at school.
2 Miguel was told off several times during classes at school.
3 Miguel and Javier entered a gaming competition together as a team.
4 The guy from London was said to be England's best player.
5 The guy from London had good skills and techniques.
6 In Javier's first game, his opponent played brilliantly.
7 Javier only just won his first game.
8 The boy is surprised that Javier did so well.
9 Javier's opponent in the final was Miguel.
10 The final was played in front of an audience.
11 Miguel came first, and Javier came second.
12 The girl thinks that Miguel and Javier's success may be thanks to her school.

EP 70 **3 Complete a summary of the conversation using the adverbs in the box. Then listen and check. Check the meaning of any adverbs that you don't understand.**

comprehensively	effectively	incredibly
individually	massively	namely	poorly
publicly	repeatedly	respectively
supposedly	technically

1 Miguel and Javier were both .... into gaming.
2 Miguel .... got into trouble for playing games during lessons.
3 Miguel and Javier were competing in the competition ....
4 Javier's first opponent was .... the top player in England – he was .... brilliant.
5 His opponent played really .... and Javier beat him ....
6 ...., Javier got through to the final.
7 He was nervous when he found out who he was against – .... his own brother.
8 The final is always staged .... and recorded.
9 Javier and Miguel came first and second ....
10 This .... means that their school produces the best gamers in the country.

4 Complete the sentences by using one pair of adverbs in each.

comprehensively / incredibly	effectively / technically
individually / massively	namely / respectively
poorly / repeatedly	supposedly / publicly

1 Isaac has finished his final exams and .... left school, as he's not required to turn up every day, although .... he'll be classed as a student there until the last day of term.
2 Sylvia got a low mark for her English literature essay, because her teacher said it was .... organised and hard to follow, plus she'd spelled 'Shakespeare' wrong .... throughout.
3 I've got my favourite then my least favourite lessons today, ... English and then maths ....
4 The prime minster of my country .... speaks amazing English, but no-one's really sure, because whenever she appears ...., she always speaks through an interpreter.
5 Our teacher said that she couldn't give us feedback on our presentations .... as it would take too long, which seems .... unfair if she expects us to improve.
6 A language learning website I use was .... redesigned at great expense, but with the new layout, it's now .... difficult to navigate. I don't know why they bothered!

5 Replace the underlined words with an adverb from the box.

incredibly	massively	namely
poorly	publicly	repeatedly

There's only one thing I detest more than going to the dentist, [1]<u>and that is</u> phoning call centres. I recently noticed that I'd been overcharged [2]<u>by a large amount</u> on my phone bill, so I called to get it sorted. Needless to say, I had to wait an [3]<u>extremely</u> long time before my call was answered. And when it was, I had to explain [4]<u>again and again</u> to different people at the call centre what the problem was, and what I wanted them to do about it. All the staff must have been really [5]<u>badly</u> trained. It was so bad that I'm going to express [6]<u>to everyone</u> how awful their service is by writing a brutally honest review of the firm online.

6 » **WORK IN PAIRS.** **TURN TO PAGE 133.**

LISTENING

1 **What might you want to say to a friend that could be**

- more appropriate in a text message than a phone call?
- best discussed face to face and in private?
- suitable for a group chat?
- suited to a phone call, but not to messaging?

2 **Work in pairs. Read the quotes and say if any of them are true for you.**

'I come across as being really confident online, whereas I'm actually quite shy in person.'

'When I'm chatting to my mates and my parents overhear us, they have no idea what we're on about.'

'I never use emojis in my social media posts because they're (a) old-fashioned and (b) childish.'

3 **You will hear a podcast discussion between two people, Harriet and Mick, who have an academic interest in how technology affects language and communication. Choose the answer (A, B, C or D) which fits best.**

71

1 Harriet says that an advantage of using electronic communication to send unwelcome news is that it
A saves people considerable time and effort.
B enables people to conceal their emotions.
C allows people to maintain good relations.
D helps people to avoid others' negative feelings.

2 Mick has learned that the way a person expresses themselves online
A may have very little to do with their age.
B is largely determined by why they first began using the internet.
C varies according to which online platform they are using.
D is affected by the time they spend socialising on the web.

3 Harriet mentions US president George Washington in order to
A demonstrate that language has changed very little over time.
B explain why the written word has always been responsible for changes in society.
C show that effective use of language can enable people to shape history.
D argue that technological changes have always influenced language.

4 When speaking about how technology may affect marriages in the future, Mick and Harriet agree that
A married couples may use technology as a way to spend less time together.
B the proportion of people who marry after meeting on a dating app will rise.
C it will be more common for people to marry without knowing the same language.
D the time between a couple first contacting each other and getting married will be shorter.

5 Mick thinks that the internet helps researchers to study language use more fully because
A people can easily see how high-profile figures express themselves.
B such enormous amounts are uploaded every day.
C data from ordinary people is publicly available.
D people use more informal language on social media.

6 Harriet says that emojis are problematic for study because
A the same ones can mean different things to different people.
B they can only be fully understood by the person the message is for.
C some experts do not consider them to be a part of written language.
D it is unclear how people who use them believe that they enhance meaning.

4 **Discuss the questions with a partner.**

1. Do you prefer to send individual messages to friends or send group messages?
2. Have you ever messaged someone instead of ringing them to avoid having to speak to them?
3. Have you ever sent a message that the recipient completely misunderstood?
4. Do you think that a friendship or a relationship conducted through a translation app could work?
5. Do you think that the popularity of messaging instead of calling or speaking face-to-face with people means that the current generation has poorer communication skills than previous generations?

SPEAKING
A DISCUSSION

1 **Discuss with a partner which of the following statements you think have been shown scientifically to be true.**

1 It's easier to tell if someone is lying by listening to them than by watching them.
2 Telling the truth leads to better mental and physical health, with less stress and fewer headaches.
3 The average person can only tell when they are being lied to 50% of the time.
4 Police officers are much better than most people at identifying when someone is lying.
5 In a study, 60% of people were found to lie at least once in a ten-minute conversation.

2 **Match 1–12 to a–l to make phrases which you can use in discussions.**

1 As far as	a a good point.
2 That's	b to a point.
3 I'm with	c you on that.
4 I'm not so	d agree more.
5 Yes, that's a	e I'm concerned …
6 I agree up	f good question.
7 I couldn't	g what you mean.
8 It depends	h to interpretation.
9 That's open	i about that before.
10 I can see where	j you're coming from, but …
11 I've never thought	k sure about that actually.
12 That's not something	l I've ever really considered.

3 **Work with a different partner. Here are some situations in which people might say things that aren't true, and a question for you to discuss. Talk to each other about why people might say things that aren't true in these situations. Try to use some of the phrases from Exercise 2.**

Why might people say things that aren't true in these situations?

- meeting someone for the first time
- talking about how good a meal was
- writing a post on social media
- speaking with family about school
- describing how they are feeling

72 **4** **Now listen to two candidates, Gerardo and Maribel, discussing the question.**

Which candidate

1 agrees with their partner's answer?
2 doesn't initially know how to answer the question?
3 gives two alternative viewpoints, then selects one of them?
4 disagrees with a statement suggested by the examiner?
5 uses an example from their own life?
6 disagrees with one of their partner's answers?

5 **Complete the *Prepare to speak* expressions with a word from the box.**

as if more so to where with

PREPARE TO SPEAK

Giving opinions

You could say … , but then again …
[1] ………… you ask me, …
I honestly think that …
As far [2] ………… I'm concerned, …
[3] ………… be honest, …

Agreeing

I'm [4] ………… you on that.
Absolutely.
Exactly.
I couldn't agree [5] ………… .

Agreeing partially

I see your point, but …
I can see [6] ………… you're coming from, but …

Disagreeing politely

I'm not [7] ………… sure about that actually.
Not for me.

72 **6** **Listen again to Gerardo and Maribel. Which of the expressions in the *Prepare to speak* box do they use? Write *G* or *M* next to the expressions.**

7 **With a partner, ask and answer the questions using expressions from the *Prepare to speak* box.**

1 Do you think it's sometimes better not to tell the whole truth? (Why? / Why not?)
2 Do you think some people are better at lying than others? (Why? / Why not?)
3 How easy is it to tell if something you read online is true or not?
4 Some people think that when small children lie, they are showing signs of intelligence. To what extent do you agree?
5 What do you imagine a world would be like in which nobody ever lied?
6 Do you think people tell the truth about their life when they write their autobiography? Would you?

8 » **WORK IN PAIRS.** **TURN TO PAGE 133.**

14 THE SOCIAL MEDIA GENERATION

? ABOUT YOU

▶ 14 **Watch the video and then answer the questions.**
Do you follow any social media influencers?
Have you ever bought something after seeing it advertised by an influencer?
Do you create original content (videos, memes, etc)?

VOCABULARY AND READING

SOCIAL MEDIA MARKETING

EP **1 Match the words and phrases to meanings a–j.**

1 How many **followers** do you have on social media?
2 The band's **fanbase** is mainly made up of teenage girls.
3 A lot of social media advertising **targets** teenagers.
4 Many companies now use influencers to **market** their products, and apparently this has really **boosted** sales.
5 Sonia loves labels like Gucci and Prada. She always has the latest **designer goods**.
6 Companies may feel that influencers can **engage with** the customer more than celebrities can, and they may be easier for people to **emulate**.
7 Fashion brands **sponsor** influencers who show their clothes and accessories to their best advantage.
8 **Product placement** on social media has become an important promotional tool for many small businesses.

a is aimed at
b supplying an item for a photo/movie so it can be noticed
c group of admirers
d try to be like someone you admire
e give money to someone in return for advertising
f expensive items made by a famous designer
g be involved and connected with
h promote, advertise
i increased
j friends or contacts

2 Complete the sentences with a word or phrase from Exercise 1. You may need to change the form.

1 Putting those sunglasses in the shot on the boat was brilliant ________.
2 You may have a lot more ________ than I do but most of them are inactive.
3 I don't waste my time trying to ________ celebrities. I prefer to just be myself.
4 Some influencers are lucky enough to be ________ by travel companies and get free holidays.
5 Some of the advertising that ________ children is quite unethical, in my view.
6 This sunny weather has helped ________ sales of garden furniture.
7 I'm not willing to pay extra for ________. Some high street brands are just as good.
8 Coca-Cola is a company who has managed to ________ successfully with consumers through their advertisements.
9 Companies need to be more and more creative when it comes to ________ their products.

3 Read the article on the opposite page quickly, ignoring the gaps. Choose the best summary.

A There need to be stricter rules governing social media influencers' promotion of potentially harmful products and their conduct in general.
B Using social media influencers to endorse products can make a lot of money for companies, but influencers have a duty to the public to behave responsibly.
C It would benefit businesses to use social media influencers to a greater extent than more traditional methods of advertising, since they have proved effective in getting results.

4 Read the notes a student has written on the parts of the article before and after the first gap. She has chosen two possible paragraphs to fill the gap: F and G. Read them carefully. Which one fits better? Highlight the words or phrases that helped you decide.

5 Choose from the paragraphs A–G the one which fits each gap (2–6). There is one extra paragraph which you do not need to use.

A On the other hand, with their well-staged photo shoots featuring perfect models, fashion magazines are too glamorous for most readers. The outfits they really want to see are those they can wear to school or work.

B Experts have responded with innovative solutions to this issue. Technological developments have made it possible to develop ways to demonstrate connections between advertising and results. One programme called RewardStyle looks particularly promising.

C Firstly, the balance between style, content and audience engagement is a challenge, and only those that achieve it will become successful. For every one that makes it, there are a hundred others that try and fail.

D Social media, with everyone potentially being a producer of content, blurs the lines between advertising and simply sharing ideas. In the absence of laws, people need to monitor their own behaviour.

How have social media influencers

CHANGED ADVERTISING?

Everyone knows how drastically the advent of the internet has changed almost every aspect of life, bringing in new concepts and terminology. Platforms, unfriending, followers, trending, hashtags and tweeting are all words or phrases that people as recently as 15 years ago would not have understood, at least not in the context they are used in today.

This gives a general introduction to the text. It might move on to a more specific aspect.

1 ____________________

It is easy to see how certain individuals manage to become popular on social media, but how they become rich is not so obvious. Why do companies sponsor relatively unknown people, sometimes with a following of less than 10,000 people? Marketing director Zoe Crosbie points out that these micro-influencers' popularity is due to their authenticity. Unlike celebrities, micro-influencers are relatable, since in spite of their enviable lifestyles and designer goods, they are accessible to their followers. She explains that they are sought after by advertisers because they are seen to be genuinely using or enjoying items, rather than simply endorsing them because they are paid to do so.

Who are these 'individuals'?

2 ____________________

They are people you can emulate with some degree of success and even have a conversation with through the platform. One fashion vlogger and influencer said that her clothes could be worn by ordinary people on the streets, which was why she enjoyed such a high degree of popularity.

3 ____________________

However, one of the dilemmas that faces brands using social media influencers is how to demonstrate that influencers' use of their products actually boosts sales. In the case of product placement, the correlation is particularly hard to prove. Marketing managers need to know whether paying a micro-influencer is boosting their brand or just keeping another millennial in designer clothes.

4 ____________________

It is able to prove that a specific sale was directly linked to an influencer's post. Several similar platforms have been created so that it is now possible for a brand to know which influencers actually generate sales. It was reported that two thirds of marketing departments were planning to increase their spending on influencer marketing since there is now sufficient evidence that it is money well spent.

There is an ethical dimension to the social influencer phenomenon, though. Whereas traditional advertising has long since been regulated by laws on what may legally be promoted, an individual's social media presence does not face the same constraints. A newspaper article revealed that criticism of social media influencers, particularly those who target pre-teens, had increased dramatically in the previous year.

5 ____________________

This example demonstrates that legislation has been unable to keep up with the rapid development of social media influencing. Each platform has its own guidelines but they only seem to be applied in extreme cases. There's a difficult balance between individual freedom to share what you choose to about your lifestyle and the need to protect vulnerable members of your audience.

6 ____________________

It is often said that with influence comes responsibility. As one blogger says, 'While it is your choice to eat junk food or take diet pills or whatever, you shouldn't encourage others to do the same.' She advised all influencers not to abuse their popularity in this way. The question is, can we trust all influencers to do what's right?

E One promotion of a slimming aid by an influencer who was pregnant at the time was the subject of a large number of complaints to the Advertising Standards Agency. The individual concerned claimed that it wasn't an advertisement and she hadn't been paid to promote the product.

F When an advertiser uses a well-known personality, such as an actor or sportsperson, in their campaign, deep down people know they are promoting the product for the income they receive from doing so. In spite of having a relatively small fan-base, micro-influencers can have significant reach and can engage with their followers.

G One phenomenon in this new world that has revolutionised both the social and business spheres is the social media influencer, an envied being with a seemingly effortless luxury lifestyle but without any particular talent.

TALKING POINTS

Who do you think should be most responsible for preventing the promotion of harmful products on social media – governments, platforms or individuals?
What are the pros and cons of being a social media influencer? Would you like to be one?

GRAMMAR
REPORTED SPEECH

1 Read the examples from the article of direct and reported speech and their equivalents. Match examples 1–4 to rules a–f. An example may match more than one rule.

1 'My clothes can be worn by ordinary people.'
One fashion vlogger and influencer said that her clothes could be worn by ordinary people.

2 'Micro-influencers' popularity is due to their authenticity.'
Marketing director Zoe Crosbie points out that these micro-influencers' popularity is due to their authenticity.

3 'While it is your choice to eat junk food or take diet pills, you shouldn't encourage others to do the same.'
A blogger said that while it was your choice to eat junk food or take diet pills, you shouldn't encourage others to do the same.

4 'Criticism of social media influencers has increased dramatically in the last year.'
A newspaper article revealed that criticism of social media influencers had increased dramatically in the previous year.

a The tense of the verb in reported speech is usually further in the past than in the spoken words.
b In reported speech, *will* changes to *would*, *can* to *could* and *must* to *had to*.
c Past perfect tenses and *would*, *could* and *should* cannot move further into the past so do not change.
d The tense of the verb in reported speech does not always change if we want to show that what the speaker said is still true now.
e Time and place adverbs change if the time or place is no longer the same.
f We often change pronouns and possessive adjectives, e.g. when the reporter is not the original speaker.

» **GRAMMAR REFERENCE AND PRACTICE PAGE 157**

2 Change the direct speech to reported speech.

1 'Ordinary people can become famous overnight.'
She said …
2 'The results of the survey will be published tomorrow.'
The evening news reported …
3 'I've got 12,000 followers on my blog.'
Mike said …
4 'I could easily get brands to sponsor me.'
Amanda said …
5 'Sales declined in the first quarter of the year.'
The manager told us that …
6 'You must finish writing your blog post by next Tuesday.'
The editor told Freya …

74 **3 Listen and complete the extracts from a conversation between two students who are members of their school's website committee. Find two examples of each of the reporting structures a–d below.**

a verb + to infinitive
b verb + object + to infinitive
c verb + ing
d verb + preposition + noun /-ing

1 Some people complained ………… to work so hard …
2 Mr Parson apologised ………… …
3 … and promised ………… us all pizza.
4 And he encouraged ………… our work on the committee on our university applications.
5 I volunteered ………… a review of the new play …
6 He suggested ………… you along too …
7 He reminded ………… all the social media sites …
8 And he recommended ………… everything up …

4 Which of the options in these sentences is *not* correct?

1 My parents *warned* / *advised* / *recommended* me not to share personal information on social media.
2 Mr Muller *told* / *reminded* / *offered* us to update our CVs.
3 Jonas *promised* / *admitted* / *denied* using his sister's password.
4 The headteacher *invited* / *encouraged* / *suggested* the parents to read the information on the website.
5 Adele always *agrees* / *volunteers* / *persuades* to endorse our products.
6 The manager *apologised for* / *promised to* / *insisted on* keeping us waiting.

5 Read the grammar rule in the box. Then find two examples of impersonal reporting structures in the article on page 105.

To report speech without saying who the reporter is, we can start sentences with *It* + a passive verb.
It has been said that the internet has turned the world into a global village.

6 Use impersonal reporting structures to avoid saying who the reporter is.

1 They say that the social media platform is worth £1 billion.
2 According to various sources, Facebook is the world's third most visited website.
3 An article in the Daily News said that more women than men use social media.
4 The prime minister announced that new laws will be introduced to protect children online.
5 People don't think there will be print newspapers for much longer.

7 Correct any mistakes in these sentences. One sentence is correct.

1 My friends advised that I become an influencer.
2 Rachel denied posting fake news on her social media platform.
3 Mike said you share his photo without asking him.
4 They agreed not publish the story.
5 Alannah said me that the event had been a great success.
6 It said that all jobs will use technology in the future.

8 » **WORK IN PAIRS. TURN TO PAGE 133.**

VOCABULARY
NEGATIVE PREFIXES

75 **1 You will hear two friends, Adrian and Teresa, discussing the article on social media influencers. What problems and solutions do they mention?**

EP 75 **2 Listen again. Which prefix was used before the words?**

1 ____ responsibly
2 ____ legal
3 ____ accessible
4 ____ obey
5 ____ precise
6 ____ do

3 Add a prefix from Exercise 2 to the highlighted words in the sentences.

1 Joanna's ____ ability to take good photos made her social media posts ____ interesting.
2 In the last few months, Dylan has become ____ mature and ____ respectful.
3 William has been behaving quite ____ rationally recently.
4 The procedure may cause some ____ comfort.
5 The children waited ____ patiently for the show to begin.
6 The ____ literacy rate is rising in most countries.

4 Complete the table using the words with negative prefixes from Exercises 2 and 3.

Nouns	Verbs	Adjectives	Adverbs
inability			

5 Look at your answers to Exercise 4 and complete the rules on negative prefixes.

1 The prefixes ____ and ____ can be used with nouns, verbs, adjectives and adverbs.
2 The prefixes *im*, *in*, *il*, *ir*, are only used with nouns, adjectives and adverbs, and not ____________.
3 The prefix ____ is often used with nouns, adjectives and adverbs beginning with *p*, *b*, *m*.
4 The prefix ____ is often used with nouns, adjectives and adverbs beginning with *l*.
5 The prefix ____ is often used with nouns, adjectives and adverbs beginning with *r*.

76 **6 Listen to the next part of Teresa and Adrian's conversation. What do they disagree about?**

EP 76 **7 Listen again. You will hear some other prefixes. Add a prefix to the highlighted words in these extracts. Say which meaning, a–d, the prefix has.**

1 So, you think influencers' accounts should be ____ activated if they break the rules?
2 The potential for ____ information being spread is huge.
3 But it seems the consequences for these people are ____ existent.
4 ... the best way to deal with ____ social behaviour online is to fine people.

a against
b absent, lacking in
c reverse, remove, reduce
d wrong or bad

SUFFIXES *-FUL* AND *-LESS*

EP **8 Work with a partner. To what extent do you agree with the statements?**

1 Fining people for breaking social media guidelines is useless.
2 It is common for influencers to be untruthful when advertising products on social media.
3 We are helpless to stop the spread of fake news online.

9 Complete the rules with adjectives from Exercise 8.

1 Many adjectives/adverbs ending in the suffix *-ful* / *-fully* can also take the suffix *-less* / *-lessly* to express the opposite meaning i.e. 'without'. For example: *useful/useless*
2 Some adjectives and adverbs take the prefix *un* to express the opposite meaning i.e. 'without'. For example ____________
3 Some adjectives/adverbs ending *-ful* / *-fully* can take both the suffix *-less* / *lessly* and the prefix *un-* but to express a different meaning. For example
____________ (willing to help) /
____________ (unwilling to help) /
____________ (powerless, incapable)

10 Read the short article below. Use the word given in capitals at the end of some of the lines to form a word that fits in the gap in the same line.

THE HISTORY OF ADVERTISING

Although it is **(0)** *impossible* to know for sure, the first printed advertisement is said to date back to the Song Dynasty in China. POSSIBLE

In England, due to the high level of **(1)** ________, much early advertising was done by town criers, who shouted out the details of products. This undoubtedly led to some degree of confusion, but the problem of **(2)** ________ in advertising didn't really become apparent until the nineteenth century. People realised that some of the claims being made for products such as medicines were, at best **(3)** ________. Due to a complete lack of relevant laws, advertisements could even be totally **(4)** ________.

LITERATE / INFORM / RELY / TRUTH

The advent of radio and, later, television in the twentieth century led to almost **(5)** ________ advertising direct to people's homes. As a result, concerns were raised about **(6)** ________ advertisements for products which were potentially harmful. As the twentieth century progressed, laws were passed to ban **(7)** ________ advertising of all types. In the twenty-first century, the internet has meant that **(8)** ________ advertisements reach us 24 hours a day, which has led to a new set of issues.

STOP / APPROPRIATE / ETHIC / END

11 » WORK IN PAIRS. TURN TO PAGE 134.

WRITING
A REPORT

1 **Discuss the questions in groups.**

1. What are the potential dangers of social media and online chat rooms?
2. What can teachers, parents and society in general do to protect young people from these dangers?
3. Have you ever received training on how to be safe online? Was it useful?

2 **Read the report writing task and answer the questions.**

1. Who is the report for? What style should it be written in?
2. What are the three things you need to cover?
3. What is the minimum number of words you should write?

> You recently took part in a course offered by your school or college called 'How to stay safe online'. Your IT teacher has asked you to write a report on the impact the course has had on the students who took part. In your report, you should evaluate the success of the course, describe any problems and make recommendations for improvements to the course programme.
>
> Write your **report** in 220–260 words.

3 **Read the report on the right, written by a student. Put a tick if the student has**

- written an appropriate introduction ☐
- written in an appropriate style ☐
- used headings ☐
- covered both positive and negative aspects of the course ☐
- made recommendations ☐
- used linking words and phrases appropriately ☐
- kept within the recommended word limit ☑

4 **Read the report again. Choose the correct sequence linker in each pair. Sometimes both are correct.**

Report on the 'How to stay safe online' course

Introduction

The school decided to run the 'How to stay safe online' programme after a number of concerns were raised about students' online activity. The programme covered the entire autumn term (3 months) and included workshops, talks by experts, reading tasks and quizzes.

Evaluation

[1] *At first / Initially*, many students were unclear about the need for such a course. The pre-programme questionnaire revealed that [2] *prior to / previously* this initiative few students had been aware of the potential hazards of online contact. The [3] *beginner / early* stages of the programme consisted of awareness-raising activities. Although most students had [4] *previously / beforehand* spent time in chat rooms, it had not occurred to most of them that people could misrepresent themselves to take advantage of vulnerable teens. [5] *Subsequently / The next stage*, case studies were introduced, which was an excellent way of making students understand that they too could become victims. When experts such as a chat room administrator and a police officer were due to come in, students had to do some reading [6] *ahead of / before* the talk.

Negative points

The quizzes were held right at the end of the programme, so students were tested on what they had learned several months [7] *before / earlier*. Although the quiz papers were [8] *eventually / at the end* returned to the students, this was [9] *at a much later date / a long time afterwards*, by which time students had forgotten about them.

Recommendations

I suggest holding the quizzes regularly. Students can mark each other's papers for immediate feedback. Also, there should be more time for questions and discussion at the end of talks by the experts.

5 **Add the words or expressions to the correct category in the *Prepare to write* box.**

afterwards at a later date during the day
later previously prior to

PREPARE TO WRITE

Sequence linkers

Adverbs: immediately, subsequently, eventually, initially, finally, beforehand, [1] ...., [2] ...., [3] ....

Prepositions + noun/pronoun: after that, before the class, [4] ....

Adjectives: earlier, next, subsequent, latter, initial, prior

Prepositional phrases: in/at the end, ahead of, [5] ...., [6] ....

6 **Complete the sentences with a word or phrase from the *Prepare to write* box. More than one answer may be possible.**

1 My parents didn't want me to join any social media sites, but I kept pestering them about it until .... they relented and I'm now on several.
2 The police ran an online safety awareness campaign last year. ...., the number of reports of fraud cases decreased dramatically.
3 After the .... enthusiasm had worn off, the students quickly lost interest in the programme.
4 Although the course was successful, it would be useful to have a follow-up session ....
5 Online crime rates were relatively low from January to August but soared in the .... part of the year.
6 Research shows that children who had had .... exposure to the internet were less likely to be tricked by online scammers.
7 The police and lawyers are busy gathering evidence .... the biggest online fraud case ever heard in the UK courts.
8 We're going to conduct a survey on attitudes to social media and .... we intend to present the findings to the rest of the class.

7 **Correct any mistakes in these sentences.**

1 We designed our survey. After we checked it with the teacher.
2 The process was very straightforward, and we eventually got our membership sorted.
3 Instagram and Facebook are both popular websites, the former with millennials and Gen Z and the later with a more mature demographic.
4 Don't worry about completing the report right now: it can be done at later date.
5 Initially, the site was popular with young people, but subsequent, it became less so.
6 First of all, we asked the participants for their ideas. Next stage we gathered all the ideas and planned the course.

8 **Discuss the questions with a partner.**

1 How many social media sites do you use?
2 How active are you on each?
3 How much time do you spend on social media?
4 Do you think you are a high, low or average social media user?

9 **Read the task. With a partner, decide how many sections you will divide your report into, what the headings will be and what you will include in each part.**

Your class has recently conducted a survey to find out about students' use of social media. Your teacher has asked you to write a report for the principal on your findings. In your report you should explain how the survey was conducted, what the main findings were and make suggestions about how the school should respond to the information.

Write your **report**.

10 **Which part of your report might the phrases in the box belong to?**

approximately 1 in 4 (students)
but only a small minority (8%) I suggest
Initially, we brainstormed ideas It would be useful if
Our class decided to set limits on slightly over half
Surprisingly The next step was
the overwhelming majority of students
We felt this was necessary We found that
Worryingly, most students

Introduction: ....
The survey: ....
Findings: ....
Recommendations: ....

11 **Write your report in 220–260 words. Use the sequence linkers from the *Prepare to write* box where appropriate.**

ONLINE PRESENCE

LIFE SKILLS

Creating a positive online presence

Everyone who uses the internet has a digital footprint – a permanent record of all activity online. You can take steps to ensure your footprint gives you a positive rather than a negative reputation, which is important not only now, but for your future as well.

1 Ask and answer these questions with a partner.

1 What sort of things do people post online?
2 Do you know exactly who can see the things you post online?
3 Have you ever regretted posting something online?

77 **2 Listen to three young people talking about the negative consequences of their online activity. Which speaker talks about consequences for**

a their employment?
b their online reputation?
c their studies?

77 **3 Listen again and answer the questions with the speakers' initials: Ben (B), Jolanta (J), Manjit (M).**

Which person

1 had and then lost an opportunity? ......
2 made inappropriate comments that others found online much later? ......
3 tried to prevent the problem getting worse? ......
4 damaged the reputation of a group? ......
5 was repeatedly unsuccessful in something? ......
6 wasn't being careful with their social media security? ......

4 Ask and answer these questions with a partner.

1 Do you know any stories similar to the ones you've just heard?
2 How can you and your friends make sure nothing similar happens to you?

5 Read the listicle quickly and match headings A–E to paragraphs 1–5.

A Don't overshare
B Put the best of yourself online
C Be kind online
D Think before you post
E Be smart when you browse

6 Read the listicle again. Which of the following is/are stated in the listicle?

1 It's possible to control who sees what you post online, but only sometimes.
2 People can avoid being insulted by not using their real name online.
3 The consequences of posting funny comments aren't always immediate.
4 If a friend is viewing inappropriate websites, you should immediately inform an adult.
5 Rather than leave a negative digital footprint, it's best not to leave one at all.

7 With a partner, put the advice in the listicle in order of usefulness. Justify your decisions.

5 ways to leave a positive digital footprint

78

Have you posted a photo on social media today, liked a friend's story, downloaded a video or done an internet search? If you have, then your digital footprint has grown. Your digital footprint is the trail of data you leave behind whenever you go online. It can tell other people all about you, from companies that want you to buy their products to potential employers who want to know what kind of person you are. What's more, your digital footprint is forever. That's why it's important to make sure it shows you in a positive light. Here are 5 ways to help you achieve that.

1 ....

Before you write that funny comment on your friend's page or upload that embarrassing video of you and your friends at a party, ask yourself these questions: How do your friends feel about the video being posted? How would you feel if your parents or grandparents saw it? What about complete strangers? If you or your friends aren't happy with something being seen by absolutely anyone at all, you shouldn't post it – because you never know who might see it. Remember that pressing 'send' means publishing. What you post will stay online forever. Even if you delete it later, someone can easily copy it and pass it on.

2 ....

Things can become nasty very quickly online, especially when people disagree. We've probably all read insulting comments about someone's appearance, background or intelligence. It can be easy to forget that behind every username there's a real person with real feelings. Never say anything to anyone online that you wouldn't say to them face to face. Remember: your comments might hurt that person more than you think, and everyone will know it's you who said those nasty things.

3 ....

If you want to leave a positive digital footprint, avoid talking too much about your feelings or your personal life, or other people's private lives. It might make you feel good in the moment to post a joke about a classmate, complain about a celebrity or share some exciting gossip, but your comments might be taken the wrong way or even used to make judgements about you by people you don't know. This can happen months or years after that moment has passed.

4 ....

Stay away from websites that make you feel nervous or uncomfortable, especially ones with violent, hateful or inappropriate content. Once you visit them, there will be a permanent record of your visit, even if you leave them immediately without reading any text or looking at any images or videos. If you see a friend looking at this kind of website, explain what the dangers are and tell them to stop. If they continue, get an adult to speak to them about it.

5 ....

Making sure you leave a positive digital footprint isn't only about avoiding negative things. You can also take control of your online reputation in other ways. Why not start a blog to show the world your creativity, let everyone know what your passions are, or talk about your achievements? How about raising money for a charity using a fundraising website, or posting a 'How to' video teaching others the skills you have? A digital footprint is inevitable, but it's also what you make it – so why not make it shine?

Project
Carrying out a survey

In groups, you're going to conduct a survey about social media use and give advice on how to achieve a more positive digital presence.

1 PLAN

In groups, create a class survey of at least six questions about social media use, based on some of these topics:

- most popular social media
- frequency and types of posts
- awareness of who sees the posts
- experience of sending/receiving negative comments
- your own ideas

2 SURVEY

Conduct the survey with the rest of the class. Summarise the results with your group.

3 DECIDE

Based on the results, choose two things your classmates can do to achieve a more positive digital presence. Use the ideas in the listicle but feel free to add your own.

4 PREPARE

Prepare a presentation about the survey results and the advice you want to share.

5 PRESENT

Give your presentation and listen to the presentations of the other groups.

6 APPLY

Start to follow the best advice.

15 EXPLOITED, ENDANGERED ... EXTINCT

? ABOUT YOU

▶ 15 **Watch the video and then answer the questions.**
How often do you spend time in nature?
What interests you most about the natural world?
Do you enjoy watching programmes about wildlife and nature?

VOCABULARY AND READING
WILDLIFE CONSERVATION

1 Look at the diagram. It shows the International Union for Conservation of Nature (IUCN) categories of the conservation status of animal species.

Extinct — Threatened — Least Concern

EX EW CR EN VU NT LC

1 What do you think the difference is between Extinct (EX) and Extinct in the Wild (EW)?
2 Can you guess what any of the other letters stand for?

2 Quickly read the text in Exercise 5 and check your answers.

3 What do you think is the conservation status of each of these animals? Write the appropriate letter (E, EW, CR, etc.) in the box.

1 lion ......

2 brown bear ......

3 grey parrot ......

4 jaguar ......

5 Amur leopard ......

6 West African black rhino ......

7 South China tiger ......

4 » Compare your answers to Exercise 3 with a partner. Go to page 134 to check your answers.

5 Read the text below and think of the word which best fits each gap. Use only one word in each gap.

EP

The **IUCN Red List** of Threatened Species

The main threat to wildlife today is **habitat loss**. As **woodland** **(0)** *is* destroyed for agriculture and human activity expands into areas of **wilderness**, many species face **declining populations**. This situation is **(1)** ...... worse by a rise in **poaching**, which people do in **(2)** ...... to sell the animals – dead or alive – for use as pets or exhibits in zoos, or as food or for medicine, or to be turned **(3)** ...... souvenirs for tourists. The International Union for Conservation of Nature (IUCN) has classified all species according to their conservation status, **(4)** ...... *Extinct* (no individuals left) to *Least Concern* (not yet under threat). In between are five statuses, the most worrying of **(5)** ...... is *Extinct in the Wild*; this means the species only exists **(6)** ...... captivity. Next come the *Critically Endangered* species, which are **on the verge of extinction**, and *Endangered* species, which face a significant risk. Species that are considered *Vulnerable* are at high risk **(7)** ...... moving into the *Endangered* category and those that are *Near Threatened* are quite **(8)** ...... to become endangered in the near future.

6 Discuss the meanings of the words and phrases in Exercise 5 with a partner. Use a dictionary to check if necessary.

7 Work with a partner. Make a list of steps people can take to help protect wildlife.

8 Read the article on the opposite page quickly and check if any of your ideas are mentioned.

9 Read the article carefully and answer the questions.

1 What is the purpose of the first paragraph?
  A to emphasise that most extinction happens naturally
  B to raise awareness of the scale of the current problem
  C to claim that human activity is not the main issue
2 What is meant by 'grazing for livestock' (line 20)?
  A land with grass for domestic animals
  B essential crops
  C forests where wild animals live
3 According to the writer, some invasive species
  A can have a positive impact.
  B were deliberately introduced to do harm.
  C were introduced due to ignorance.
4 Why should we 'shop mindfully'?
5 Why might the writer disagree with the view that 'we should eat meat because our ancestors ate it'?
6 How might inhabitants of cities help protect wildlife?

PROTECTING WILDLIFE: *What can I do?*

Extinction is a normal part of evolution. 99.9% of animal species that ever existed are now extinct, largely as a result of naturally occurring catastrophic events. Our planet has experienced five mass extinctions during its existence. The last of these, the K-T Mass Extinction, happened almost 65 million years ago and resulted in the disappearance of the dinosaurs. Many scientists believe that what is happening now is the sixth mass extinction, and the first caused by humans. The UN Environmental Programme estimates that between 150 and 200 species of plants and animals die out every day.

The main cause of species becoming extinct in our time is loss of natural habitats due to human activity:

- Urbanisation and the construction of dams and roads lead to the fragmentation of habitats, cutting animals off from their homes and food sources.
- Woodland is destroyed to provide grazing for livestock to feed the growing human population and also in order to grow crops to feed the livestock.
- According to the National Wildlife Federation, 42% of endangered animals are threatened by non-native species, which were introduced by humans, either intentionally or accidentally, due to a lack of awareness of the issues they would create. These invasive species can reduce biodiversity and physically change eco-systems.
- The use of pesticides in order to increase the profitability of farming is killing off populations of bees and other insects.

This can seem overwhelming, but there are actions every one of us can take to help protect our wildlife. Here's what YOU can do.

SHOP MINDFULLY

Check food and cosmetics labels and avoid items containing palm oil, which is produced by stripping rainforests, unless you are sure it is from a sustainable source. Avoid excess packaging and try to buy locally sourced produce where possible. When on holiday, never buy souvenirs made from ivory, tortoise shell or coral. Remember that certain types of alternative medicines may contain ingredients that come from endangered animals.

CUT DOWN ON MEAT AND FISH

While it is true that our ancestors ate meat, what we don't always realise is that they ate much less of it. Our grandparents, for whom meat was a special treat, ate smaller portions and had many meatless days. Nowadays, many people eat meat up to three times a day, and it is this demand that leads to destruction of the rainforests. In addition, overfishing has led to several species of fish becoming near threatened or vulnerable. Eating more locally grown food is better for the planet, and people whose diet is largely plant-based tend to be healthier. Swap meat and fish for pulses, like lentils and chickpeas, nuts, tofu and other meat-alternatives at least a few times a week.

START AT HOME

One third of the food that we eat is the result of pollination. If we don't make an effort to protect the bees and insects who pollinate our crops, then we are threatening our own species. If you are lucky enough to have a garden, create a wilderness area, where local birds and insects can live naturally. Hang bird feeders or a bee hotel, which provides an environment for bees to breed. Plant native plants and trees and avoid the use of pesticides. Those of you who live in an apartment and only have a balcony can feed birds and have some eco-friendly plants. At school, ask whether you can create a wilderness area in the school garden. Keep your dustbins and sheds secure to avoid wild animals accidentally eating something that is poisonous to them.

RAISE AWARENESS

Start by reading as much as you can about different species and their habitats and how human activity threatens them. Use your social media presence to share articles and information about what people can do to prevent species going extinct or to share plant-based recipes. Petition the politicians who represent you to support laws which protect animals. Promote the idea that other species are worthy of respect and are not to be exploited for human gain.

JOIN AN ORGANISATION

Fortunately, there are several organisations that focus on helping species whose populations are in decline. The ones that most people know about include the World Wildlife Fund (WWF) and the Wildlife Conservation Society (WCS). Others concentrate on one species, such as the Jane Goodall Institute, which protects chimpanzees, and the International Rhino Fund (IRF). Join one of these and help support their efforts to make a better world for animals.

These may seem like small steps but if everyone does them, they will make a genuine difference to animals and the natural world.

10 Discuss the questions with a partner.

1. Which of the facts in the text surprised you most?
2. How realistic/useful are the suggestions made in the text?
3. Do any of the suggestions appeal to you? Might you do any of them?

TALKING POINTS

How important do you consider preventing the extinction of endangered species?
How much responsibility should governments have to protect endangered species?
To what extent do you think vegetarian/vegan diets might help protect the environment and endangered species?

GRAMMAR
RELATIVE CLAUSES

1 Look at these sentences from the article. Which sentence contains a defining relative clause and which contains a non-defining relative clause? Then complete rules a–c.

1 Petition the politicians who represent you to support laws which protect animals.
2 Check food and cosmetics labels and avoid items containing palm oil, which is produced by stripping rainforests, unless you are sure it is from a sustainable source.

> **a** We use relative clauses to give more information about a *noun* / *verb* or *noun* / *verb* phrase.
> **b** We use defining relative clauses to give *essential* / *extra* information.
> **c** We use non-defining relative clauses to give *essential* / *extra* information.

» **GRAMMAR REFERENCE AND PRACTICE PAGE 158**

2 Do the sentences contain defining (D) or non-defining (ND) relative clauses?

1 Those of you who live in an apartment and only have a balcony can feed birds and have some eco-friendly plants.
2 The ones that/which most people know about include the World Wildlife Fund (WWF) and the Wildlife Conservation Society (WCS).
3 If you are lucky enough to have a garden, create a wilderness area, where local birds and insects can live naturally.
4 Eating more locally grown food is better for the planet, and people whose diet is largely plant-based tend to be healthier.

3 Look at the sentences in Exercise 2 and complete the rules for relative clauses with words from the box. There is one word you don't need.

defining	non-defining	object	subject	that
when	where	which	who	whose	why

> 1 .... relative clauses are surrounded by commas.
> 2 In defining relative clauses, the relative pronoun .... can replace *who* or *which*.
> 3 .... is the most common relative pronoun used for people.
> 4 .... is the most common relative pronoun used for things.
> 5 Other relative pronouns are .... (to show possession), ... (for place), ... (for time) and .... (for reason).
> 6 The relative pronoun can sometimes be omitted in .... relative clauses when the noun it refers to is the .... of the relative clause.

» **GRAMMAR REFERENCE AND PRACTICE PAGE 158**

4 Rewrite the sentences using a relative clause. Can the relative pronoun be omitted from any of the sentences?

1 Jane Goodall founded a centre in the Congo. Orphaned chimpanzees are cared for at the centre.
Jane Goodall ....
2 I admire the work of the natural historian David Attenborough.
Someone ....
3 Gerald Durrell wrote a very funny book called *My Family and Other Animals*. He founded Jersey Zoo.
Gerald Durrell ....
4 The Serengeti National Park is home to all of Africa's 'big five'. It is in Tanzania.
The Serengeti National Park ....
5 We can help endangered species by protecting their habitats.
Something ....

5 Which sentence in each pair is more formal? Complete the rules.

1 **a** The place **to which** we were travelling is famous as a leopard sanctuary.
b The place (**which**) we were travelling **to** is famous as a leopard sanctuary.
2 **a** The woman (**who**) you spoke **to** is known for her work with pandas.
b The woman **to whom** you spoke is known for her work with pandas.

> **i** To make a sentence more formal, put the preposition .... the relative pronoun.
> **ii** *Whom* is used instead of *who* after a preposition and is used in .... situations.

6 Correct any mistakes in these sentences. One sentence is correct.

1 The Major Oak is said to have sheltered Robin Hood, which is in Sherwood Forest.
2 Cherry blossom, which it is the national flower of Japan, is found all over the Northern Hemisphere.
3 Nowadays people, who want to celebrate an event, do so by planting trees.
4 The tulip is a flower for which the Netherlands are famous.
5 Jane Goodall, who is a British anthropologist.
6 Leonardo Da Vinci was a botanist, which he was not famous for it.

7 » **WORK IN PAIRS. TURN TO PAGE 134.**

VOCABULARY

ADVERB AND ADJECTIVE COLLOCATIONS

1 **Identify the adverb–adjective collocation in the quote. Do you agree with the quote?**

> The truth is: the natural world is changing. And we are totally dependent on that world. It provides our food, water and air. It is the most precious thing we have, and we need to defend it.

Sir David Attenborough

80 **2** **You will hear a talk on recent efforts to protect wildlife. What pieces of good news are mentioned?**

EP 80 **3** **Listen again and match the adverbs in Column A to the adjectives in Column B.**

A	B
rapidly	important
virtually	recognised
officially	selected
equally	increasing
universally	different
naturally	impossible
noticeably	occurring
randomly	accepted

4 **Complete the sentences with an adverb–adjective collocation from Exercise 3.**

1 In my view, it is ________ ________ to educate people about wildlife conservation as it is to pass laws on it.
2 Unfortunately, it is still not ________ ________ that all species are worthy of protection.
3 A ________ ________ chemical is one obtained from the earth, the sea, plants or animals with no processing at all.
4 Subjects for the medical trial were ________ ________ to ensure the accuracy of the results.
5 The Indian Elephant is ________ ________ in size and shape from its counterpart, the African Elephant.
6 A ________ ________ number of fish species are dying out due to overfishing.
7 It is ________ ________ for scientists to keep track of all the species that are becoming extinct.
8 The Arctic has now been ________ ________ as a special place by the global scientific community because of its unspoiled ecosystem.

INTENSIFYING ADVERBS

EP **5** **Look at the examples. Which same word could be used instead of the intensifying adverbs in all three sentences? Why are the intensifying adverbs used instead of this word?**

1 It's **highly** unlikely that household recycling alone will be enough to tackle climate change.
2 Wildlife campaigners are **bitterly** disappointed about the government's decision to allow houses to be built in the middle of the national park.
3 The documentary about Jane Goodall's chimpanzee sanctuary was **deeply** moving.

EP **6** **Complete the sentences with the correct intensifying adverbs.**

1 It's *deeply / highly / utterly* unusual for it to snow in Sydney. The last time it happened was in 1836!
2 Harry was *dangerously / deeply / fully* offended by the negative comments some followers left on his recent TikTok videos.
3 Night-time temperatures in the desert are *bitterly / fully / perfectly* cold – often falling below zero degrees.
4 You shouldn't give chocolate to dogs – it can make them *bitterly / seriously / utterly* ill.
5 Greta Thunberg warns that people are not *dangerously / fully / seriously* aware of the consequences of climate change.
6 My friend sent me a video about people who believe the *deeply / highly / utterly* ridiculous theory that the Earth is flat.
7 In towns in some tropical regions it's *perfectly / seriously / utterly* normal to see giant lizards walking around on the streets.
8 The number of Amur leopards left in the wild is *dangerously / deeply / bitterly* low and scientists fear the species could soon become extinct.

7 **Complete the sentences with an adjective from the box.**

clear	concerning	disappointing	likely
prepared	stupid	underweight	unwell

1 Swimming in the sea when a red flag is flying is utterly ________ behaviour.
2 It's highly ________ the Maldives will soon disappear if sea levels keep rising at the current rate.
3 Gabriel received some bitterly ________ news this morning: he had failed to get into the university he really wanted to go to.
4 The recent news that African elephants are facing extinction is deeply ________.
5 It's perfectly ________ that climate change cannot be tackled unless countries work together.
6 Due to the melting of the ice caps, some polar bears are dangerously ________.
7 My grandmother's goat became seriously ________ after eating a tyre.
8 The mayor said she was fully ________ to ban cars from the city centre if it would help reduce pollution.

8 **Think of an example of:**

1 an idea or scientific theory that is universally accepted
2 an environmental problem that is rapidly increasing
3 something you find it virtually impossible to do
4 two things which are equally important to you
5 something you've been bitterly disappointed about

Share your ideas with a partner.

LISTENING

1 **Look at the photos. Why do you think the people are interacting with animals in this way? Would you like to be in any of these situations?**

2 **Look at the introduction and Tasks One and Two. Which task**

1 focuses on the speakers' attitudes and opinions?
2 focuses on identifying what the speakers are talking about?

You'll hear five short extracts in which people are talking about experiences relating to animals.

TASK ONE

Choose from the list (A–H) the problem related to animals that each speaker describes.

A an animal causing illness		
B a misbehaving animal	**1** Speaker 1 ....
C a natural disaster	**2** Speaker 2 ....
D illegal activity	**3** Speaker 3 ....
E destruction of habitat	**4** Speaker 4 ....
F losing an animal	**5** Speaker 5 ....
G a risky encounter	
H homeless animals	

TASK TWO

Choose from the list (A–H) the feeling expressed by each speaker.

A shock at the vast scale of the problem	
B anger at others' behaviour	**6** Speaker 1 ....
C frustration with an outcome	**7** Speaker 2 ....
D confusion about a reaction	**8** Speaker 3 ....
E amusement caused by an event	**9** Speaker 4 ....
F fear for their life	**10** Speaker 5 ....
G sympathy towards an animal	
H satisfaction with their efforts	

81 **3** **Listen to Speaker 1 and answer these questions.**

1 What did the goat do to the child's doll?
2 What did the speaker think the girl's reaction was? What was it really?

81 **4** **Look at Tasks One and Two. Listen again and choose the answers for Speaker 1.**

5 **Look at what Speaker 1 says. Underline the parts of the script that provide the answer to each task. Use a different colour for each.**

> We run an animal sanctuary and to make ends meet we are open to visitors. Children usually enjoy getting close to the animals, who are all pretty tame. One day a little girl sat her doll down in the pasture while she went to stroke the kids – you know, the baby goats – who are very cute and friendly. Meanwhile, Nancy, one of the goats, found the abandoned doll. She must have been a bit peckish because she ate its fingers! Hearing a loud noise from the child, I came running over. I felt terrible because I thought the little girl was upset, but it turned out she was crying with laughter – she thought it was hilarious!

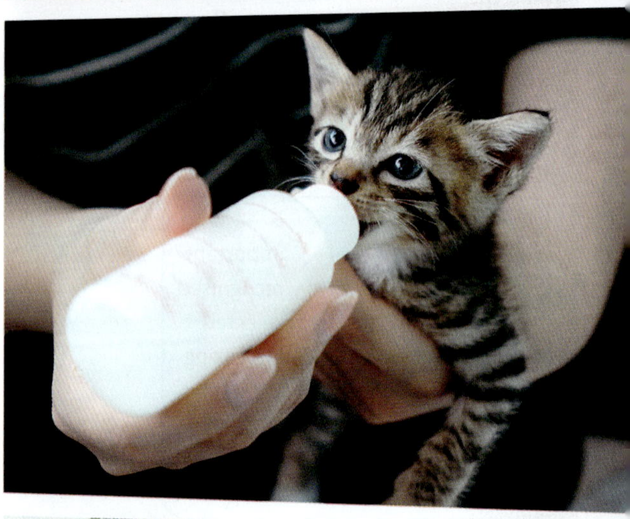

82 **6** **Listen to Speakers 2–5 and complete both tasks. Which answers are you most/least sure of?**

82 **7** **Listen to Speakers 2–5 again and check your answers, focussing on the answers you were least sure of.**

8 **Discuss the questions with a partner.**

1 Have you ever considered working with animals or volunteering at an animal shelter?
2 Have you ever been on a safari? If not, would you like to? Do you think safaris are ethical? Why? / Why not?
3 What punishments do you think should be enforced for poaching endangered animals?
4 Have you had any interesting encounters with animals?

SPEAKING
COMPARING AND DESCRIBING

1 Work with a partner. Use the words and phrases in the box to talk about the photos.

clean up conservation deserted litter-picking planting trees reforestation release into the wild shoreline threatened volunteers

1

2

3

83 **2** You will hear a student called Jorge. What questions do you think he was asked?

83 **3** Look at the *Prepare to speak* box. Listen again and tick the expressions Jorge uses.

PREPARE TO SPEAK

Explaining your opinion

The reason I say this is …
They look like they are …
They might feel that …
It looks as if …
I'm wondering if they …
What I mean by that is …
Why I think that is …
Since …
In other words, …
After all, …

4 Does Jorge

- answer both questions?
- give equal attention to both photos?
- use a good range of vocabulary and sentence structure?

84 **5** You will now hear another student, Rosa, answering a question about Jorge's photos. What do you think she was asked? Did she answer well?

6 Add expressions from the *Prepare to speak* box to an extract from another speaker's answer.

While the people in the first picture are likely to be volunteers, I'd say the person – I think it's a woman – In the third photo is probably releasing the … er … they're kind of like tortoises but they're sea creatures … she's probably releasing them into the sea as part of her job. [1] ________ that there are many conservation organisations involved in this kind of activity. [2] ________ she's involved in breeding the creatures – the *turtles*! – she might be a zoology graduate or something like that. [3] ________ that it's probably not a very straightforward process and might need specialist knowledge. I'm sure she's feeling extremely focused. [4] ________ that is she needs to concentrate to make sure all the turtles make their way into the sea rather than wandering off in the wrong direction.

7 » WORK IN PAIRS. TURN TO PAGE 134.

16 WHO DO YOU LOOK UP TO?

? ABOUT YOU

▶ 16 **Watch the video and then answer the questions.**
Who do you particularly admire, and why?
Is there anything you've always dreamed of doing?

VOCABULARY AND READING
ROLE MODELS

EP **1 Read the sentences and try to work out the meaning of the phrases.**

1. My cousin **Dave** had been saying for years he wanted to travel in a hot-air balloon, and this year he finally fulfilled his ambition and flew in one over Bryce Canyon in the USA.
2. **Elly's older sister** finished school with good grades and is now doing really well at medical school. She's a good role model for **Elly**, who really looks up to her, and also wants to train as a doctor.
3. **Azeem** has said he's going to devote himself to learning Italian so that he knows enough to get by when he goes to Tuscany on holiday next month. He certainly likes to take on a challenge! And he's really throwing himself into it, getting up early each day to study.
4. All the teachers think highly of **Liza**, as she's good at all subjects. And now they've decided to nominate her for the Outstanding Pupil of the Year award.
5. **Poppy** is campaigning against the use of cars for short journeys and wants to raise awareness of the harm they cause and get more people to walk to school or work.
6. When the **headteacher** suggested starting the school day half an hour earlier from next year onwards, she came up against a lot of opposition from pupils and their parents.

2 Which person in Exercise 1

1. respects and admires another person?
2. did something they had always wanted to do?
3. is a good example of how to live your life?
4. hopes to persuade people to do something less often?
5. has started doing something with great effort and energy?
6. was faced with people who were against their idea?
7. has decided to spend time doing a specific activity?
8. wants to enable people to learn more about something?
9. is going to try and do something which might not be easy?
10. is someone that people have a high opinion of?

3 Insert the missing preposition(s) in the correct place. Then discuss with a partner which statements you agree with and why.

1. It's pointless to look up pop stars, as they are rarely suitable role models young people.
2. The best way to raise awareness an important global issue is to make a video which goes viral.
3. You can learn a lot from reality shows where contestants take a challenge, like singing a solo in public.
4. While you're at school, your top priority should be devoting yourself your academic work.

An inspiration to us all

Someone I've always [1] __________ is the television presenter Sir David Attenborough, who [2] __________ making wildlife documentaries, starting when my grandparents were kids in the 1950s. People then didn't think much about how man-made pollution affects other species. But David Attenborough did a great deal to [3] __________ how our actions can destroy animal habitats and endanger species. Offscreen and onscreen, he [4] __________ dumping plastic in the oceans because of the damage it is causing. David Attenborough will always [5] __________ for our local Environment Action group.

My best friend **the superhero**

My friend Holly and two other classmates decided to [6] __________ – they entered a triathlon event. It was something Holly had always wanted to do. They knew they needed to get super-fit, so they immediately [7] __________ an intensive training schedule. When I asked Holly what they'd do if they [8] __________ a problem, such as getting injured, during the event, she just said, 'No way is that going to happen to me!' I've always [9] __________ Holly and admired her self-belief, but this time I wondered if she was being over-confident. But she proved me wrong, and I'm really pleased for her that she was able to [10] __________. It goes to show, it's worth chasing your dreams!

4 Complete the two short articles above with phrases from Exercise 1 in the correct form.

5 Quickly read the profiles of some remarkable people on the opposite page. Identify the two people you admire the most and explain why.

6 Read the profiles again. Which person (A–E)

1. has prompted other people to take action?
2. inspires others to feel more independent?
3. managed to deal with a variety of major challenges on their own?
4. found a way to correctly identify where something is?
5. has similar tastes to others of the same age?
6. is sceptical about something that was said about them?
7. acknowledges the help they've received?
8. does the writer say is likely to be remembered as an influential person?
9. combined two interests to find a solution to a problem?
10. considered it unfair that they were prevented from doing something?

INSPIRING **YOUNG** PEOPLE

A LAURA DEKKER

What do you do when you've already fulfilled your life's ambition in your teens? That's something Laura Dekker will have to figure out, having sailed solo around the world aged just 16. She came up against some serious difficulties, taking on six-metre waves, mending ripped sails unaided, avoiding near collisions with cargo ships, and surviving weeks of solitude. All that – plus getting her school homework finished. But that was nothing compared to the setback she endured when a Dutch court ruled that her voyage was unsafe given her age (she was 14 at the time) and vetoed her trip. Given that her parents supported her, Laura felt the court ruling to be an injustice. But she had no option but to wait, and in the meantime devoted herself to preparations for her round-the-world adventure. Later, the authorities lifted the restrictions and she set off shortly before she turned 15. The journey took her 518 days, and she became the youngest person to sail solo round the world.

B BILLIE EILISH

To get a feel for the impact that American pop star Billie Eilish has had, you only need look at the comments on social media. It's clear that her music really speaks to young people and that they look up to her. 'Her lyrics are so raw and honest,' says 15-year-old Joelie from Australia. 'They serve as a warm hug and have taught me to not care about what others think and instead to be my own person.' In an industry obsessed with image, in which women are expected to look and dress a particular way, Eilish, with her baggy clothing, colourful hair and distinctive style, is considered by many to be a role model. Some of her fans go further still, seeing her as the voice of a generation, a charge the singer dismisses with a roll of the eyes. 'I don't know what that even means,' she says.

C GRETA THUNBERG

If there's one person who has won everyone's admiration, it's Greta Thunberg. The young Swede has campaigned tirelessly against the indifference shown by world leaders to the crisis of climate change. She has spoken out against injustice and inactivity, and is bound to go down in history as a crucial figure in the battle against pollution and global warming. She achieved a great deal while still very young and her age has been a key factor in her ability to raise awareness of ecological issues, and get young people on board; it's largely thanks to her that so many worldwide have enthusiastically thrown themselves into the climate struggle. She's a person with well-researched views and persuasive arguments on environmental concerns, which she uses in discussions with world leaders and experts alike.

D CHLOE KIM

If you met Chloe Kim without knowing who she was, she'd probably chat to you about her love of fast food and Lady Gaga, much like any other young woman her age. But she's actually a champion snowboarder. She won her first X Games at the age of 14 and started to push back the boundaries of the sport. A year later, she managed to land back-to-back 1080 spins, a move requiring such power and skill that none of the snowboarders competing against her had ever managed to bring it off. Although Chloe was born and raised in the United States, her parents came from Korea, and her father is on the road with Chloe much of the time. Chloe accepts that her father sacrificed a great deal for her, quitting his job in order to accompany her, enabling her to chase her dream.

E RISHAB JAIN

Rishab Jain's life changed when he was 13, and a family friend was diagnosed with pancreatic cancer. 'I found out about the low survival rate and how deadly the disease was,' Jain says. At the time he was learning about programming and Artificial Intelligence, so, wanting to help, he decided to put both of these areas of knowledge together to take on the challenge of fighting pancreatic cancer. The disease is difficult to treat effectively with radiation, because of the pancreas's proximity to the stomach and other organs. Rishab created an algorithm using AI which was able to pinpoint the organ with an impressive 98.9% accuracy. Winner of the Top Young Scientist award at such a young age, Rishab is highly thought of in the scientific community, and is someone we can expect to see saving lives in the future.

TALKING POINTS

Do you think people who become successful as teenagers would be equally well known if they weren't so young? Would you want to become famous in your teens? Why? / Why not?

GRAMMAR
PARTICIPLE CLAUSES

1 Complete sentences 1–6 with participle clauses a–f.

1 Greta Thunberg has campaigned tirelessly against the indifference ______.
2 Laura Dekker will now have to figure out what to do with her life, ______.
3 Laura came up against some serious difficulties, ______ in the middle of the ocean.
4 None of the snowboarders ______ had ever managed to bring off such a spectacular jump.
5 ______, Rishab decided to take on the challenge of fighting pancreatic cancer.
6 If you met Chloe Kim ______, she'd probably chat to you about her love of fast food.

a competing against Chloe
b taking on six-metre waves
c having sailed solo around the world aged just 16
d shown by world leaders to the crisis of climate change
e without knowing who she was
f Wanting to help

2 Complete the rules with a word or phrase from the box.

at the same time | *because* | before | passive | prepositions | a relative clause

a Present participle clauses are used to describe something that happens ______ as the action in the main clause.
*Our teacher walked along the corridor **whistling** a tune.*

b Present participle clauses can be used with conjunctions and ______.
*I was in trouble because I stayed out late without **telling** anyone beforehand.*

c Perfect participle clauses are used to mention something that happened ______ the action in the main clause.
***Having won** Wimbledon five times, tennis star Björn Borg retired.*

d Past participle clauses are used when the meaning is ______.
***Eaten** in moderation, chocolate is good for you.*

e Participle clauses can be used instead of ______.
The course is aimed at people trying to build up their fitness levels. (= who are trying to build up)

f Participle clauses can be used instead of reason clauses that begin with ______ or *as*.
***Not realising** that the shop closed at 4pm, she arrived too late to buy a present.*

3 Match sentences 1–6 in Exercise 1 to rules a–f in Exercise 2.

» **GRAMMAR REFERENCE AND PRACTICE PAGE 159**

4 What do you know about the system of reading and writing shown in Exercise 5?

86 **5 Listen to the recording, noticing how the wording differs from the written version. Don't fill the gaps yet.**

The system of writing which was invented [0] *invented* by Louis Braille two hundred years ago is still used today. When he was blinded [1] ______ in one eye following a childhood accident, Braille suffered greatly, as the blindness gradually spread to the other eye. Because he didn't understand [2] ______ what had happened to him, Braille would often ask his parents why it was dark. But he soon began to accept his condition, and by using a stick which was made [3] ______ for him by his father, he learned to navigate the lanes in his village outside Paris. As they realised [4] ______ that Louis was very bright, his parents sent him to the school for the blind in Paris. There, the children learned to read using a system that had been created [5] ______ by the school's founder, which consisted [6] ______ of raised letters. Readers would move their fingers over each letter, and slowly work out [7] ______ the meaning. The system had drawbacks, though, not least the fact that the blind could read, but not write, when they were using [8] ______ this system. The teenage Braille invented an alternative system, which represented [9] ______ each letter as a series of raised dots which were stamped [10] ______ onto the paper, which enabled [11] ______ the reader to identify each letter through a single touch.

Braille's system wasn't widely used in his lifetime, and it wasn't even adopted by the blind school where Braille later taught. It did, however, find fame after his death, and eventually became [12] ______ accepted all over the world. It has proved to be lasting and versatile, adapting to the digital era as Robobraille, a translation service to and from Braille in a range of languages.

86 **6 Replace the underlined phrases in the text above with the words used by the speaker. Listen again to check.**

7 Correct any mistakes in these sentences. Two are correct.

1 Graduating from university at the age of ten in 1994, Michael Kearney is the youngest person ever to receive a degree.
2 A new planet discovered by 17-year-old Wolf Cukier while he was an intern with NASA has been given the name TOI 1338 b, although Cukier had hoped to call it Wolftopia.
3 Knowing not the area very well, I got lost three times before finally arriving at my destination.
4 I had the amazing experience of meeting poet Benjamin Zephaniah, looked up to him all my life.
5 In 2000, Bill Gates pledged to give a proportion of the money was earned by Microsoft to charity.
6 After watching the Michelle Obama film *Becoming*, I decided to read the book as well.

8 » **WORK IN PAIRS. TURN TO PAGE 135.**

VOCABULARY

DEPENDENT PREPOSITIONS

1 **When you were a child, what job did you want to do?**

87 **2** **Listen to a careers advisor giving a talk to students at a school. Are the statements true or false?**

1 When he was young, Michaela's brother realised he was unlikely to become an astronaut.
2 Michaela thinks that children aspiring to dream jobs is an important part of the process of maturing.
3 Children's ability to select suitable careers becomes much better as they get older.
4 Michaela has noticed that the jobs young people want are different from the jobs that are available.
5 In sectors like sport and media there are a large number of jobs available.

EP 87 **3** **Complete the sentences summarising the talk with one adjective and one preposition from the box. Then listen again and check. The prepositions can be used more than once.**

apparent	capable	compatible	integral
mistaken	notable	thankful	unaware
for	in	of	to	with

1 Michaela says that she is .... the chance to speak to the students.
2 As a young child, Michaela's brother would have been .... the tiny number of people actually working as astronauts.
3 Michaela acknowledges that she was .... her belief that she could be a professional dancer.
4 Some people think that children imagining themselves doing a particular job in the future is .... their development.
5 There is an argument that, as young people grow up, they become more .... picking a career that is .... society's needs.
6 It is .... Michaela that there aren't many jobs in some highly sought-after sectors.
7 Sport is one field that is .... having fewer jobs than jobseekers.

4 **Add the missing prepositions and match the sentence halves. Then discuss which statements you agree with.**

1 Anyone who goes to school should be thankful ......
2 A lot of social media influencers seem to be completely unaware ......
3 Air pollution in this town is easily apparent ......
4 The internet has become so integral ......
5 Anyone who's into astrology is seriously mistaken ......
6 A lot of YouTubers are notable ......
7 The use of bad language is simply not compatible ......

a a kind and respectful school environment.
b how their actions may affect their followers.
c their belief that it's possible to predict the future.
d anyone who simply looks out of the window.
e everything we do, that it's hard to imagine life without it.
f the opportunity that an education will give them in life.
g being famous without being particularly good at anything!

PHRASAL PREPOSITIONS

EP **5** **Complete the extracts from the talk with a phrasal preposition from the box.**

aside from	contrary to	in common with
in the region of	let alone	with regard to

1 I've been asked to come in today and speak to you .... your career aspirations.
2 My older brother, ... many other young boys, wanted to be an astronaut.
3 .... a handful of people working for NASA and other agencies, there aren't many professional astronauts.
4 Once they're .... ten or twelve years old, they'll be much more capable of selecting more realistic jobs for themselves.
5 Well, ... what some people might think, it's actually, wrong!
6 Most of us are highly unlikely to become professional sports players, ... astronauts.

6 **Read the text below and think of the word which best fits each gap. Use only one word in each gap.**

Growing up with ***the heroes of literature***

The home my sisters and I grew up in was notable **(0)** *for* its vast collection of books. We never knew just how many there were, but it must have been **(1)** .... the region of 5,000. Tales of Don Quixote, Sherlock Holmes and Maigret dominated **(2)** .... only our home, but our childhoods too. Shelves filled every wall, so there was hardly enough space for a TV, let **(3)** .... any other furniture. Unsurprisingly, my sisters and I, in common **(4)** .... our parents, were all avid readers. At an early age, provided a book's central character was someone inspirational (like Robinson Crusoe), I was quite capable **(5)** .... reading it from cover to cover in one sitting – **(6)** .... from regular trips to the fridge of course. And contrary **(7)** .... what you might expect twenty-first century teenagers to be into, we all preferred the old stuff. Those literary figures experienced all the **(8)** .... dilemmas and emotions as people of our age do today. They were the heroes we grew up with.

WRITING
A PROPOSAL

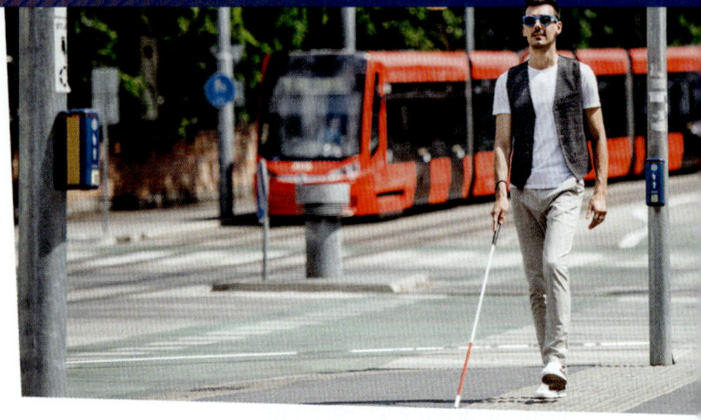

1 Look at the picture and discuss these questions.

1. What disability does the man have?
2. What is he using, and in what way might this help the man to get about?
3. What limitations might his device have, and how could these be overcome?

2 Read the task, then tell another student who you would choose and why.

> You receive this email from your school principal.
>
> Dear Students,
> I'd like to invite a prominent person to come and give a talk to all the pupils to prepare them for work or higher education after school. I'd like you to nominate a suitable speaker, say why they would be suitable, and suggest how this person's talk might be able to inspire the audience.
>
> Write your **proposal**.

3 Read a student's proposal. How is the photograph at the top of this page connected to it?

PROPOSAL FOR SPEAKER

The purpose of this proposal is to nominate a suitable role model to visit the school in order to address and motivate the students. The person I would like to suggest is Riya Karumanchi, a young Canadian entrepreneur and designer. I would like to outline why.

RIYA'S ACHIEVEMENTS

In a short time, Riya has revolutionised something that millions of blind and visually impaired people around the world use every day – the white cane. When she was 15, she saw a friend's grandmother using one, and was dismayed that its design had not changed in 100 years. For this reason, she applied her knowledge of coding and technology to create the SmartCane, which exploits sensors and GPS technology. SmartCane is designed so that visually impaired users can identify and avoid obstacles, recognise people's faces and in particular, plan safe routes. What particularly impresses me is how Riya is endeavouring to make the world a better place by enabling people to overcome a disability.

HOW A TALK BY RIYA COULD MOTIVATE STUDENTS

Riya is an engaging and articulate speaker. I am convinced that if she was to come and give a talk to the school, her story could be an inspiration to pupils. She would be able to demonstrate how having a great idea, determination and know-how can make a vast improvement to people's lives. Not only could a talk by Riya be of great interest to students, but it could also help some of them decide that this is what they too want to spend their lives doing.

4 Which of these comments on the proposal do you think are correct?

1. The student has done exactly what the task asks them to do.
2. The student should have used three headings which more closely replicate the three parts of the task.
3. The task asks for a 'prominent person'. Many people have never heard of Riya, and so the student has misunderstood a key aspect of the task.
4. Formal language is used effectively throughout the answer.
5. The proposal is a suitable length.

5 Read these statements about writing proposals. Which ones do you agree with? What would you say in response to the statements you don't agree with?

1. Proposals are similar to reports insofar as both are formal and usually have headings.
2. One difference between a proposal and a report is that reports summarise factual information, whereas a proposal must recommend something and persuade the reader that it is a good idea.
3. While reports tend to focus on past or present situations, proposals mostly refer to the future.
4. You need to argue forcefully in proposals, in order to destroy the argument of anyone who might disagree with you.
5. The first section of a proposal should always be headed 'Introduction' and the final section should always be headed 'Conclusion'.
6. Impersonal structures can be useful in proposals, such as *It is recommended that …* and *One possible solution would be …*
7. It's best to use bullet points as much as you can, because then you don't have to worry about writing sentences that are grammatically correct.

6 Select the most suitable verb to complete each sentence. Did you select the word in order to be correct, or to be polite?

1. I would like to *outline* / *urge* some of the benefits that cookery classes with a celebrity chef could have for the pupils.
2. This proposal will *nominate* / *put forward* two suggestions for enhancing the fitness levels of the community.
3. After consultation with my classmates, we have decided to *demand* / *propose* that it is named the Stephen Hawking Science Room.
4. The person I would like to *nominate* / *advise* for the School Hero Award this year is my French teacher, Mrs Pike.
5. For these reasons, I *insist* / *suggest* that a School Careers Day be held once a year from now on.

7 **Complete the extracts with the most suitable phrase for justifying what you propose.**

but it could also | for these reasons | in order to | not least | so that | would ensure that

1. I would like to propose that the school should organise an art competition ______ pay tribute to the amazing work done by our town's doctors and nurses.
2. Delaying the start of the school day until 10.30 ______ all pupils are sufficiently rested and alert during lessons.
3. A 'safe cycling' training session is desirable, ______ all students can minimise the risk of being involved in accidents.
4. Not only would nominating a Recycling Champion help pupils reduce their carbon footprint, ______ inspire other schools to do something similar.
5. The purchase of an electric minibus would have several advantages, ______ a reduction in air pollution around the school.
6. The school library is outdated and under-used. ______, I am in favour of having it converted into a café.

8 **Complete the advice in the *Prepare to write* box with these words.**

clear | connected | impersonal | main | polite

PREPARE TO WRITE

Recommendations

- Be [1] ______: suggest things to the reader, and don't tell them what to do.
  We would like to propose a college sports day.
  NOT ~~*There must be a college sports day.*~~
- Use [2] ______ language.
  A new approach is strongly recommended.
  NOT ~~*You've got to totally rethink the way you do things.*~~
- Make it [3] ______ why you make certain recommendations.
  Holding bike safety classes for all students would help to minimise the risk of pupils being involved in accidents while cycling.
  Not only would a whole school picnic be great fun, but it would also provide an opportunity for pupils to say their goodbyes before leaving.
- Link your ideas, so that your clauses and sentences are [4] ______ to each other.
  For these reasons …; so that …; in order to …; not least …

Headings

Using three or four headings can help you to organise your proposal and can help your reader to quickly identify your [5] ______ points. Headings can be:

- *Wh-* clauses: *Why the school would benefit from more sports classes; How the school can save money*
- Noun phrases: *Current problems with the school library; The advantages of buying tablets for pupils*

9 **Do you recognise the people below? What places do you think might have been named after them? Where do you think these places might be?**

10 **Discuss the questions with a partner.**

1. Can you think of any places which are named after famous people?
2. What kind of people should/shouldn't places be named after?

11 **Read the question, plan your answer, then write your proposal in 220–260 words.**

> Your local town council wants to name a park after a real person (living or dead). Suggest an appropriate person, say in what way they would be suitable, and explain what it would mean for local people to have the park named after this person.
>
> Write your **proposal**.

LIFE SKILLS COLLABORATION

TEAMWORK

LIFE SKILLS

Working effectively together

We often have to collaborate with others to solve a common problem or achieve a common goal. In order to do this well, we have to share our skills and experience and make sure we work together with honesty and respect.

1 Tell your partner about a time you worked with others to achieve something together.

1 What was it? What did you personally have to do?
2 How successful were you?
3 How challenging was it to work with the other people?
4 What advice would you give to others for how to work well in a team?

2 Read the magazine article and match the interviewer's questions a–e to Rita's answers 1–5.

a All of that requires good communication, I imagine?
b How should we deal with unexpected problems then?
c Rita, you've said that collaboration is increasingly important. Why is that?
d What advice would you give to team leaders?
e But collaboration is more than just working together, isn't it?

3 Read the article again and answer the questions. According to Rita,

1 which two areas of life are young people likely to have to collaborate in?
2 what might you sometimes need to do to help the rest of your team?
3 what should you expect to happen in any project?
4 how can team members from different parts of a project help one another?
5 what happens when people aren't aware of why they are necessary?

4 Think about the advice in green in the article. With a partner, put the advice in order from the most important to the least.

88 **5 Andy, Cathy and Ben are collaborating to raise money for environmental organisations. Listen to some of their conversations. What kind of event are they organising?**

88 **6 Listen again. Are these statements true (T) or false (F)?**

1 Andy isn't happy with his part in organising the event.
2 They can't use the hall because it's closed on Friday 7th.
3 They have to print the posters again.
4 Cathy assumed Andy knew about the change of date.
5 They find a simple solution to the problem with the tickets.
6 Andy offers to translate for the singer.

7 Thinking about Rita's advice in the article, what do the students do well? What do they do badly?

THE ART OF COLLABORATING

89

This week we asked Rita Charlesworth, company trainer and author of several books on the art of collaborating, how we can all learn to work together better. Here's what she had to say to our questions.

1 ....

Most people today, especially young people, are going to find themselves working with others to achieve a common goal at some point in their lives. This might be in further education, working on research projects with other students, or organising an event, or in the world of work, where it's extremely common for people to work in teams. What's more, people are collaborating more than ever online, and this is only going to become more common.

2 ....

Absolutely. For a start, nobody can do everything, so it's important to **allocate roles according to people's talents and experience**, although I'd say you also need to **be prepared to step outside your usual role** sometimes, depending on the circumstances, in order to assist the other people involved. Of course, when there are lots of people working on one project, each doing their own thing, it's essential that everyone should **take responsibility** for their particular part in a project. Just like in a sports team, you really have to **trust one another** to do what you're supposed to do.

3 ....

Exactly. You can't have trust without it. Good collaborators **talk to one another regularly**. It's also much easier to avoid problems when everyone is fully aware of what's happening in the project. Having said that, it's unlikely there won't be at least one unexpected problem on the way. Some of these will be out of your control, but others will be down to mistakes that people have made. My advice here is to **avoid blaming one another**. That won't solve anything. It will just make it harder for the team to work together.

4 ....

There's a saying that 'two heads are better than one'. Well, if there are five or six of you, that's even better. In other words, to collaborate successfully, you have to **solve problems together**. You can brainstorm ideas in a group. You can get creative. In fact, when things go wrong in one part of a project, you'll often find that someone working on a completely different part of the project will come up with a way around it. It's part of the beauty of teamwork.

5 ....

I would tell them to get to know their team members. Find out everyone's strengths as soon as possible and make sure you build the team based on those strengths. You also need to **make sure everyone understands the importance of their part in the project**, no matter how small. If you can't see how you fit into the bigger picture, it's hard to stay motivated. I really think it all comes down to the same basic idea: if you want your team to work, if you want to collaborate successfully, you really need to communicate with one another every step of the way.

Project
Planning an event

Work in groups and follow these steps to plan a fund-raising event.

1 THINK
Brainstorm together to decide what your event will be.

2 ASSIGN ROLES
Work out together which roles are needed and assign them to the group members.

3 PLAN
Each group member plans what they need to do and how they will do it.

4 SHARE
Group members come together and share their ideas with the group, who have to discuss and agree or improve the ideas and work out all the details.

5 PRESENT
Groups then present their ideas to the class and listen to their classmates' presentations.

6 DECIDE
Decide which team you think is the best example of successful collaboration.

7 APPLY
Perhaps the class could even hold the fund-raising event in real life!

REVIEW 4 UNITS 13–16

VOCABULARY

1 Replace the words in bold with a word or phrase from the box.

boost emulate fanbases followers
market sponsor target

People have always found creative ways to [1]**advertise** the products they want to sell. Many companies are skilful at using different media to [2]**aim for** those most likely to become their customers. One successful way of promoting products has been to [3]**pay** famous people to wear or use their products. This tactic is especially popular in the world of sport, where it has been shown to [4]**increase** the sales of many famous brands of sportswear, especially among those who wish to [5]**be like** their sporting idols. Social media has made it possible for advertisers to reach the [6]**admirers** of celebrities, who typically have well over 10 million [7]**contacts** on each platform.

2 Choose the correct adverbs in these sentences.

1. Some say that it is *officially / virtually* impossible to become fluent in a language if you start learning it as an adult.
2. The trial used *randomly / naturally* selected subjects to ensure they represented the whole population.
3. It's surprising that the concept of climate change is not *virtually / universally* accepted.
4. It's good when nurses and firefighters are *noticeably / officially* recognised for their hard work.
5. The size and weight of the company's latest smartphone is *noticeably / equally* different from the previous model.
6. Linguists may use *rapidly / naturally* occurring data, such as conversations in a café, to study the way language is used.

3 Are the phrasal verbs used correctly in these sentences? Change any that are incorrect.

1. Will you please stop getting on about Ed Sheeran? We know he's your hero.
2. Tom was going to post that picture on Instagram but his friends managed to talk him into it.
3. Sophie can read Italian quite well but she needs to brush up on her speaking.
4. I was watching a documentary on rising sea levels but to be honest, I wasn't really taking it all on.
5. Let's switch channels and watch the news. I need to catch into what's happening in the world.
6. I just couldn't understand what the teacher was going at when she made that comment.
7. When I was younger, I could just about get by in Arabic, but I'm not sure that I could nowadays.
8. I hate it when people come down to me in the street and ask me to take part in a survey.

4 Complete the extract with phrases from the box.

be a role model campaigns against
coming up against devoted herself
fulfil their ambitions look up to
raise awareness took on the challenge

You don't have to be an adult to [1] .... for young people. Take Yash Gupta. Yash broke his glasses while doing martial arts and realised how hard it was to live without them. He learned that over 12 million children were unable to [2] .... because they didn't have the glasses they needed. Aged just 14, Yash founded SightLearning to [3] .... of the issue and he [4] .... of getting people's old glasses to those who needed them. He has so far provided $1.5 million worth of glasses to children across the world.

Another teenager that others can [5] .... is Anoyara Khatun. Aged 12, Anoyara was forced into domestic labour, but managed to escape and return home. Since then she has [6] .... to helping other children in a similar situation. She [7] .... child labour and child marriage. Despite [8] .... opposition, Anoyara has been able to negotiate with local leaders and prevent many early marriages.

5 Eight prepositions are missing from this text. Put them in the correct place.

for from in (x2) of (x2) with (x2)

Most people are unaware the various sub-species of gorilla, such as eastern and western lowland gorillas and mountain gorillas. There are the region of 5,000 eastern lowland gorillas left in the jungles of Africa. They are on the verge of becoming extinct in the wild, which is something they have common with mountain gorillas. Regard to western lowland gorillas, there are close to 100,000 individuals, which still means that they are critically endangered.

Whereas lowland gorillas can thrive in zoos, mountain gorillas are incompatible life in captivity. Older male mountain gorillas are notable their silver fur, which gives them the nickname silver-backs.

While mountain gorillas are mostly terrestrial, lowland gorillas are capable swinging vast distances through the trees to get to the fruit they want to eat. Aside that, it is size that differentiates the lowland and mountain gorillas, the latter weighing up to 50kg more than the former.

GRAMMAR

1 **Add a relative clause a–f to the correct place in sentences 1–6. Are they defining (D) or non-defining (ND) relative clauses? Add commas where necessary.**

1 A wilderness is an environment
2 Many young people have aspirations
3 Actor Cillian Murphy is a speaker of Irish Gaelic.
4 One species is the sea turtle mainly because of their shells.
5 One linguist is David Crystal.
6 Rowan Atkinson has also played a few serious roles.

a that poachers target most
b whose films include the *Dark Knight* trilogy
c on which humans have not had a significant impact
d who is best known for playing Mr Bean
e to whom I will refer frequently in these lectures
f that are utterly unrealistic

2 **Which TWO sentences are correct? Correct the others, making sure the new sentence contains a causative structure.**

1 The number of companies that have their websites translated into different languages is rapidly increasing.
2 We have had our brand of cosmetics officially recognise as environmentally friendly.
3 The headteacher is planning to have teachers used only English in the classroom.
4 Ben couldn't believe it when he had his account deactivated for not following the site's guidelines.
5 The WWF has managed to get passed laws which prevent trafficking of wildlife.
6 Andrés was absolutely delighted that he managed to have Mo Salah to sign his shirt.

3 **Complete the sentences with the correct form of the verb in brackets.**

1 .... by stories of teenage millionaires, Khalid started his own business at the age of 17. (motivate)
2 The charity gratefully accepted our donation, ... us that every penny would be used to help animals. (reassure)
3 Young people .... to be social media influencers should focus on one main area. (aspire)
4 .... its declining population, the ICUN has decided to change the status of the red panda to endangered. (give)
5 By the age of 12, Corinne was competing in adult competitions, ... her own against tennis players twice her age. (hold)
6 The guidelines .... in place by social media sites are designed to keep all users safe. (put)
7 .... French at school, Jo found it comparatively easy to learn Spanish. (study)

4 **Read the text below and decide which answer (A, B, C or D) best fits each gap.**

GENTOO PENGUINS

Gentoo penguins are the third-largest species of penguin. Living just beyond the Antarctic Circle, there are **(0)** *B* to be around 300,000 breeding pairs. Those living in the northern part of the region are slightly larger than their southern **(1)** .... All Gentoo penguins are **(2)** .... well adapted to harsh climates.

The penguins' diet is **(3)** .... solely of sea animals. They have no land-based predators except humans; their eggs and chicks, however, are **(4)** .... to birds of prey. Gentoo penguins usually mate for life. The female usually **(5)** .... two eggs, only one of which hatches.

The Gentoo penguin was **(6)** .... Near Threatened in 2007, although in 2019 this was updated to Least Concern. The species used to be common on islands and it was due to **(7)** .... populations on these that there was some concern over the species. However, with numbers rising **(8)** .... on the mainland, the Gentoo is safe for the time being.

	A	B	C	D
0	**A** guessed	**(B)** estimated	**C** researched	**D** revealed
1	**A** opposites	**B** parallels	**C** equals	**D** counterparts
2	**A** totally	**B** greatly	**C** extremely	**D** hugely
3	**A** comprised	**B** involved	**C** consisted	**D** included
4	**A** available	**B** endangered	**C** vulnerable	**D** sensitive
5	**A** lays	**B** sets	**C** passes	**D** puts
6	**A** stated	**B** claimed	**C** published	**D** declared
7	**A** decaying	**B** degrading	**C** declining	**D** deteriorating
8	**A** intensely	**B** considerably	**C** highly	**D** heavily

5 **Read the text below. Use the word given in capitals at the end of some of the lines to form a word that fits in the gap in the same line.**

Children of courage

We often assume children are **(0)** *helpless* and dependent on others to look after them, but all over the world they have been recognised for a wide range of **(1)** .... acts, including taking care of parents and siblings. Many countries hold annual **(2)** .... to honour these special young people. — HELP, COURAGE, CELEBRATE

In India, a National Bravery Award was given to Sebastian Vincent, a boy who saved his friend from being hit by a train. He was granted financial **(3)** .... to finish his education. In the UK, a child named Oliver Van Berckel was rewarded for **(4)** .... supporting his brother Kit, who has cerebral palsy. He even gave up his own football training so that Kit could join Adversity United, an **(5)** .... team for the disabled. — ASSIST, SELF, INCLUDE

In spite of their own physical **(6)** .... , children as young as eight act as the main carers for their parents. Others bravely cope with injuries, illness and other **(7)** .... without complaint. It is wonderful to see these **(8)** .... youngsters receive the credit they deserve. — MATURE, HARD, INSPIRE

EXTRA ACTIVITIES

UNIT 1 PAGE 8 VOCABULARY AND READING

2

PERSONALITY TEST RESULTS

For the questions to which you answered *Yes*, these are your personality characteristics.

If you answered Yes to question 1 you may be **extroverted**.

2 **open-minded**
3 argumentative
4 **self-conscious**
5 **introverted**
6 **trustworthy**
7 **conscientious**
8 sympathetic

UNIT 1 PAGE 10 GRAMMAR

7 Ask and answer the questions with a partner.

1 Who's the best friend you've ever had?
2 What games did you use to play when you were younger?
3 When did you last have a disagreement with a friend? What about?
4 How long have you been living in your current house or flat?
5 Had you ever done a personality test before the one in this unit?

UNIT 2 PAGE 16 GRAMMAR

7 Complete the sentences so that they are true for you.

1 The older I get, …
2 The more I study, …
3 The hotter it is, …
4 The less I sleep, …
5 The more I exercise, …

Compare and discuss your sentences with a partner.

UNIT 2 PAGE 17 VOCABULARY

7 Complete the questions with an idiom from page 17 in the correct form.

1 What can you do to avoid all your work ______ if your computer crashes?
2 Do you agree that it is hard for women in some professions to ______, but not for those in areas such as teaching?
3 Would you ______ in a holiday job which involved speaking in English all day?
4 Have you ever met anyone with whom you ______ from the very beginning? And are you still in touch today?
5 When it's your birthday, are you more likely to have a quiet get-together with your immediate family or really ______ and throw a huge party?
6 Which days of the week do you have to do homework? Is that ______, or does it vary each week?
7 What's the minimum that visitors to your town would have to pay to get ______ for the night?
8 Have you ever ______ with someone and regretted it later?

Ask and answer the questions with a partner.

UNIT 3 PAGE 24 GRAMMAR

6 Read the three posts from users of a well-being blog. Which person is describing

1 stress? 2 fatigue? 3 insomnia?

Night after night, I lie awake and I just can't get to sleep. I often read something on my tablet in the hope that it will make me tired, but it doesn't help at all. What can I do?

OLIVIA B LIKE | REPLY

I've got lots going on at school each day, and then handball or judo practice immediately after lessons most days. Then on Saturday, I do a 10-hour shift at a local supermarket. By the time Sunday comes, I'm shattered, but then in no time it's Monday, and I've got to do it all again. Any suggestions?

NICO J LIKE | REPLY

I recently started a new job, which I love. I'm 100% committed to it and bring work home with me in the evenings and at weekends. I'm concerned my boss might think I'm not doing well enough if I don't do this. And I can't stop thinking about work, it all gets too much sometimes.

LORENA P LIKE | REPLY

UNIT 3 PAGE 24 GRAMMAR

10 **What problems might these people have? And what advice would you give them? Use some of the modal and auxiliary verbs from page 24.**

A

B

C

UNIT 3 PAGE 27 SPEAKING

7 **Work in pairs. Now look at the second group of three photos and take turns to complete the task.**

- How might these activities affect the health of the people?
- Why might these people find it difficult to do these activities regularly?

UNIT 4 PAGE 30 GRAMMAR

8 **Tell your partner about a time when**

1 you should have done something to help someone.
2 you shouldn't have done something and you feel bad about it.
3 you might have made the wrong decision.
4 you could have put more effort into something.
5 you had to apologise for something.
6 you were angry that you weren't allowed to do something.
7 you were frustrated that you weren't able to do something.

UNIT 4 PAGE 31 VOCABULARY

8 **Discuss the questions with a partner.**

1 How do you feel about leaving school?
2 What do you think will be the deciding factor in your choice of career?
3 What decisions do you have to make in the immediate future?
4 Would you consider doing an apprenticeship? In what?

UNIT 5 PAGE 40 GRAMMAR

7 **In pairs or small groups, make predictions about**

- something you use now which will have become obsolete by 2030.
- something you'll be spending more money on in five years' time.
- someone you know who's going to be famous within the next ten years.
- what energy your vehicle will be running on in 2030.

Respond to your partner's/group's predictions with some of these expressions.

That's way off the mark!
We'll have to wait and see!
That one's almost there!
I think that's spot on!

EXTRA ACTIVITIES

UNIT 5 PAGE 41 VOCABULARY

6 Complete the sentences with a phrasal verb from the box. Then discuss whether you agree with the statements and why.

catch on | check out | do away with | lie ahead | look upon

1 In order to create a cleaner world, everyone should ________ their cars and buy a bicycle instead.
2 Driverless vehicles will never really ________, as humans like to feel that they are fully in control.
3 Difficult times ________ for the human race unless our carbon footprint can be reduced drastically.
4 Most people ________ environmental activists as eccentric, and don't take them seriously.
5 You should ________ the carbon footprint of absolutely any product before you buy it.

UNIT 5 PAGE 41 VOCABULARY

8 Complete the questions in any way you like. Then select any three to ask a partner.

1 Do you think that ________ will ever catch on?
2 Are you in favour of doing away with ________ in order to save the planet?
3 Is there anything you reckon I should check out on ________?
4 Do you know anyone who's notorious for ________?
5 How likely is it that there will ever be a car that runs entirely on ________?

UNIT 5 PAGE 43 SPEAKING

8 Discuss this question. Make sure you involve your partner by using some of the expressions in *Prepare to speak*.

Looking ahead, how likely is it that the following things will happen in your lifetime?

- people settling on Mars
- someone living to 150 years of age
- life being discovered on another planet
- all energy coming from renewable sources
- all the ice on the polar ice caps melting

UNIT 6 PAGE 46 GRAMMAR

9 Complete the sentences about yourself. Then share your ideas with a partner.

1 I try to avoid …
2 I hate …
3 I remember …
4 I would like to be famous for …
5 I'm very good at …
6 I find it difficult to …

UNIT 6 PAGE 47 VOCABULARY

9 Work with a partner. Make quiz questions using the prompts.

0 world-famous actor, director or author
Which world-famous director directed films such as Jurassic Park and the Indiana Jones series?
1 action-packed film
2 thought-provoking book
3 critically acclaimed film
4 Oscar-nominated actor/actress
5 internationally successful film
6 best-paid actor/actress

Give your quiz to another pair to do.

UNIT 7 PAGE 54 GRAMMAR

10 Complete the sentences so that they are true for you.

1 If I didn't spend so much time …, I could have …
2 If I hadn't … I could have …
3 If I were better at … I could …
4 If I …, I will …
5 I would be … if I had …

Share your completed sentences with a partner. Were any of your sentences similar?

UNIT 7 PAGE 55 VOCABULARY

7 Complete the questions by adding a suffix.

1 What sports did you enjoy during your child____?
2 What is your main motiva____ for learning English?
3 Why do some people have a fascina____ with the lives of sports stars?

Ask and answer the questions with a partner.

UNIT 8 PAGE 60 GRAMMAR

9 **What might the people in the pictures be thinking? Use *I wish* or *if only* and a range of tenses.**

1 

2 

3 

4 

UNIT 9 PAGE 71 VOCABULARY

7 **Complete the sentences with your own ideas.**

1 In the future, I hope to gain a better understanding of …
2 One day, I will fulfil my dream of …
3 After we break up from school, I usually …
4 One topic I'm keen to read up on is …
5 I'm not sure if I'll be able to get through …

Compare your completed sentences with a partner.

UNIT 9 PAGE 73 SPEAKING

11 **Student A, paraphrase these words. Your partner should try to guess the words.**

Example
0 racket
It's the thing you hit the ball with when you play tennis.

1 sequel
2 scholarship
3 masterpiece
4 Oscar
5 trainee
6 discrimination

Now think of some words yourself, paraphrase them and ask your partner to guess them.

UNIT 10 PAGE 76 GRAMMAR

8 **Work with a partner. Imagine that you are a politician writing a speech on how to tackle crime. How could you express the following ideas forcefully? Begin each sentence with a phrase from the box.**

~~Never~~ No way Not only … but also Only when Under no circumstances

0 Crime is a more serious problem now than it's ever been.
Never has crime been a more serious problem than it is now.

1 Building more prisons is the only way to make the streets safer.
2 Criminals won't be able to get away with light punishments for repeat offences.
3 I'm going to be tough on crime. But that's not all. I'm going to be tough on the causes of crime.
4 Criminals have no chance of getting let off with a warning any more – anyone found guilty will be punished.

9 **Write a short statement of about three sentences as a politician who is explaining their policy on crime. Incorporate two or three suitable structures with inversion. Consider the following ideas:**

- how you propose to stop kids getting involved in crime
- what kinds of offences people should be imprisoned for
- how you will deal with vandalism
- what improvements you will make to the prison service

Present your policy to the class. Have a class vote on whose policy is the best.

UNIT 11 PAGE 84 GRAMMAR

9 **Complete the questions using the verb in brackets in the passive. Then ask and answer them with a partner.**

1 Have you ever eaten anything which .... ? (undercook)
2 When you go to a supermarket, would you say that too much plastic packaging .... ? (use)
3 Do you think people would eat less meat if a meat tax .... ? (introduce)
4 Some people think it's morally wrong that so much food .... long distances by plane. What's your opinion? (transport)
5 Would you ever eat meat or fish that .... at all? (not cook)

EXTRA ACTIVITIES

UNIT 9 PAGE 73 SPEAKING

11 **Student B, paraphrase these words. Your partner should try to guess the words.**

Example

0 racket

It's the thing you hit the ball with when you play tennis.

1 blockbuster
2 apprenticeship
3 extroverted
4 gap year
5 networking
6 setback

Now think of some words yourself, paraphrase them and ask your partner to guess them.

UNIT 11 PAGE 87 SPEAKING

7 **Use the words in brackets to make these comments more tactful.**

1 Let's have a party. (thinking / maybe)
2 I forgot to do my homework. (seem / forgotten)
3 I'm too tired to meet you after school today. (honest / a bit)
4 You haven't given me enough change. (sorry / seem)
5 I'm busy now – call me later, OK? (thing / could)
6 You just made a grammar mistake. (hope / saying / little)

8 **Work as Student A and Student B. Read the information, prepare what to say, and then role play the conversations.**

Student A

You work in a bakery. The manager has just announced that they may need to reduce the number of staff. You are worried that your friend Ali may lose his/her job for the following reasons:

- usually late for work
- sometimes has dirty hands
- calls colleagues 'mate', which isn't always appropriate
- often makes private phone calls while at work, which is against the rules

Give Ali feedback as tactfully as you can, to help him/her improve. Start and end on these positive notes.

- is hardworking
- is always willing to learn

Student B

You and your friend Frankie work in a restaurant, and you have just heard that they are planning to cut down on the number of waiting staff. You want to warn Frankie that he/she needs to stop

- telling 'jokes' to customers, which they don't find funny
- taking breaks which are longer than they should be
- complaining to the manager about the rates of pay
- looking untidy (shoelaces untied, hair not brushed)

Give Frankie feedback as tactfully as you can. Start and end on these positive notes.

- always cheerful
- quick and efficient at their job

UNIT 11 PAGE 86 LISTENING

6 **They are all true. In D, builder's glue is a purer white than milk, and doesn't make food such as cereal go soggy.**

UNIT 12 PAGE 90 GRAMMAR

9 **Complete the questions with the correct form of the verb in brackets.**

0 Have you ever been forced *to go* on a trip you didn't want to go on? (go)
1 What kind of things have people in your country been asked ________ to protect the environment? (do)
2 How important do you think it is for holidays ________ greener? (make)
3 Can you remember ________ about climate change at school? (teach)
4 How concerned are you about your country ________ by tourism? (damage)
5 Do you know of any countries that are in danger of ________ by rising sea levels? (submerge)

Discuss the questions with a partner.

UNIT 12 PAGE 91 VOCABULARY

10 **Complete the sentences in the extracts from tour guidebooks (1–4) and conversations (5–8) with an appropriate way of expressing quantity from Exercises 6 to 9.**

1 ________ people enjoy cruises because of the on-board activities.
2 ________ countries offer as much to the tourist as Spain.
3 ________ attempts have been made to make the tourist industry in this country more eco-friendly.
4 ________ increasing the cost of flying would help protect the environment.

5 There isn't ________ interest in green travel in my country.

6 Trekking holidays are ________ exciting. You should try them.

7 There are ________ things to do in the area where I live.

8 There's usually ________ of a delay on trains in the rush hour.

Give your view on three statements above and ask your partner if they agree.

UNIT 13 PAGE 100 GRAMMAR

5 Use the phrases in the box with a causative structure to complete the sentences.

classmate / proofread / homework
classmate / explain
eyes / test
friend / give / lift to school
parent / take you out in the car / practise
pupils / study
students / use

0 If you're ever confused about a phrasal verb, it's worth *having a classmate explain it to you*.
1 When you're in your teens, you should ______ regularly.
2 ______ each morning is a great way to reduce your carbon footprint.
3 Teachers should ______ phones and tablets in class.
4 If you're learning to drive, it's useful ______.
5 If you can ______ before you hand it in, this can help get rid of errors.
6 Schools should ______ the history of their country up until school leaving age.

Discuss with a partner whether you agree with the statements. Change any you disagree with so that they are true for you.

UNIT 13 PAGE 101 VOCABULARY

6 Complete the statements with the adverbs in the box.

comprehensively effectively individually
publicly respectively supposedly

1 Spending too much time online is ______ bad for you, but there's no real evidence that it causes any harm.
2 Anyone aged 16 and over is ______ an adult, and should be free to decide whether they want to go to school or not.
3 For a corporation to proclaim ______ that they're committed to helping the environment means nothing; they need to get out there and do something.
4 The key thing for students of English is to learn all twelve tenses ______, and make sure you use them accurately.
5 The best ever decades for music and films were the 1970s and the 2010s ______.
6 To really learn effectively, school students should be taught ______ and not in large groups.

Discuss with a partner whether you agree with the statements.

UNIT 13 PAGE 103 SPEAKING

8 Work with a different partner. Here are some situations in which you might need to think carefully about the way you communicate and a question for you to discuss. Talk to each other about why people might have to think carefully about the way they communicate in these different situations.

Why might people have to think carefully about the way they communicate in these different situations?

- in a job interview
- talking to a friend about a problem
- talking to someone who is learning your language
- on social media
- dealing with young children

In which of these situations do you think it's most important to communicate effectively?

9 With a partner, ask and answer the questions using expressions from the *Prepare to speak* box.

1 Do you think that social media has had a positive effect on the way we communicate? (Why?/Why not?)
2 How important is body language to effective communication? (Why?/Why not?)
3 Is it possible for people to learn to improve their communication skills? (Why?/Why not?)
4 'Good communication skills are the most important things that a child can learn.' To what extent do you agree? (Why?/Why not?)
5 Do you think too much importance is given to the way we communicate in formal situations such as job interviews? (Why?/Why not?)
6 In what ways can a good knowledge of foreign languages be a benefit to people?

UNIT 14 PAGE 106 GRAMMAR

8 Complete the sentences so that they are true for you.

1 A website I visited recently advised people …
2 I strongly believe we should encourage students …
3 People in my town are always complaining …
4 I have volunteered …
5 An advert I saw recently claimed that …

Compare your sentences with a partner. Ask each other follow-up questions.

EXTRA ACTIVITIES

UNIT 14 PAGE 107 VOCABULARY

11 Complete the questions with the correct prefix.

1 Do you think it's ____ moral to misrepresent yourself on social media?
2 Do you think influencers should show themselves consuming ____ healthy food and drinks?
3 Why might influencers be happy to have ____ active or 'ghost' followers?
4 What do you think the ____ advantages of being an influencer might be?
5 Do you think young people need to be taught how to identify ____ leading information on the internet?

Ask and answer the questions with a partner.

UNIT 15 PAGE 112 VOCABULARY AND READING

4 Key to Exercise 3

1 V Lion – There are fewer than 40,000 mature individuals left in the wild
2 LC Brown bear – It is estimated that there are 110,000 mature individuals – a stable population.
3 EN The grey parrot was declared endangered in 2016 due to rapidly declining populations.
4 NT The jaguar was listed as near threatened in 2016 due to decreasing populations.
5 CR Amur leopard – There are fewer than 100 mature individuals left in the wild.
6 EX The West African black rhino was declared extinct by ICUN in 2011
7 EW The South China tiger has been Critically endangered since 1996. It is considered 'extinct in the wild' as no individual has been seen in the wild since the 1970s.

UNIT 15 PAGE 114 GRAMMAR

7 Use the prompts to make sentences with relative clauses which express your own ideas.

0 A wildlife programme …
A wildlife programme that I really enjoyed was Spy in the Wild.
1 The animal …
2 The time …
3 The place …
4 A country …
5 A person …

Compare your ideas with a partner. Ask him or her for more information.

UNIT 15 PAGE 117 SPEAKING

7 Practise with a partner. Student A, choose TWO pictures to talk about. Try to use language from the *Prepare to speak* box. Student B, answer the question at the end.

A's question: I'd like you to compare two of the pictures and say why the people might have chosen to spend time with these animals, and how you think the people might be feeling.

B's question: Who do you think is benefiting most from spending time with animals in this way?

Now swap roles. Student B, don't choose the same two pictures as A.

LIFE SKILLS PAGE 80

Scores for the quiz in Exercise 1

1 **a** 0
b 1 point
c 2 points
2 1 point for each
3 1 point for each correct answer:
b/c = because
e.g. = for example (exempli gratia)
prob = probably
w/o = without
s/b = somebody
s/t = something

Results

0–4 You're not a great notetaker. It's high time you changed that!
5–11 Your notetaking is OK, but it could be a lot better.
12–15 You're a notetaking superstar!

LIFE SKILLS PAGE 94

Scores for the quiz in Exercise 1

Calculate your score:
a=3 points, b=2 points, c=1 point

Results

1–3 You're not green at all – but that can change!
4–6 You're good, but you could be greener.
7–9 You're green and that's great! Now what else can you do?

UNIT 16 PAGE 120

GRAMMAR

8 Complete the sentences with a participle clause using the words in brackets and any other words necessary.

1 What do you think is the funniest film ________? (ever / made)
2 ________, would you say it is a good place for children? (grow up / this town)
3 ________, if you could go on holiday anywhere in the world right now, where would you go? (put aside practical considerations / cost)
4 When ________, what kind of things do you usually talk about? (meet somebody / first time)
5 ________, what do you think the single most difficult thing about English is? (look at it / a foreign learner / point of view)
6 Have you ever woken up ________? (not remember / where you are)
7 ________, do you ever wish that you could go straight back there again? (just return / holiday)
8 If ________, could fast food actually be good for us? (eat / small quantities)

Ask and answer the questions with a partner.

EP VOCABULARY LIST

adj = adjective *adv* = adverb *n* = noun *v* = verb
pv = phrasal verb *prep* = preposition *phr* = phrase
id = idiom *conj* = conjunction *pron* = pronoun
det = determiner

UNIT 1

PERSONALITY

clash (with) /klæʃ/ *v* to fight or argue

come across as /ˌkʌm əˈkrɒs əz/ *pv* to behave in a way that makes people believe that you have a particular characteristic

conscientiously /ˌkɒnʃiˈenʃəsli/ *adv* in a careful way that involves a lot of effort

extroverted /ˈekstrəvɜːtɪd/ *adj* energetic and enjoying being with other people

feel left out /fiːl left ˈaʊt/ *phr* to feel that you are not included in something

introverted /ˈɪntrəvɜːtɪd/ *adj* shy, quiet and preferring to spend time alone rather than often being with other people

open-minded /ˌəʊpənˈmaɪndɪd/ *adj* willing to consider ideas and opinions that are new or different to your own

relate to /rɪˈleɪt tu/ *pv* to understand a situation or someone's feelings because you have experienced a similar situation or similar feelings

rely on /rɪˈlaɪ ɒn/ *pv* to need a particular thing or the help and support of someone or something in order to continue to work correctly or to succeed

self-conscious /ˌselfˈkɒnʃəs/ *adj* nervous or uncomfortable because you are worried about what people think about you or your actions

trustworthy /ˈtrʌstˌwɜːði/ *adj* able to be trusted

ADJECTIVE SUFFIXES

careless /ˈkeələs/ *adj* not taking or showing enough care and attention

chatty /ˈtʃæti/ *adj* liking to talk a lot in a friendly, informal way

judgemental /dʒʌdʒˈmentəl/ *adj* too quick to criticise people

knowledgeable /ˈnɒlɪdʒəbəl/ *adj* knowing a lot

narrow-minded /ˌnærəʊˈmaɪndɪd/ *adj* not willing to accept ideas or ways of behaving that are different from your own

optimistic /ˌɒptɪˈmɪstɪk/ *adj* hoping or believing that good things will happen in the future

respectful /rɪˈspektfəl/ *adj* showing admiration for someone or something

selfish /ˈselfɪʃ/ *adj* Someone who is selfish thinks only of their own advantage.

sensible /ˈsensəbəl/ *adj* based on or acting on good judgement and practical ideas or understanding

supportive /səˈpɔːtɪv/ *adj* showing agreement; giving encouragement or help

ADVERB SUFFIXES

bad-temperedly /ˌbædˈtempədli/ *adv* in an angry or annoyed way

beautifully /ˈbjuːtɪfəli/ *adv* in a way that is attractive or pleasant

falsely /ˈfɒlsli/ *adv* wrongly

happily /ˈhæpəli/ *adv* in a happy way

knowledgeably /ˈnɒlɪdʒəbli/ *adv* in a way that suggests that you know a lot

realistically /ˌrɪəˈlɪstɪkəli/ *adv* accepting things as they are in fact and not making decisions based on unlikely hopes for the future

UNIT 2

CITIES

densely populated /ˌdensli ˈpɒpjəleɪtɪd/ *adj* with a lot of people living close together

derelict /ˈderəlɪkt/ *adj* Derelict buildings or places are not cared for and are in bad condition.

green space /ˌgriːn ˈspeɪs/ *n* an area of grass, trees or other vegetation set apart for leisure purposes in an urban environment

high-rise /ˈhaɪraɪz/ *adj* with many floors

pedestrianised /pəˈdestriənaɪzd/ *adj* made into an area where vehicles are not allowed to go

ring road /ˈrɪŋ ˌrəʊd/ *n* a main road that goes around the edge of a town, allowing traffic to avoid the town centre

slum /slʌm/ *n* a very poor and crowded area, especially of a city

suburb /ˈsʌbɜːb/ *n* an area on the edge of a large town or city where people who work in the town or city often live

transport link /ˈtrænspɔːt ˌlɪŋk/ *n* a way of travelling between two places, especially by public transport

urban sprawl /ˌɜːbən ˈsprɔːl/ *n* the spread of a city into the area surrounding it, often without planning

BUILDINGS AND PLACES: IDIOMS

break the glass ceiling /ˌbreɪk ðə ˌglɑːs ˈsiːlɪŋ/ *id* to go past a point that was preventing you from progressing, usually in relation to your position at work

burn your bridges /ˌbɜːn jə ˈbrɪdʒɪz/ *id* If you are in a situation and you burn your bridges, you destroy all possible ways of going back to that situation.

feel at home /ˌfiːl ət ˈhəʊm/ *id* to feel comfortable and relaxed

get on like a house on fire /get ˌɒn laɪk ə ˈhaʊs ɒn ˌfaɪə/ *id* If two people get on like a house on fire, they like each other very much and become friends very quickly.

go down the drain /gəʊ ˌdaʊn ðə ˈdreɪn/ *id* If you say that something has gone down the drain, it has been destroyed or wasted.

go to town /ˌgəʊ tə ˈtaʊn/ *id* to do something in a detailed and enthusiastic way, especially by spending a lot of money

have a roof over your head /ˌhæv ə ˈruːf ˌəʊvə jə ˈhed/ *id* to have a place to live

hit a brick wall /ˌhɪt ə ˈbrɪk ˈwɔl/ *id* to encounter something that prevents you from doing something

hit the roof /ˌhɪt ðə ˈruːf/ *id* to get very angry

set in stone /ˌset ɪn ˈstəʊn/ *id* very difficult or impossible to change

UNIT 3

THE HUMAN BODY

choke /tʃəʊk/ *v* If you choke, or something chokes you, you stop breathing because something is blocking your throat.

exhale /eksˈheɪl/ *v* to send air out of your lungs

germ /dʒɜːm/ *n* a very small organism that causes disease

inhale /ɪnˈheɪl/ *v* to breathe air, smoke or gas into your lungs

joint /dʒɔɪnt/ *n* a place in your body where two bones are connected

left-handed /ˌleftˈhændɪd/ *adj* using your left hand to write and do most things

limb /lɪm/ *n* an arm or leg of a person or animal

lung /lʌŋ/ *n* either of the two organs in the chest with which people and some animals breathe

nerve /nɜːv/ *n* a long, thin fibre (= structure like a thread) that carries information or instructions between the brain and other parts of the body

numb /nʌm/ *adj* If a part of your body is numb, you are unable to feel it, usually for a short time.
poorly /'pɔːli/ *adj* ill
spine /spaɪn/ *n* the line of bones down the centre of the back that provides support for the body and protects the spinal cord
sweat /swet/ *n* the clear, salty liquid that you pass through your skin

HEALTH: PHRASAL VERBS

black out /blæk 'aʊt/ *pv* to become unconscious suddenly but for a short period
break out (in a sweat/fever) /breɪk 'aʊt/ *pv* to suddenly have sweat appear on your skin / have a fever
burned out /ˌbɜːnt 'aʊt/ *adj* ill or very tired from working too hard
come round /kʌm 'raʊnd/ *pv* to become conscious again after an accident or medical operation
fight off (an illness) /faɪt 'ɒf/ *pv* to free yourself from an illness
freak out /friːk 'aʊt/ *pv* to become extremely emotional
nod off /nɒd 'ɒf/ *pv* to begin sleeping, especially not intentionally
pass away /pɑːs ə'weɪ/ *pv* to die (polite)
pass on (an illness) /pɑːs 'ɒn/ *pv* to give an illness to someone, after someone else gave it to you
sleep (something) off /sliːp 'ɒf/ *pv* If you sleep something off, you go to sleep so that you will feel better when you wake up.

HEALTH: EXPRESSIONS

all in one piece /'ɔːl ɪn wʌn 'piːs/ *phr* not damaged or hurt
cause for concern /ˌkɔːz fə kən'sɜːn/ *phr* a reason to worry
not sleep a wink /ˌnɒt ˌsliːp ə 'wɪŋk/ *phr* to not sleep at all
on the mend /ˌɒn ðə 'mend/ *phr* becoming healthy after an illness or injury
right as rain /'raɪt əz 'reɪn/ *phr* healthy or well (usually after an illness)
under the weather /ˌʌndə ðə 'weðə/ *phr* If someone feels under the weather, they feel ill.

UNIT 4

MAKING DECISIONS

be in doubt about /biː ɪn 'daʊt əˌbaʊt/ *phr* to not know what to do about something, to be unsure
be in two minds about /biː ɪn ˌtuː 'maɪndz əˌbaʊt/ *phr* to be unable to decide about something
be undecided about /biː ˌʌndɪ'saɪdɪd əˌbaʊt/ *phr* If you are undecided about something, you have not yet made a decision or judgement about it.
be unsure about /biː ʌn'ʃɔːr əˌbaʊt/ *phr* If you are unsure about something, you are not certain about it or have doubts about it.
brainstorm ideas /ˌbreɪnstɔːm aɪ'dɪəz/ *phr* to think of a lot of ideas for a future activity very quickly before considering some of them more carefully
come to a decision /ˌkʌm tu ə dɪ'sɪʒən/ *phr* to make a choice about something after thinking about several possibilities
consider your options /kən'sɪdə jɔːr 'ɒpʃənz/ *phr* to think about a set of possibilities or choices in a situation
make up your mind /ˌmeɪk ʌp jɔː 'maɪnd/ *phr* to decide
reconsider /ˌriːkən'sɪdə/ *v* to think again about a decision or opinion and decide if you want to change it
seek advice /ˌsiːk əd'vaɪs/ *phr* to ask someone their opinion about what you should do or how you should act in a particular situation
think (something) through /θɪŋk 'θruː/ *pv* to carefully consider the possible results of doing something
weigh up the pros and cons /'weɪ ʌp ðə 'prəʊz ən 'kɒnz/ *phr* to think carefully about the advantages or disadvantages of a situation before making a decision

LIFE EVENTS: VERB AND NOUN COLLOCATIONS

accept (a place at university) /ək'sept/ *v* to say yes to an offer or invitation
apply for (a job / a place at university / an apprenticeship) /ə'plaɪ fɔː/ *v* to request something, usually official, especially by writing or by sending in a form
be a huge step /biː ə ˌhjuːdʒ 'step/ *phr* to be a major stage in a process
be offered (a job / a place at university) /biː 'ɒfəd/ *v* to be asked if you would like to have something
choose (a path / a career) /tʃuːz/ *v* to decide what you want from two or more possibilities
do (a course / an apprenticeship) /duː/ *v* to take part in a set of classes or work for a skilled person in order to learn, usually leading to a qualification
fail (an exam) /feɪl/ *v* to be unsuccessful in a test or exam
follow the path /ˌfɒləʊ ðə 'pɑːθ/ *phr* to do a particular set of actions, especially ones that lead to a goal or result
get good grades /get gʊd 'greɪdz/ *phr* to receive high marks for an exam or piece of work
get into (a school / university) /get 'ɪntu/ *pv* If you get into a school or university, you are accepted to study there.
graduate (from university) /'grædʒueɪt/ *v* to complete a first university degree successfully
leave home /liːv 'həʊm/ *phr* to go away permanently from the place where you grew up with your family
leave university / college / school /liːv ˌjuːnɪ'vɜːsəti / 'kɒlɪdʒ / 'skuːl/ *phr* to finish a course of study at university / college / school
mark (an exam) /mɑːk/ *v* to correct mistakes in and give points for work
pass (an exam) /pɑːs/ *v* to be successful in
resit (an exam) /ˌriː'sɪt/ *v* to take an exam again, usually because you failed or did not do well the first time
set (an exam) /set/ *v* to give someone an exam to do
sit (an exam) /sɪt/ *v* to take an exam
take a gap year /teɪk ə 'gæp ˌjɪə/ *phr* to have a year between leaving school and starting university that is usually spent travelling or working
take an exam /ˌteɪk ən ɪg'zæm/ *phr* to do a test of your knowledge or skill in a particular subject

ADJECTIVE AND NOUN COLLOCATIONS

big changes /ˌbɪg 'tʃeɪndʒɪz/ *phr* important differences in something
big decision /ˌbɪg dɪ'sɪʒən/ *phr* an important choice that you make about something after thinking about several possibilities
clear understanding /ˌklɪər ʌndə'stændɪŋ/ *phr* certain knowledge about a subject, situation, etc., with no doubt
deciding factor /dɪˌsaɪdɪŋ 'fæktə/ *phr* a fact or situation which is more important than others because it influences the result of something more and the final decision or choice is changed by it
immediate future /ɪˌmiːdiət 'fjuːtʃə/ *phr* a period of time that is to come very soon
major changes /ˌmeɪdʒə 'tʃeɪndʒɪz/ *phr* important differences in something
major role /ˌmeɪdʒə 'rəʊl/ *phr* an important position or purpose that something has in a situation
mixed feelings /ˌmɪkst 'fiːlɪŋz/ *phr* If you have mixed feelings about something, you feel both pleased and not pleased about it at the same time.
near future /ˌnɪə 'fjuːtʃə/ *phr* a period of time that is to come quite soon
strong feelings /ˌstrɒŋ 'fiːlɪŋz/ *phr* powerful emotions
strong influence /ˌstrɒŋ 'ɪnfluəns/ *phr* the power to have a big effect on people or things, or a person or thing that is able to do this
strong understanding /ˌstrɒŋg ʌndə'stændɪŋ/ *phr* certain knowledge about a subject, situation, etc., with no doubt

VOCABULARY LIST

vital factor /ˌvaɪtəl ˈfæktə/ *phr* a fact or situation which is very important in the way it influences the result of something
vital role /ˌvaɪtəl ˈrəʊl/ *phr* an extremely important position or purpose that something has in a situation

UNIT 5

TECHNOLOGY AND PROGRESS

advance /ədˈvɑːns/ *n* the forward movement of something, or an improvement or development in something
breakthrough /ˈbreɪkθruː/ *n* an important discovery or event that helps to improve a situation or provide an answer to a problem
cutting edge /ˌkʌtɪŋ ˈedʒ/ *adj* very modern and with all the newest features
development /dɪˈveləpmənt/ *n* the process in which someone or something grows or changes and becomes more advanced
drawback /ˈdrɔːbæk/ *n* a disadvantage or the negative part of a situation
launch /lɔːntʃ/ *v* to begin something such as a plan or introduce something new such as a product
market /ˈmɑːkɪt/ *v* to make goods available to buyers in a planned way that encourages people to buy more of them, for example by advertising
obsolete /ˌɒbsəlˈiːt/ *adj* not in use any more, having been replaced by something newer and better or more fashionable
prototype /ˈprəʊtətaɪp/ *n* the first example of something, such as a machine or other industrial product, from which all later forms are developed
radical /ˈrædɪkəl/ *adj* extreme
trigger /ˈtrɪgə/ *v* to cause something to start

ADJECTIVES AND DEPENDENT PREPOSITIONS

apparent (to) /əˈpærənt/ *adj* able to be seen or understood
appropriate (for) /əˈprəʊpriət/ *adj* suitable or right for a particular situation or occasion
conscious (of) /ˈkɒnʃəs/ *adj* If you are conscious of something, you notice that it exists or is present.
hostile (towards) /ˈhɒstaɪl/ *adj* unfriendly and not liking something or someone
inferior (to) /ɪnˈfɪəriə/ *adj* not good, or not as good as someone or something else
notorious (for) /nəˈtɔːriəs/ *adj* famous for something bad
toxic (to) /ˈtɒksɪk/ *adj* poisonous
vulnerable (to) /ˈvʌlnərəbəl/ *adj* able to be easily physically, emotionally or mentally hurt, influenced or attacked

PHRASAL VERBS

catch on /kætʃ ˈɒn/ *pv* to become fashionable or popular
cater for /ˈkeɪtə fɔ/ *pv* to provide what is wanted or needed by someone or something
check out /tʃek ˈaʊt/ *pv (informal)* to have a good look at something or someone
do away with /ˌdu əˈweɪ wɪð/ *pv* to get rid of or remove something
lie ahead /ˌlaɪ əˈhed/ *pv* to be in the future
look upon /ˈlʊk əˌpɒn/ *pv* to consider or think of someone or something as something
run on /ˈrʌn ɒn/ *pv* If an engine runs on something, it uses it as a fuel to make it work.
rush into /ˌrʌʃ ˈɪntu/ *pv* If you rush into something such as a job, you start doing it without having really decided if it is the right thing to do or having considered the best way to do it

UNIT 6

FILMS AND BOOKS

blockbuster /ˈblɒkbʌstə/ *n* a book or film that is very successful
blurb /blɜːb/ *n* a short description of a book, film, etc., written by the people who have produced it, and intended to make people want to buy it or see it
box-office flop /ˌbɒks ˌɒfɪs ˈflɒp/ *n* a film that is a financial failure
cinemagoer /ˈsɪnəməˌgəʊə/ *n* a person who regularly goes to watch films at the cinema
instalment /ɪnˈstɔːlmənt/ *n* one of several parts into which a book or film has been divided, so that each part is released at a different time until the end is reached
main character /ˌmeɪn ˈkærəktə/ *n* the most important person (or one of the most important people) represented in a film, play or story
masterpiece /ˈmɑːstəpiːs/ *n* a work of art, such as a painting, film or book, that is made with great skill
remake /ˈriːmeɪk/ *n* a film that has a story and title similar to an old one
revenue /ˈrevənjuː/ *n* the income that a company receives regularly
sequel /ˈsiːkwəl/ *n* a book, film or play that continues the story of a previous book, etc.
set (in) /set/ *v* If a story, film, etc. is set in a particular time or place, the action in it happens in that time or place.
trailer /ˈtreɪlə/ *n* an advertisement for a film or a television or radio programme, consisting of short parts taken from it

ENTERTAINMENT: ADVERB AND ADJECTIVE COLLOCATIONS

critically acclaimed /ˌkrɪtɪkli əˈkleɪmd/ *phr* attracting approval and praise from the people whose job is to write or speak about literature, film, etc.
highly anticipated /ˌhaɪli ænˈtɪsɪpeɪtɪd/ *phr* If a film or book is highly anticipated, it is one that people have been eagerly waiting for and expect to be very good.
hysterically funny /hɪˈsterɪkəli ˈfʌni/ *phr* extremely funny
internationally successful /ˌɪntəˈnæʃənəli səkˈsesfəl/ *phr* being very popular and/or making a lot of money in several different countries
largely unknown /ˈlɑːdʒli ʌnˈnəʊn/ *phr* almost completely unfamiliar or not known
painfully slow /ˌpeɪnfəli ˈsləʊ/ *phr* If something is painfully slow, it is very slow, in an unpleasant or unwanted way.

ENTERTAINMENT: COMPOUND ADJECTIVES

action-packed /ˈækʃənˌpækt/ *adj* full of exciting events
award-winning /əˈwɔːdˌwɪnɪŋ/ *adj* having won a prize or prizes for being of high quality or very skilled
best-known /ˈbest ˌnəʊn/ *adj* the most known or recognised by many people
highest-paid /ˈhaɪəst ˌpeɪd/ *adj* earning the most amount of money for doing something
low-budget /ˌləʊ ˈbʌdʒɪt/ *adj* If a film is low-budget, not much money has been spent on making it.
Oscar-nominated /ˈɒskə ˈnɒmɪneɪtɪd/ *adj* on the shortlist of candidates to win a prize at the annual awards ceremony held by the Academy of Motion Picture Arts and Sciences in the US
record-breaking /ˈrekɔːdˌbreɪkɪŋ/ *adj* better, bigger, longer, etc. than anything else before
thought-provoking /ˈθɔːt prəˈvəʊkɪŋ/ *adj* making you think a lot about a subject
world-famous /ˌwɜːld ˈfeɪməs/ *adj* known about by many people from most parts of the world

UNIT 7

ACHIEVEMENTS

adversity /əd'vɜːsəti/ *n* a difficult or unlucky situation or event
against all odds /ə'genst ɔːl 'ɒdz/ *id* If you do or achieve something against all odds, you do or achieve it although there were a lot of problems and you were not likely to succeed.
break down barriers /ˌbreɪk daʊn 'bæriəz/ *id* to improve understanding and communication between people who have different opinions
endurance /ɪn'dʒʊərəns/ *n* the ability to keep doing something difficult, unpleasant or painful for a long time
overcome /ˌəʊvə'kʌm/ *v* to defeat or succeed in controlling or dealing with something
self-belief /ˌself bɪ'liːf/ *n* trust in your own abilities
self-discipline /ˌself 'dɪsəplɪn/ *n* the ability to make yourself do things you know you should do, even when you do not want to
setback /'setbæk/ *n* something that happens that delays or prevents a process from developing
suffer defeat /'sʌfə dɪ'fiːt/ *phr* to experience losing against someone in a fight or competition, or being made to fail
thrive /θraɪv/ *v* to grow, develop or be successful

NOUN SUFFIXES

acceptance /ək'septəns/ *n* general agreement that something is satisfactory or right, or that someone should be included in a group
aggression /ə'greʃən/ *n* spoken or physical behaviour that is threatening or involves harm to someone or something
apprenticeship /ə'prentɪsʃɪp/ *n* a period of time working as an apprentice
courtesy /'kɜːtəsi/ *n* polite behaviour, or a polite action or remark
disapproval /ˌdɪsə'pruːvəl/ *n* the feeling of having a negative opinion of someone or something
freedom /'friːdəm/ *n* the condition or right of being able or allowed to do, say, think, etc. whatever you want to, without being controlled or limited
inaccuracy /ɪn'ækjərəsi/ *n* a situation in which a fact or measurement is not completely correct or exact
interference /ˌɪntə'fɪərəns/ *n* an occasion when someone tries to interfere in a situation
motivation /ˌməʊtɪ'veɪʃən/ *n* enthusiasm for doing something
negativity /ˌnegə'tɪvəti/ *n* an attitude that is not hopeful or enthusiastic
neighbourhood /'neɪbəhʊd/ *n* the area of a town that surrounds someone's home, or the people who live in this area
replacement /rɪ'pleɪsmənt/ *n* the process of substituting something with something else
unfairness /ʌn'feənəs/ *n* the quality or fact of not treating people in an equal way, or of being morally wrong

UNIT 8

MONEY AND WEALTH

allowance /ə'laʊəns/ *n* money that you are given regularly, especially to pay for a particular thing; an amount of money that parents regularly give to their child to spend as they choose
broke /brəʊk/ *adj* without money
fund /fʌnd/ *v* to provide the money to pay for an event, activity or organisation
rip-off /'rɪpɒf/ *n* something that is not worth what you pay for it
support /sə'pɔːt/ *n* financial, emotional or practical help
take out a loan /ˌteɪk aʊt ə 'ləʊn/ *phr* to arrange to borrow money from a company, bank, etc. which has to be paid back, together with an extra charge for borrowing it
unaffordable /ˌʌnə'fɔːdəbəl/ *adj* too expensive for people to be able to buy or pay for
well-off /wel 'ɒf/ *adj* rich
withdraw /wɪð'drɔː/ *v* to take out (e.g. money from a bank account)

MONEY: IDIOMS

break the bank /ˌbreɪk ðə 'bæŋk/ *id* to cost too much
daylight robbery /ˌdeɪlaɪt 'rɒbəri/ *id* a situation in which you have to pay far too much money for something
false economy /ˌfɒls ɪ'kɒnəmi/ *id* an action that saves money at the beginning but, over a longer period of time, results in more money being wasted than saved
go from rags to riches /ˌgəʊ frəm 'rægz tə 'rɪtʃɪz/ *id* to be very poor and then become very rich
make ends meet /ˌmeɪk endz 'miːt/ *id* to have just enough money to pay for the things that you need
pour money down the drain /pɔː 'mʌni daʊn ðə 'dreɪn/ *id* to waste money

MONEY: PHRASAL VERBS

come down (in price) /kʌm 'daʊn/ *pv* If a price comes down, it becomes lower.
come into (money) /ˌkʌm 'ɪntu/ *pv* If someone comes into money, they receive it as a result of the death of someone, usually a relation.
get by (on) /get 'baɪ/ *pv* to be able to live by having just enough money
put (money) aside /ˌpʊt ə'saɪd/ *pv* to save money, usually for a special purpose
rip (someone) off /rɪp 'ɒf/ *pv* to cheat someone by making them pay too much money for something
share out /ʃeər 'aʊt/ *pv* to divide something between several people
shop around /ˌʃɒp ə'raʊnd/ *pv* to compare the price and quality of the same or a similar object in different shops before you decide which one to buy
splash out (on) /splæʃ 'aʊt/ *pv* to spend a lot of money on something, especially something that is pleasant to have but that you do not really need

UNIT 9

EDUCATION

aspirations /ˌæspɪ'reɪʃənz/ *n* things that you hope to achieve
career path /kə'rɪə pɑːθ/ *n* the way that you progress in your work, either in one job or in a series of jobs
careers advice /kəˌrɪərz ə'dvaɪs/ *n* advice given about the best type of job or career for you
critical thinking /ˌkrɪtɪkəl 'θɪŋkɪŋ/ *n* the process of thinking carefully about a subject or idea, without allowing feelings or opinions to affect you
internship /'ɪntɜːnʃɪp/ *n* a period of training during which someone works for a company or organisation in order to get experience of a particular type of work
leadership /'liːdəʃɪp/ *n* the set of characteristics that make a good leader; the position or fact of being the leader
networking /'netwɜːkɪŋ/ *n* the activity of meeting people who might be useful to know, especially in your job
scholarship /'skɒləʃɪp/ *n* an amount of money given by a school, college, university or other organisation to pay for the studies of a person with great ability but little money
social skills /'səʊʃəl skɪlz/ *n* the skills that you need to communicate and interact successfully with other people
trainee /ˌtreɪ'niː/ *n* a person who is learning and practising the skills of a particular job

VOCABULARY LIST

EDUCATION: PHRASAL VERBS

break up /breɪk ˈʌp/ *pv* When schools and colleges break up, their classes stop and the holidays start.

catch up (with) /kætʃ ˈʌp/ *pv* to reach the same quality or standard as someone or something else

drop out /drɒp ˈaʊt/ *pv* If a student drops out, they stop going to classes before they have finished their course.

fall behind (with) /ˌfɔːl bɪˈhaɪnd/ *pv* to fail to do something fast enough or on time

get through (an exam) /get ˈθruː/ *pv* to succeed in an exam

go over /gəʊ ˈəʊvə/ *pv* to check or repeat something

hand in /hænd ˈɪn/ *pv* If you hand in something, e.g. homework, you give it to your teacher.

read up on /riːd ˈʌp ɒn/ *pv* to spend time reading in order to find out information about something

EDUCATION: VERB AND NOUN COLLOCATIONS

fulfil (an ambition, a dream, a goal, requirements) /fʊlˈfɪl/ *v* to do something that is expected, hoped for or promised, or cause it to happen

gain (experience (in), insight (into), understanding (of)) /geɪn/ *v* to get something that is useful, that gives you an advantage, or that is in some way positive, especially over a period of time

pay a visit (to) /ˌpeɪ e ˈvɪzɪt/ *phr* to go to a place in order to look at it

pay attention /ˌpeɪ əˈtenʃən/ *phr* to watch, listen to or think about something or someone carefully or with interest

pay (school) fees /peɪ ˈfiːz/ *phr* to pay a specified amount of money for education

set (a goal, homework, a standard) /set/ *v* to establish or decide something

submit (an application, an essay, homework, a proposal) /səbˈmɪt/ *v* to give or offer something for assessment by others

UNIT 10

PUNISHMENT FOR CRIME

arrest (someone) on suspicion of /əˈrest ɒn səˈspɪʃən əv/ *phr* If the police arrest someone on suspicion of a crime, they take them away to ask them about it because they have reason to believe that they have committed it.

be found guilty of /bi ˌfaʊnd ˈgɪlti əv/ *phr* If someone is found guilty of a crime, a court of law decides that they were responsible for that crime.

be issued with (a fine) /bi ˈɪʃuːd wɪð/ *pv* to be given (by an official)

be prosecuted for /bi ˈprɒsɪkjuːtɪd fə/ *v* to be officially accused in a law court of committing a crime

charge (someone) with (a crime) /ˈtʃɑːdʒ wɪð/ *v* to make a formal statement saying that someone is accused of a crime

pay damages (to) /ˌpeɪ ˈdæmɪdʒɪz/ *phr* to pay money to a person to compensate them for injury or loss

plead guilty to (a crime) /ˌpliːd ˈgɪlti tu/ *phr* to make a statement in a law court saying that you were responsible for a crime

report (someone) to the police /rɪˈpɔːt tu ðə pəˈliːs/ *phr* to make a complaint about someone to the police

sentence (someone) to /ˈsentəns tu/ *v* to decide and say officially what a punishment will be

CRIME AND PUNISHMENT: COLLOCATIONS

community service /kəˌmjuːnəti ˈsɜːvɪs/ *n* work done without payment to help other people. Criminals whose crime was not serious enough for them to be put in prison are sometimes ordered to do community service.

jail sentence /ˈdʒeɪl ˌsentəns/ *n* Someone who receives a jail sentence is sent to prison for a specified length of time.

light (punishment/sentence) /laɪt/ *adj* not severe, short

minor (crime/offence) /ˈmaɪnə/ *adj* having little importance, influence or effect, especially when compared with other things of the same type

organised crime /ˈɔːgənaɪzd ˈkraɪm/ *n* criminal behaviour that is planned and carried out by a group of people on a regular basis

petty (crime/theft) /ˈpeti/ *adj* not considered serious when compared with other crimes, etc.

repeat (offence/offender) /rɪˈpiːt/ *n* when someone commits a similar crime again and again

CRIME AND PUNISHMENT: SUFFIXES

burglary /ˈbɜːgləri/ *n* the crime of illegally entering a building and stealing things

crime /kraɪm/ *n* illegal activities; an illegal act

criminal /ˈkrɪmɪnəl/ *n* someone who commits a crime

cruelty /ˈkruːəlti/ *n* cruel behaviour or a cruel action

imprison /ɪmˈprɪzən/ *v* to put someone in prison

imprisonment /ɪmˈprɪzənmənt/ *n* the act of putting someone in prison or the condition of being kept in prison

offence /əˈfens/ *n* an illegal act; a crime

offender /əˈfendə/ *n* a person who is guilty of a crime

offensive /əˈfensɪv/ *adj* causing offence; unpleasant; used for attacking

prison /ˈprɪzən/ *n* a building where criminals are forced to live as a punishment

shoplift /ˈʃɒplɪft/ *v* to take goods illegally from a shop without paying for them

shoplifting /ˈʃɒplɪftɪŋ/ *n* the illegal act of taking goods from a shop without paying for them

steal /stiːl/ *v* to take something without the permission or knowledge of the owner and keep it

theft /θeft/ *n* (the act of) dishonestly taking something that belongs to someone else and keeping it

vandalism /ˈvændəlɪzəm/ *n* the crime of intentionally damaging property belonging to other people

vandalise /ˈvændəlaɪz/ *v* to intentionally damage property belonging to other people

UNIT 11

DESCRIBING FOOD

bland /blænd/ *adj* not having a strong taste

fatty /ˈfæti/ *adj* containing a lot of fat

high in /ˈhaɪ ɪn/ *adj* containing a large quantity of something

in season /ɪn ˈsiːzən/ *phr* If fruit and vegetables are in season, they are being produced in the area and are available and ready to eat.

junk food /ˈdʒʌŋk ˌfuːd/ *n* food that is unhealthy but is quick and easy to eat

low in /ˈləʊ ɪn/ *adj* containing a small quantity of something

organic /ɔːˈgænɪk/ *adj* not using artificial chemicals in the growing of plants and animals for food and other products

preservative /prɪˈzɜːvətɪv/ *n* a chemical used to stop food from decaying

produce /ˈprɒdʒuːs/ *n* food or any other substance or material that is grown or obtained through farming

ready meal /ˈredi ˌmɪəl/ *n* a meal cooked and bought at a shop but taken somewhere else, often home, to be heated and eaten

rich /rɪtʃ/ *adj* If food is rich, it contains a large amount of oil, butter, eggs or cream.

DESCRIBING FOOD: COLLOCATIONS

free-range /ˌfriː' reɪndʒ/ *adj* relating to or produced by farm animals that are allowed to move around outside and are not kept in cages

freshly baked /ˌfreʃli 'beɪkt/ *adj* Something that is freshly baked has been recently cooked inside an oven, without using added liquid or fat.

gluten-free /ˌgluːtən 'friː/ *adj* containing no gluten (= a protein contained in wheat and some other grains)

homemade /ˌhəʊm'meɪd/ *adj* made at home and not bought from a shop

locally sourced /ˌləʊkəli 'sɔːst/ *adj* If something is locally sourced, it is obtained from the particular small area that you are talking about.

pan-fried /'pænfraɪd/ *adj* cooked in a pan in a small amount of oil or fat

slow-roasted /ˌsləʊ 'rəʊstɪd/ *adj* If something is slow-roasted, it is cooked in an oven or over a fire over a long period of time.

sun-dried /'sʌndraɪd/ *adj* Sun-dried vegetables have been dried by leaving them in the sun so that their flavour becomes much stronger.

FOOD AND DRINK: EXPRESSIONS

go easy on (something) /ˌgəʊ 'iːzi ɒn/ *phr* to not use too much of something

go halves (on) /ˌgəʊ 'hɑːvz/ *phr* If two people go halves, they each pay half the price of something.

have a sweet tooth /ˌhæv ə ˌswiːt 'tuːθ/ *phr* If you have a sweet tooth, you like eating sweet foods, especially sweets and chocolate.

I could eat a horse. /aɪ ˌkʊd 'iːt ə 'hɔːs/ *id* I am really hungry.

It's on the house. /ɪts ˌɒn ðə 'haʊs/ *id* If you have something on the house, it is given to you free by a business.

Say when. /seɪ 'wen/ *id* said when you are pouring a drink or serving food for someone and you want them to tell you when to stop

Tuck in! /tʌk 'ɪn/ *id* said when you want someone to start eating

Your eyes are bigger than your stomach. /jɔːr ˌaɪz ə 'bɪgə ðən jɔ 'stʌmək/ *id* said to someone who has taken more food than they can eat

UNIT 12

TRAVEL

bound for /'baʊnd fə/ *adj* going to

carbon neutral /ˌkɑːbən 'njuːtrəl/ *adj* If a person, organisation, event, etc. is carbon neutral, it does things such as planting trees to reduce carbon dioxide by the same amount as it produces it.

clean up /kliːn 'ʌp/ *pv* to remove harmful substances or chemicals from a place or the environment

itinerary /aɪ'tɪnərəri/ *n* a detailed plan or route of a journey

off the beaten track /ˌɒf ðə ˌbiːtən 'træk/ *id* not known or popular with many people

offset your carbon footprint /ɒfˌset jɔː ˌkɑːbən 'fʊtprɪnt/ *phr* to pay for things that will reduce carbon dioxide in order to reduce the damage caused by carbon dioxide that you produce

self-catering /ˌself'keɪtərɪŋ/ *adj* (of a holiday) having cooking facilities available so that you can cook meals for yourself rather than having them provided for you

staycation /steɪ'keɪʃən/ *n* a holiday that someone spends in their own country or at home, rather than travelling somewhere else

sustainable /sə'steɪnəbəl/ *adj* causing little or no damage to the environment and therefore able to continue for a long time

tourism tax /'tʊərɪzəm ˌtæks/ *n* (an amount of) money paid to the government by tourists to help offset their impact on the environment

FORMAL *(F)* AND INFORMAL *(INF)* LANGUAGE

become *(f)* /bɪ'kʌm/ *v* to start to be
  get *(inf)* /get/ *v*

child *(f)* /tʃaɪld/ *n* a boy or girl from the time of birth until he or she is an adult; a son or daughter of any age
  kid *(inf)* /kɪd/ *n* child

commence *(f)* /kə'mens/ *v* to begin something
  start *(inf)* /stɑːt/ *v*

dishonest *(f)* /dɪ'sɒnɪst/ *adj* not honest
  dodgy *(inf)* /'dɒdʒi/ *adj*

express *(f)* /ɪk'spres/ *v* to show a feeling, opinion or fact in words
  say *(inf)* /seɪ/ *v*

friend *(f)* /frend/ *n* a person who you know well and who you like a lot, but who is usually not a member of your family
  mate *(inf)* /meɪt/ *n*

incorrect *(f)* /ˌɪnkər'ekt/ *adj* not correct or not true
  wrong *(inf)* /rɒŋ/ *adj*

investigate *(f)* /ɪn'vestɪgeɪt/ *v* to examine a crime, problem, statement, etc. carefully, especially to discover the truth
  look into *(inf)* /lʊk 'ɪntu/ *pv*

permit *(f)* /pə'mɪt/ *v* to allow something
  let *(inf)* /let/ *v*

purchase *(f)* /'pɜːtʃəs/ *v* to get something by paying money for it
  buy *(inf)* /baɪ/ *v*

resign (from) *(f)* /rɪ'zaɪn/ *v* to give up a job or position by telling your employer that you are leaving
  quit *(inf)* /kwɪt/ *v*

return *(f)* /rɪ'tɜːn/ *v* to send, take, give, put, etc. something back to where it came from
  give back *(inf)* /gɪv 'bæk/ *pv*

succeed in (doing) *(f)* /ˌsək'siːd ɪn/ *pv* to achieve something that you have been aiming for, especially something difficult
  manage to (do) *(inf)* /'mænɪdʒ tu/ *v*

virus *(f)* /'vaɪərəs/ *n* an extremely small piece of organic material that causes disease in humans, animals and plants
  bug *(inf)* /bʌg/ *n*

UNIT 13

COMMUNICATION: PHRASAL VERBS

brush up on /brʌʃ 'ʌp ɒn/ *pv* to improve your knowledge of something already learned but partly forgotten

burst out (laughing) /bɜːst 'aʊt/ *pv* If you burst out laughing, you suddenly start laughing.

catch up on /kætʃ 'ʌp ɒn/ *pv* to learn about (recent events)

come up to (someone) /kʌm 'ʌp tə/ *pv* to move towards someone

get at /'get ət/ *pv* to suggest or express something in a way that is not direct or clear

get by /get 'baɪ/ *pv* to be able to live or deal with a situation with difficulty, usually by having just enough of something you need, such as money or a skill

go on about /gəʊ 'ɒn əˌbaʊt/ *pv* to talk in an annoying way about something for a long time

take (something) in /teɪk 'ɪn/ *pv* to understand completely the meaning or importance of something

talk (someone) into /tɔːk 'ɪntu/ *pv* to persuade someone to do something, or to decide to do something

talk (someone) out of /tɔːk 'aʊt əv/ *pv* to persuade someone not to do something, or to decide not to do something

VOCABULARY LIST

ADVERBS

comprehensively /ˌkɒmprɪˈhensɪvli/ *adv* completely
effectively /ɪˈfektɪvli/ *adv* used when you describe what the real result of a situation is
incredibly /ɪnˈkredəbli/ *adv* extremely
individually /ˌɪndɪˈvɪdʒuəli/ *adv* separately
massively /ˈmæsɪvli/ *adv* extremely or very much
namely /ˈneɪmli/ *adv* used when you want to give more detail or be more exact about something you have just said
poorly /ˈpɔːli/ *adv* not well, badly
publicly /ˈpʌblɪkli/ *adv* If something is done publicly, it is done so that everyone can know about it.
repeatedly /rɪˈpiːtɪdli/ *adv* many times
respectively /rɪˈspektɪvli/ *adv* in a way that relates or belongs to each of the separate people or things you have just mentioned
supposedly /səˈpəʊzɪdli/ *adv* used to show that you do not believe that something you have been told is true
technically /ˈteknɪkəli/ *adv* according to an exact understanding of the rules, facts, etc.

UNIT 14

SOCIAL MEDIA MARKETING

boost (sales) /buːst/ *v* to improve or increase sales
designer goods /dɪˈzaɪnə ˈgʊdz/ *n* items for sale or possessions made by a famous or fashionable designer
emulate /ˈemjəleɪt/ *v* to copy something achieved by someone else and try to do it as well as they have
engage with /ɪnˈgeɪdʒ wɪð/ *v* to become involved, or have contact, with someone or something
fanbase /ˈfænbeɪs/ *n* the fans of a singer, group, team, etc. considered as a group
follower /ˈfɒləʊə/ *n* someone who chooses to see a particular person's posts (= messages) on social media
market /ˈmɑːkɪt/ *v* to make goods available to buyers in a planned way that encourages people to buy more of them, for example by advertising
product placement /ˈprɒdʌkt ˌpleɪsmənt/ *n* a way of advertising a product by supplying it for use in films, TV or the media
sponsor /ˈspɒnsə/ v to support a person, organisation or activity by giving money, encouragement or other help
target /ˈtɑːgɪt/ *v* to direct advertising or a product at someone

NEGATIVE PREFIXES

antisocial /ˌæntiˈsəʊʃəl/ *adj* harmful to society
deactivate /ˌdiːˈæktɪveɪt/ *v* to cause something to be no longer active or effective
disobey /ˌdɪsəˈbeɪ/ *v* to refuse to do something that you are told to do
illegal /ɪˈliːgəl/ *adj* not allowed by law
imprecise /ˌɪmprɪˈsaɪs/ *adj* not accurate or exact
inaccessible /ˌɪnəkˈsesəbəl/ *adj* very difficult or impossible to travel to or reach
irresponsibly /ˌɪrɪˈspɒnsəbli/ *adv* in a way that shows that you are not thinking or worrying enough about the possible results of what you do
misinformation /ˌmɪsɪnfəˈmeɪʃən/ *n* wrong information, or the fact that people are misinformed
non-existent /ˌnɒnɪgˈzɪstənt/ *adj* Something that is non-existent does not exist or is not present in a particular place.
undo /ʌnˈduː/ *v* to remove the good or bad effects of an action or several actions

SUFFIXES *-FUL* AND *-LESS*

helpful /ˈhelpfəl/ *adj* willing to help, or useful
helpless /ˈhelpləs/ *adj* unable to do anything to help yourself or anyone else
unhelpful /ʌnˈhelpfəl/ *adj* not wanting to help someone, in a way that seems unfriendly; not improving a difficult situation
truthful /ˈtruːθfəl/ *adj* honest and not containing or telling any lies
untruthful /ʌnˈtruːθfəl/ *adj* not honest
useful /ˈjuːsfəl/ *adj* effective; helping you to do or achieve something
useless /ˈjuːsləs/ *adj* of no use; not working or not achieving what is needed; not at all good at doing something

UNIT 15

ENDANGERED ANIMALS

declining population /dɪˈklaɪnɪŋ ˌpɒpjəˈleɪʃən/ *n* a group of people or animals of a particular type or group who live in one country, area or place, that is gradually becoming less
endangered /ɪnˈdeɪndʒəd/ *adj* Endangered animals may soon not exist because there are very few now alive.
extinct /ɪkˈstɪŋkt/ *adj* not now existing
habitat loss /ˈhæbɪtæt ˈlɒs/ *n* when there is less of the natural environment in which an animal or plant usually lives than there was before
on the verge of extinction /ɒn ðə ˈvɜːdʒ əv ɪkˈstɪŋkʃən/ *phr* If an animal is on the verge of extinction, it is very close to no longer existing.
poaching /ˈpəʊtʃɪŋ/ *n* catching and killing animals without permission on someone else's land
threatened /ˈθretənd/ *adj* likely to be harmed or damaged
vulnerable /ˈvʌlnərəbəl/ *adj* able to be easily physically, emotionally or mentally hurt, influenced or attacked
wilderness /ˈwɪldənəs/ *n* an area of land that has not been used to grow crops or had towns and roads built on it, especially because it is difficult to live in as a result of its extremely cold or hot weather or bad earth
woodland /ˈwʊdlənd/ *n* an area of land on which many trees grow

ADVERB AND ADJECTIVE COLLOCATIONS

equally important /ˈiːkwəli ɪmˈpɔːtənt/ *phr* necessary or of great value to the same degree as something else
naturally occurring /ˈnætʃərəli əˈkɜːrɪŋ/ *phr* Something that is naturally occurring can be found existing as part of nature and not made or done by people.
noticeably different /ˈnəʊtɪsəbli ˈdɪfərənt/ *phr* not the same in a way that is easy to see or recognise
officially recognised /əˈfɪʃəli ˈrekəgnaɪzd/ *phr* If someone or something is officially recognised, it is accepted by people in positions of authority that that person or thing has a particular position or quality.
randomly selected /ˈrændəmli sɪˈlektɪd/ *phr* chosen in way that happens or is done by chance rather than according to a plan
rapidly increasing /ˈræpɪdli ɪnˈkriːsɪŋ/ *phr* becoming larger in amount or size in a fast or sudden way
universally accepted /juːnɪˈvɜːsəli əkˈseptɪd/ *phr* generally agreed to be satisfactory or right by everyone
virtually impossible /ˈvɜːtʃuəli ɪmˈpɒsəbəl/ *phr* If an action or event is virtually impossible, it is extremely unlikely to happen or be achieved.

INTENSIFYING ADVERBS

bitterly /'bɪtəli/ *adv* in a way that shows strong negative emotion such as anger or disappointment; If it is bitterly cold, the weather is extremely and unpleasantly cold.
dangerously /'deɪndʒərəsli/ *adv* in a way that could put someone or something in danger or cause harm
deeply /'diːpli/ *adv* extremely or strongly
fully /'fʊli/ *adv* completely or totally
highly /'haɪli/ *adv* very, to a large degree, or at a high level
perfectly /'pɜːfɪktli/ *adv* completely or totally
seriously /'sɪəriəslɪ/ *adv* badly or severely; in a serious way, not joking
utterly /'ʌtəli/ *adv* completely or extremely

UNIT 16

ROLE MODELS

campaign for/against (something) /kæm'peɪn fə/əˌgenst/ *v* to organise a series of activities to try to achieve or stop something
come up against (a difficulty) /kʌm 'ʌp əˌgenst/ *pv* to have to deal with a problem
devote yourself to (something) /dɪ'vəʊt jəˌself tu/ *v* to give your time or effort completely to something you believe in, or to use a particular amount of time or energy doing something
fulfil an ambition /fʊl'fɪl ən æm'bɪʃən/ *phr* to do something that you have had a strong wish to achieve, or cause it to happen
look up to (someone) /lʊk 'ʌp tu/ *pv* to admire and respect someone
raise awareness of /reɪz ə'weənəs əv/ *phr* to increase knowledge and understanding of a particular activity, subject, etc.
role model /'rəʊl ˌmɒdəl/ *n* a person who someone admires and whose behaviour they try to copy
take on a challenge /teɪk 'ɒn ə 'tʃælɪndʒ/ *phr* to accept something that needs great mental or physical effort in order to be done successfully and therefore tests a person's ability
think highly of (someone) /θɪŋk 'haɪli əv/ *phr* to have a good opinion of someone
throw yourself into (something) /'θrəʊ jəˌself 'ɪntu/ *pv* to do something actively and enthusiastically

DEPENDENT PREPOSITIONS

apparent to (someone) /ə'pærənt tu/ *adj* able to be seen or understood by someone
capable of (something) /'keɪpəbəl əv/ *adj* having the ability, power or qualities to able to do something
compatible with (something) /kəm'pætəbəl wɪð/ *adj* able to exist, live or work successfully with something else
integral to (something) /'ɪntɪgrəl tu/ *adj* necessary and important as part of something else
mistaken in (something) /mɪ'steɪkən ɪn/ *adj* wrong in what you believe about something, or based on a belief that is wrong
notable for (something) /'nəʊtəbəl fə/ *adj* important and deserving attention for something
thankful for (something) /'θæŋkfəl fə/ *adj* happy or grateful because of something
unaware of (something) /ˌʌnə'weər əv/ *adj* not understanding or realising something

PHRASAL PREPOSITIONS

aside from /ə'saɪd frəm/ *adv* except for
contrary to /'kɒntrəri tu/ *adj* opposite from, in a different way
in common with /ɪn 'kɒmən wɪð/ *phr* in the same way as someone or something
in the region of /ɪn ðə 'riːdʒən əv/ *phr* approximately
let alone /let ə'ləʊn/ *id* and to an even greater degree do something (used to emphasise the extreme nature of an action)
with regard to /wɪð rɪ'gɑːd tu/ *phr* in connection with

GRAMMAR REFERENCE AND PRACTICE

UNIT 1 PAST TENSE REVIEW

Past simple

- We use the past simple for completed past actions. These can be single actions or repeated past actions.
  *What **happened** to you?*
  *I **fell off** my bike, but I **didn't hurt** myself.*
  *The three friends **walked** to school together every day last week.*

Past continuous, *used to*, *would*

- We use the past continuous for actions in progress at a point in the past.
  *What **were you doing** in my room this morning?*
  *I **wasn't doing** anything wrong. I **was looking** for my phone.*
- We use ***used to*** (+ the infinitive) for past states
  *People **used to believe** the Earth was flat.*
  and for past habits and routines that are no longer current.
  *My brother and I **used to play** football every Saturday morning.*

> **Note** In questions and negative sentences which include the auxiliary verbs *did* and *didn't*, **use** not **used** *is the correct form.*

*Where **did you use to** live?*
*I **didn't use to** drink coffee.*

- We use ***would*** (+ the infinitive) for habitual past actions (but not states).
  *Every time we got together, we **would argue** about something trivial.*
  But we can't say
  *When I was a child, **I would have** blond curly hair.*
  Used to is the correct form here.
  *When I was a child, **I used to have** blond curly hair.*

Present perfect simple

- We use the present perfect simple for actions that took place at an unspecified time in the past.
  ***Have you** ever **visited** South America?*
  *Yes. **I've visited** most countries in South America but I **haven't been** to Argentina.*

> **Note** Although we cannot specify a time with the present perfect verbs, we can use these time adverbs to indicate a link between the past and present time.

already	*I've **already** read that book.*
never	*I've **never** ridden a horse.*
ever	*Have you **ever** met anyone famous?*
just	*He's **just** passed his driving test.*
yet	*I haven't spoken to my parents about it **yet**.*

Past perfect simple

- We use the past perfect simple for states which existed up to a point in the past
  ***I'd always wondered** what my cousin looked like. **I hadn't expected** her to be so tall.*
  and for actions which took place before a point in the past.
  *Jorge **had finished** his homework by 7 o'clock.*

Present perfect continuous

- We use the present perfect continuous for actions that started in the past and continued up to the present time.
  ***We've been waiting** for the concert to start for nearly an hour – and we're still waiting.*

Past perfect continuous

- We use the past perfect continuous for actions in progress up to a point in the past.
  *They **had been planning** to join the gym for ages.*

Practice

1 Choose the correct options.

1. Larissa can't play tennis this weekend because she *has injured / had injured* her wrist. She *fell over / was falling over* while she *ran / was running* for a train yesterday.
2. Could you get me a bandage, please? *I'd cut / I've cut* my finger.
3. While I *had / was having* lunch, my phone *rang / was ringing* six or seven times.
4. It wasn't the first time Jess *had broken / has broken* the law. When she *was / was being* a child, she *would often steal / was often stealing* sweets in shops.
5. What time *did you get / have you got* home last night?
6. Ben *had been playing / has been playing* computer games all morning. He must be hungry by now.

2 Choose the correct options in the conversation.

Anna: You look pretty rough. [1]*Did you have / Have you had* any breakfast yet?
Sofia: No – I'm not hungry.
Anna: What's the matter? Are you OK?
Sofia: No, I feel terrible. [2]*I didn't sleep / I haven't slept* a wink last night.
Anna: What's the problem?
Sofia: I should be getting my exam results any day now. It's Thursday already. [3]*I looked / I've looked* online every morning this week. I must get them soon.
Anna: Calm down! You'll just have to be patient.
Sofia: But it's nearly three months since [4]*I took / I've taken* the exams. [5]*I never had / I've never had* to wait as long as this before. It's absolute torture.
Anna: I'm sure you'll be OK. [6]*You revised / You've been revising* for months.
Sofia: I know, but geography and music aren't my strongest subjects. [7]*I failed / I've failed* every geography exam [8]*I ever took / I've ever taken.*
Anna: What was that noise?
Sofia: An email arriving. It could be the message [9]*I've waited for / I've been waiting for*. Can you check it for me, Anna?
Anna: Sure! Brilliant! [10]*You passed! / You've passed!* Congratulations!
Sofia: That's amazing – [11]*I really thought / I've really thought* that [12]*I've failed / I'd failed.*

3 **Decide if it is possible to use both *used to* and *would* in these sentences. Cross out any wrong forms.**

1. Life is quite different from what it *used to* / *would* be like 50 years ago.
2. The majority of people *didn't use to* / *wouldn't* have as much free time as we have today.
3. Most of them *used to* / *would* work for six full days a week.
4. If they were fortunate enough to have a summer holiday, people *used to* / *would* spend it in their own country. Hardly anyone *used to* / *would* go abroad.

UNIT 2 COMPARATIVES AND SUPERLATIVES

Comparative and superlative adjectives

- We use comparative adjectives to compare two people or things and superlative adjectives to compare more than two.
  Comparative adjectives end in *-er* OR are preceded by ***more*** and both forms are followed by ***than***.
  Superlative adjectives are preceded by ***the*** and end in ***-est*** OR are preceded by ***the most***.
- Adjectives of one-syllable end in ***-er*** /***-est***.
  wide *Rivers are **wider than** streams. The Amazon is **the widest river** in the world.*
  tall *My sister is **taller than** me, but our brother is **the tallest** of us all.*
  big *Your house is **bigger than** ours. The President's palace is **the biggest** private residence in the country.*
- Adjectives of three or more syllables are preceded by ***more*** or ***most***.
  expensive *An Audi is **more expensive** than a Ford, and a Bugatti is probably **the most expensive** car you can buy.*
- Adjectives of two syllables follow one of the two rules above.
  healthy – healthier – healthiest
  angry – angrier – angriest
  common – more common – the most common
  honest – more honest – the most honest
- ***less / least***
  less and ***least*** are the opposites of ***more*** and ***most***.
  These two sentences have the same meaning.
  *You are **more interested** in art / **keener** on art than Jan or me.*
  *I am **less interested** in art / **less keen** on art than you, but Jan is **the least interested**.*

Irregular adjectives

good *Ben is **a better** writer than me, but Sam is **the best** writer in the class.*

bad *The weather today is **worse** than yesterday, but Sunday was **the worst** weather we've had all year.*

far *Anne's house is **further** / **farther** from school than mine, but Jo's is **the furthest** / **the farthest**.*

Comparative and superlative adverbs

- We use adverbs to qualify verbs (actions) and adjectives.
  *I can speak French **more fluently** than I could last year, but Fran speaks it **the most fluently** of us all.*
  *That was **the most beautifully decorated** building (that) I have ever seen.*
- **Adverbs with the same form as adjectives**
  Many adverbs are formed by adding *-ly* to an adjective.
  warm – warmly
  But a few adverbs, e.g. ***hard, right, tough, quick, late,*** have the same form as adjectives.
  *He's a **hard** worker. / He works **hard**.*
  The comparative and superlative forms of these adverbs are also the same as the adjectives.
  *He's works **harder than** me. But Jeremy works **the hardest**.*

Qualifying comparative and superlative structures

- We can use these words and phrases to qualify comparative adjectives and adverbs: ***a bit, a little, slightly, much, a lot***
  *I'm **a bit** /**a little** / **slightly** / **much** / **a lot warmer** than I was earlier.*
  *You're walking **a bit** / **a little** / **slightly** / **much** / **a lot faster** than me.*
  *We'll be catching a **slightly later** train than we expected.*
- We can use these words and phrases to qualify superlative adjectives and adverbs: ***by far, nearly, easily, one of***
  *He's **easily** / **by far** the best singer / He's **one of** the best singers I've ever heard.*
  *Ben is **nearly the oldest** person working here, but he works **by far the hardest**.*
- We can also add comment adverbs to qualify comparative adjectives and adverbs.
  *Manuel was **noticeably more nervous** than Mario at the interview.*
  *Suzi was running **significantly faster** than her brother.*

Double comparatives – adjectives and adverbs

- We use phrases like these to describe something which is changing.
  *The climate is getting **hotter and hotter**. I'm getting **more and more worried**.*
  *She ran **faster and faster**.*
  *The snow was getting heavier, so we drove **more and more cautiously**.*
- We use phrases with ***the … / the …*** to describe situations which are changing in parallel.
  ***The older** he gets, **the lazier** he becomes.*
  ***The faster** I run, **the sooner** I arrive.*
  ***The more impatient** he gets, **the more irritating** he becomes.*

Practice

1 **Choose the correct word.**

1. James has worked in our department *much* / *more* longer than anyone else.
2. Jed is the *more* / *most* irritating person I know.
3. Out of everyone I know, Jack works the *harder* / *hardest*.
4. My headache is *bit* / *slightly* better than it was this morning.
5. This year we have had by far the *hottest* / *hotter* summer I can remember.
6. People today are driving *fast* / *faster* and faster.
7. Mark and Ed are both good tennis players but Mark is *better* / *best*.
8. I hope our new office computers are *efficienter* / *more efficient* than the old ones.

2 Complete the sentences with the comparative or superlative form of the word in brackets. The answers can be adjectives or adverbs. Add *than* if necessary.

1 TV programmes are never very good in the summer, but this year they were even ______ usual. In fact they were ______ I can remember. (bad)
2 I go to the gym much ______ I used to. I'm there nearly every day! (frequent)
3 Last December it poured down every day. Experts say it was ______ December on record. (wet)
4 Some people say that London is ______ city in the world, but for me Istanbul is much ______. (exciting)
5 Out of all my friends, Kirsten writes ______. (clear)
6 This has been a good year for me. I'm much ______ I was last year. In fact I think I'm ______ I have ever been! (happy)
7 She felt terrible all weekend, but she seems much ______ this morning. (good)
8 The ______ I run, the ______ I feel. (far / fit)

3 Rewrite the sentences using the words in brackets.

1 Every time I hear that name I get really worried. (the more)
2 I've never seen a funnier film than that. (funniest)
3 Finding a new job was easier than I had expected. (difficult)
4 Petrol is becoming increasingly expensive. (more and)
5 We didn't expect the journey to take so long. (longer)
6 The maths homework was easier than I expected. (not as)

UNIT 3 MODAL VERBS: REVIEW

The future forms of these modal verbs are written in red. If no future form is suggested, this is because the form given applies to both the present and the future.

Speculation and deduction: *must, can't, might, could, may*

- We use ***must*** + **infinitive without *to*** when we are almost sure something is true.
  *Look! People are putting their umbrellas up. **It must be** raining.*
- We use ***can't*** + **infinitive without *to*** when we are almost sure something is impossible.
  *He's isn't wearing a uniform, so **he can't be** a police officer.*
- We use ***may (not)*** / ***might (not)*** / ***could (not)*** + **infinitive without *to*** when we are not sure.
  *She looks terrible, but **she may** / **might** / **could** just **need** a good night's sleep.*
  *He's never as late as this. I suppose he **may not** / **might not be** coming.*

Permission: *can, could, may*

- We use *can* / *could* / *may* + **infinitive without *to*** to ask for permission.
  ***Can I leave** early this evening, please?*

> **Note** *Could* or *may* can be used in this sentence to make the request sound more polite.

- We use ***can*** to give permission and ***can't*** for lack of permission or prohibition.
  *You **can leave** at any time you like.*
  *Students **can't use** mobile phones in the college library.*
  *You **can't go out** until you've done your homework.*

Obligation: *must, have to, need (to)*

- We use *must* / *mustn't* + **infinitive without *to*** for rules and laws.
  *Passengers **must keep** / **will have to keep** their seat belts on at all times.*
  *Drivers **must not exceed** 90 km on this road.*
- We can also use *must* / *mustn't* to express a personal feeling of obligation or a feeling that something is important.
  *I **must phone** / **will have to phone** my brother tomorrow.*
  *You **mustn't worry** about paying the rent on time.*
  Note the opposites of *must*:
  *You **must wear** / **will have to wear** a tie for work.* This is a rule.
  *You **mustn't wear** jeans for work.* This is also a rule.
  *You **don't have to wear** / **won't have to wear** a tie.* You can wear a tie if you like. It is your choice.
- We use ***have to*** + **infinitive** to express duties or obligations from an external source.
  *He **has to attend** / **will have to attend** a meeting at 8.30 in the morning.*
- We use **need to** / **don't need to** + **infinitive** to express necessity or lack of necessity.
  *You **need to get** / **will need to get** more sleep.*
  *You **don't need to hurry** / **won't need to hurry** / **needn't hurry**.*

Advice: *should, ought to*

- We use ***should*** / ***shouldn't*** + infinitive without *to* to give advice.
  *You **should see** the dentist if you have toothache.*
  *You **shouldn't eat** too much sugar.*
- We use ***ought to*** / ***ought not to*** + **infinitive** to give strong advice or to express moral obligation or responsibility.
  *People **ought to set** a good example to children.*
  *You **ought not to drive** if you feel tired.*
  It is also used to remind someone, including yourself, about a responsibility.
  *I really **ought to finish** my homework, but I'm too tired.*

Practice

1 Choose the correct verbs.

1 Sorry, I can't come out with you this evening. I *must* / *have to* finish this essay.
2 I *don't need to* / *can't* catch a train home. My brother's picking me up.
3 He *can* / *must* stay for 90 days with this type of visa if he wants to.
4 You *mustn't* / *don't have to* go to the lecture this afternoon. It's optional.
5 If you don't understand, you *should* / *may* ask your teacher to explain it again.
6 In Britain, you *can't* / *needn't* leave school until you're 18.
7 These tablets will make you feel better, but you *mustn't* / *don't have to* take more than two at a time.
8 The meeting will be quite informal, so you *mustn't* / *needn't* wear a suit.

2 **Complete the conversation with *can*, *can't*, *have to* or *mustn't*.**

A: Do you [1] ______ wear a school uniform, or [2] ______ you wear what you like?

B: At my last school, I could wear whatever I liked, but at this school, we [3] ______ wear an old-fashioned uniform.

A: What about jewellery?

B: No, we [4] ______ wear any kind of jewellery. It's completely prohibited.

A: So you [5] ______ even wear a simple gold chain that you received as a present?

B: No, unfortunately not.

3 **Complete the sentences with *must*, *can't*, *might* and one of these verbs: *be*, *have*, *live*, *want*.**

1. You've lost your keys. You are almost sure your sister Julie has them.
   'Julie ______ my keys. I'll go and check.'
2. There's a lot of noise coming from next door. It's possibly a party.
   'My neighbours ______ having a party.'
3. You hear someone who sounds like your brother, but that's impossible. Your brother is on holiday.
   'It ______ my brother – he's on holiday.'
4. Don't turn the water heater off. Tanya ______ to have a shower later.
5. He walks to work, so he ______ far away.
6. If Ben gave you the information, it ______ true. He never tells lies.

UNIT 4 MODALS IN THE PAST

Speculation and deduction: *must have, can't have, may have, might have, could have*

- We use ***must have*** + **past participle** when we are almost certain that something happened.
  There are students everywhere. Their lectures ***must have finished*** *early today.*
- We use ***can't have*** + **past participle** when we are almost certain that something did not happen.
  That's Matt's bike over there, so he ***can't have cycled*** *to college this morning.*
- We use ***may not*** / ***might (not) have*** + **past participle** when we are not sure whether something happened or not.
  He isn't normally as late as this. He ***may*** / ***might have missed*** *his train.*
- We can also use ***could have*** with this meaning, but not in the negative.
  Pete ***may*** / ***might*** / ***could have phoned*** *while I was in the shower.*
  I wonder why Mandy hasn't phoned me back. I suppose she ***may not*** / ***might not have heard*** *my message.*

Permission: *could / couldn't, was/were allowed to*

- We use ***could*** / ***couldn't*** + **infinitive without *to*** to refer to actions that were/weren't permitted.
  During the holidays I ***could go*** *to bed as late as I liked, but I* ***couldn't get up*** *late.*
- Alternatively we can use ***was/were allowed to***.
  We ***were allowed to take*** *water into the library, but we* ***weren't allowed to eat*** *anything.*

Obligation: *had to, needed to* + infinitive

- There is no past form of the verb *must*, so we use ***had to*** / ***needed to*** for rules or personal feelings.
  We ***had to keep*** *our seat belts on for the whole flight.*
  I felt I ***had to*** / ***needed to explain*** *what I'd done.*
- We use the negative form ***didn't have to*** or ***didn't need to*** to refer to lack of obligation or necessity.
  On Friday mornings we ***didn't have to*** / ***didn't need to dress*** *formally for work.*
- We use ***didn't need to*** for actions that were not necessary.
  We had lots of coffee, so we ***didn't need to buy*** *any. (We didn't buy coffee.)*
- We use ***needn't have*** + **past participle** for actions that were unnecessary but actually happened.
  We had plenty of coffee, so we ***needn't have bought*** *any more.* (We bought coffee, but we didn't need it.)

Advice: *should have / ought to have* + past participle

- We use ***should have*** / ***ought to have*** + **past participle** to describe mistakes, regrets or to give retrospective advice (advice after the event) to other people or ourselves.
  You ***should have*** / ***ought to have told*** *me you had no money. I'd have lent you some.*
  Everything was fine. I ***shouldn't have*** / ***oughtn't to have worried***.

Ability: *could / couldn't, was able to / was unable to*

- We use ***could*** / ***couldn't*** + **infinitive without *to*** for natural or learned abilities. We can also use ***was/were able to*** *or* ***was/were unable to*** + **infinitive**.
  I ***could/couldn't ride*** *a bicycle OR I* ***was able/unable to ride*** *a bicycle.*
- For specific past actions we can use the negative ***couldn't*** but not the affirmative ***could***. Instead, we use ***was/were able to*** or ***managed to***.
  I ***couldn't get in*** *because I'd lost my key, but in the end* ***I was able to*** / ***managed to climb in*** *through a broken window.*

Practice

1 **Rewrite these sentences so that they refer to the past.**

1. At my school, everyone must study maths and English until they are 16.
   At my last school, everyone ______.
2. We needn't study history or geography if we don't want to.
   We ______.
3. Older students don't have to arrive before their first lesson.
   Older students ______.
4. They can drive to school in their cars or on their motorbikes if they wish.
   They ______.
5. This means that students do not need to catch buses or trains.
   This meant that ______.

2 **Choose the correct verb.**

1. We knew there'd be plenty of food at the party, so we *didn't need to eat* / *needn't have eaten* before we came.
2. I was going to take my computer somewhere to be repaired, but in the end I *could fix* / *managed to fix* it myself.

3 I wish Tom hadn't turned up. I *mustn't have told / shouldn't have told* him where we were going.
4 I *couldn't swim / couldn't have swum* until I was nearly nine.
5 Maria *didn't need to buy / needn't have bought* any bread but she didn't know her flatmate had already bought some the day before.

3 Rewrite the second sentence in each set using *must have*, *can't have* or *might have*.

1 a Helena is usually here by now. Maybe she has overslept.
Helena *might have overslept.*
b Helena is a light sleeper. So it's extremely unlikely that she has overslept.
She ______
c Helena has a bad memory. It's certain that she has forgotten to come.
She ______
2 a Tom's looking happy. You are sure that he has won an important competition.
Tom ______
b He didn't go in for the competition, so you know he didn't win.
He ______
c It's possible that Tom has just heard the results of his college application.
He ______

UNIT 5 THE FUTURE

Present tense for future

We use the **present simple**

- for future actions or events which are timetabled or scheduled.
*Our flight **takes off** at 10.25 on Saturday morning.*
*My driving lesson **starts** at 9.00 and **finishes** at 9.45.*
- in subordinate clauses which refer to the future and begin with time phrases.
***As soon as we arrive**, I'll give you a call.*
***When Leo sees** what you've done, he'll be so grateful.*

We use the **present continuous**

- for fixed future arrangements.
*I'**m meeting** my sister for lunch at the weekend.*
*I'**m not doing** anything interesting this evening.*

Future simple: *will* + infinitive

We use ***will* + the infinitive**

- for predictions and expectations.
*Hopefully, we'**ll meet** again soon.*
*I'm sure you'**ll enjoy** the course you've chosen.*
- for future facts and theoretical certainties.
*On his next birthday Stan **will be** seven.*
*The sun **will rise** at 6.43 in the morning.*
- for promises, offers and refusals.
*I'**ll close** all the windows if you like.*
*I'**ll never do** that again, I promise.*
*It doesn't matter what I say, he **won't go** to sleep.*
- for sudden responses or instant decisions.
***Jo:** Oh no! We've run out of coffee.*
***Sam**: Don't panic. **I'll go** and get some.*

going to + infinitive

We use ***going to* + the infinitive**

- for intentions, plans or resolutions.
*Dave **is going to work** really hard for next month's exams.* (He's determined.)
*Eva's **going to stop** playing computer games before she goes to bed.* (It's a bad habit.)
- for making predictions when there is evidence.
*Hold my coffee. **I'm going to** sneeze.* (Evidence: a tickly nose)
*It's **going to snow** tonight.* (Evidence: dark clouds in the sky and it's very cold)

be about to + infinitive

We use this structure to refer actions that we expect to happen very soon. It is often used with *just* to emphasise how imminent the action is.

*Can we talk later? I'**m (just) about to leave** for work.*
*It looks like it'**s about to** rain.*

It can also be used in the past.

*That's a coincidence. I **was (just) about to phone** you.*

Future continuous: *will be* + *-ing*

We use the future continuous to predict an activity in progress in the future.

*This time next year, I'**ll be studying** drama in London.*
*In the future, more people **will be working** from home.*

We can also use this form to refer to future events that we expect to happen. This use does not refer to an activity in progress.

*I'**ll be seeing** my grandparents at the weekend.*

Future perfect: *will have* + past participle / *will have been* + *ing*

We use the future perfect, simple and continuous forms, to predict an action that will already be completed.

*By this time next year, I hope I'**ll have found** somewhere to live.* (future perfect simple)
*On March 10th, we'**ll have been living** here for three years.* (future perfect continuous)

was/were going to + infinitive; *would* + infinitive

We use these forms to talk about predictions made in the past.

*Sarah was sure she **was going to pass** all her exams.* (the past form of *going to*)
*I didn't know that I'**d spend** six years in Berlin.* (the past form of *will* – *would*)

We can also use ***was/were going to*** + infinitive for plans in the past which didn't happen.

*They **were going to have** a picnic but the weather was awful.*

Practice

1 Complete the predictions with *will* or *going to*.

1 I feel dizzy. I think *I'll faint / I'm going to faint.*
2 You can use Omar's desk. I'm sure he *won't mind / isn't going to mind.*

3 We can't wait for Mike. I expect *he'll be / he's going to be* late again.
4 Watch out! *We'll crash / We're going to crash.*
5 If all goes well, *we'll get / we're going to get* there with time to spare.

2 Complete the sentences with the correct form of the verb in brackets.

1 I ______ (leave) for the airport in a minute. I ______ (fly) to Moscow this afternoon. My plane ______ (leave) at 2.15. Let's meet up when I ______ (get) back. ______ (you do) anything on Saturday evening?
2 My family ______ (take) me out this evening to celebrate my passing my exams. After my gap year I ______ (apply) to study medicine at university. When I ______ (graduate), I ______ (be) a doctor. I ______ (probably work) in a hospital.
3 Tomorrow, I ______ (watch) a basketball match with my friend, Jason. Our team ______ (play) for a place in the final. The match ______ (start) at 4 o'clock.

3 Complete the sentences with the verbs in the box. Use the future continuous or future perfect only.

bring	clear	eat	finish	forget	make
sunbathe	work	write			

1 I hope I ______ my assignment by the deadline tomorrow. It looks like I ______ on it all night!
2 Just think. This time tomorrow, I ______ on a beautiful beach and you ______ emails and ______ phone calls.
3 I'm sure Jack (not) ______ it's your birthday today. I expect he ______ your present round later.
4 Don't come before 7 o'clock. We (still) ______ . Come any time after 8.00. We ______ everything away by then.

UNIT 6 GERUNDS AND INFINITIVES

Gerunds (*-ing* forms) and infinitives are used in a number of ways.

After verbs

- Verbs which are always followed by ***to* + infinitive**
  afford, agree, arrange, appear, attempt, choose, claim, decide, expect, happen, help, hope, intend, learn, manage, offer, pretend, promise, refuse, seem, want
  We can't ***afford to go*** *on holiday this year.*
  I'm ***learning to play*** *the saxophone.*
- Verbs which are always followed by **the gerund** (*-ing* form)
  admit, avoid, carry on, consider, delay, deny, dislike, enjoy, feel like, finish, can't help, imagine, keep, look forward to, miss, practise, put off, risk, can't stand, recommend, suggest
  I don't ***feel like going*** *swimming today.*
  Don't you ***miss spending*** *time with your friends?*
- Verbs which can be followed by ***to* + infinitive or the gerund** (*-ing* form)
  – with no difference in meaning:
  begin, can't bear, continue, intend, start
  Things will ***continue to improve / continue improving.***
  – with a change of meaning:
  forget, go on, mean, remember, stop, try
  I ***forgot to phone.*** (I did not do this.)
  I'll ***never forget arriving*** *home.* (I remember this clearly.)
  John went to Oxford University and then ***went on to study*** *at Yale.* (Studying at Yale was the next thing he did.)
  They ***went on playing*** *even after the referee had blown the whistle.* (They, didn't stop playing.)
  I ***meant to phone*** *you earlier, but I was very busy.* (I intended to …)
  Cancelling our flight now will ***mean losing*** *our deposit.* (This will involve losing …)
  I ***remember buying*** *the tickets.* (remember = recall)
  I ***remembered to buy*** *the tickets.* (remember = did not forget)
  I've ***stopped drinking*** *coffee.* (stop = do it no longer)
  We ***stopped to ask*** *the way.* (stop = interrupt one action to do another)
  I ***tried to phone*** *you all week.* (try = make an effort to do something but not succeed)
  Have you ***tried taking*** *those tablets for your headache?* (try = experiment)

After adjectives

- Adjectives which are followed by ***to* + infinitive**
  afraid, anxious, certain, difficult, happy, impossible, pleased, ready, right, shocked, stupid, surprised, welcome
  Everyone was really ***surprised to see*** *me at the party.*
  I'm ***pleased to tell*** *you that you've passed your driving test.*
- Adjectives which are followed by a **preposition + gerund** (*-ing* form)
  accustomed to, afraid of, ashamed of, bored of, capable of, different from, enthusiastic about, excited about, famous for, fond of, good at, interested in, keen on, proud of, responsible for, tired of, worried about
  Are you ***interested in joining*** *our squash club?*
  I'm quite ***capable of finding*** *my own way home.*

After all prepositions

- Gerunds are used after all prepositions.
  after, before, by, instead of, on, while, without, etc.
  Instead of catching *the bus, I walked home.*
  We found our way there ***without looking*** *at a map.*

As nouns

- Gerunds can also be used like nouns, as the subject of a sentence or as the complement of the verb *be*.
  Flying *is much less expensive than it used to be.*
  My favourite method of relaxation is ***reading*** *a good novel.*

Practice

1 Choose the correct form of the verb – infinitive or gerund.

I'd always refused [1]*to buy / buying* lottery tickets because I thought they were a waste of money. But last week, for the first time in my life, I decided [2]*to get / getting* just one. It was just a bit of fun and I didn't really expect [3]*to win / winning*, but despite this I couldn't help [4]*to think / thinking* about how I'd spend the money if I actually won. My brother had won £1000 the year before, and I had really enjoyed [5]*to see / seeing* the expression on his face when he realised. All week I looked forward to [6]*watch / watching* the TV programme when the winning numbers were announced, but that evening I was so busy that I forgot [7]*to put / putting* the TV on. I checked my numbers on the website the next day – and of course I hadn't won. At that moment I promised myself never [8]*to buy / buying* another lottery ticket. I couldn't risk [9]*to be / being* so disappointed again.

2 Complete the sentences with the correct preposition.

1 You shouldn't be afraid ______ saying what you think.
2 I must admit I'm not very good ______ remembering people's names.
3 I'm really keen ______ getting into the school football team.
4 I'm ashamed ______ making such a basic mistake.
5 Working from home is very different ______ working in a large office.

3 Correct any mistakes in the sentences. Two are correct.

1 I suggest to take the overnight train to Vienna.
2 Part of my job is helping maintaining the machinery in good working order.
3 I would strongly recommend going by plane.
4 If I were you, I'd consider to spend less time at work.
5 I found it impossible sleeping because of the noise.
6 I nodded and smiled and pretended understanding what she was saying.
7 I remember to see that show in New York. It was incredible.
8 I didn't mean to break the TV. It was an accident.

UNIT 7 CONDITIONALS

Conditional sentences consist of a subordinate clause beginning with *if* and a main clause. The *if* clause can come before or after the main clause. When the *if* clause comes first, it is separated from the main clause by a comma.

Zero conditional

- ***If*** + **present simple** (comma) … **present simple**
  This form is used when the result always occurs. In these sentences, ***if*** means the same as *when* or *whenever*.
  If I'm *thirsty,* ***I drink*** *water.*
  I get up *later than usual* ***if I have*** *a day off.*

First conditional

- ***If*** + **present simple** (comma) … ***will / may / might*** + **infinitive**
  This form is used when the result is quite likely to happen in the future.
  If I get *money for my birthday,* ***I'll put*** *it straight into the bank.*
  I might go out *on my bike* ***if it's*** *sunny tomorrow.*
- ***Unless*** + present simple affirmative verb can often replace ***if*** + negative verb. Sentences like these refer to the future.
  Wild animals ***won't attack*** *people* ***unless they feel threatened.***
  (= *Wild animals* ***won't attack*** *people* ***if they do not feel threatened.***)
  Unless you have *a valid passport,* ***they will stop*** *you entering the country.*
  (= *If you do not have a valid passport,* ***they will stop*** *you entering the country.*)

Second conditional

- ***If*** + **past simple** (comma) … ***would / could*** + **infinitive**
  This form is used to describe possible but unlikely future events.
  If I won *the lottery,* ***I could buy*** *my friends and family new cars.*
  I would contact *the police* ***if someone stole*** *my phone.*
  This form is also used to describe impossible or hypothetical conditions.
  If I were *ten years younger,* ***I'd sail*** *round the world.*
  I could join *the basketball team* ***if I were*** *half a metre taller.*

Third conditional

- ***If*** + **past perfect simple/continuous** (comma) … ***would / might / may / could*** + ***have*** + **past participle**
  This form is used to describe hypothetical past actions.
  If I had known *your address,* ***I would have emailed*** *you.*
  You might not have had *the accident* ***if you had been driving*** *more carefully.*

Mixed conditionals

- Present affected by past
  If + **past perfect** (comma) … ***would / might / could*** + **verb**
  This form is used to describe an imaginary present or future action which is impossible because of a past action or event.
  If I hadn't broken *my arm,* ***I'd be playing*** *in the tennis finals tomorrow.*
  (I broke my arm, so I can't play in the tennis finals tomorrow.)
  Ella ***would/could/might be*** *a doctor now if she* ***hadn't failed*** *medical school.*
  (Ella failed medical school, so she can't be a doctor now.)
- Past affected by present
  If + **past simple** (comma) … ***would / might / could*** + ***have*** + **past participle**
  If I wasn't *so busy,* ***I might have*** *come camping with you.*

Practice

1 Match the sentence halves.

1. Unless you turn the music down,
2. If he wasn't afraid of water,
3. If I had told you the story,
4. If I'd known you didn't like Max,
5. If we had left earlier,
6. If you stay outside for too long,
7. If you look at the sun,
8. If she practised more often,

a. I wouldn't have invited him to my party.
b. you may damage your eyes.
c. the neighbours will complain.
d. you wouldn't have believed it.
e. we wouldn't have missed our train.
f. he'd learn to swim.
g. she'd be a better tennis player.
h. you'll get sunburnt.

2 Complete the sentences with the correct form of the verb in brackets.

1. Unless you ________ (train) harder, you'll never get a place in the team.
2. If I ________ (have) a better voice, I'd be in the school choir.
3. If I ________ (think) an email might contain a virus, I don't open it.
4. I would still be lying in bed if you ________ (not phone).
5. If she'd had her phone with her when her car broke down, she ________ (be able) to phone the breakdown services.
6. She won't understand what you're saying unless you ________ (speak) more clearly.
7. If he ________ (not work) so hard, he wouldn't always be exhausted.
8. If he didn't like animals, he ________ (not choose) to be a vet.

3 Correct the mistakes in these sentences.

1. If you haven't taken these photographs, I wouldn't have remembered our holiday.
2. I'd tell you if I see anything unusual.
3. If I felt tired, I usually go to bed early.
4. If we don't reduce our dependence on fossil fuels in the near future, global warming would have become a more serious problem.
5. If the petrol engine hadn't been invented, there will still be plenty of oil left.

UNIT 8 *WISH* AND *IF ONLY*

Wish

We use *wish* with various verb forms to express the following ideas.

- We use *wish* + **past simple** or **past continous** to express unhappiness about a situation which is impossible to change.
  I was so carefree when I was younger. ***I wish I were/was*** *a teenager again.*
  I wish I wasn't *an only child. I'd love to have a brother or sister.*
  I wish I didn't have to *go to school today.*
  Jan wishes the wedding ***was taking place*** *in the spring.*
- We use *wish* + **past perfect** to express regret for something in the past which is impossible to change.
  She wishes *her brother* ***had told*** *the truth.*
  We wished we hadn't spent *so much money on that holiday.*
  Don't you wish we hadn't arranged *to go away at the weekend?*
  Peter ***wished he hadn't arranged*** *to go out that evening.*
- We use *wish* + *could* + **infinitive** to express frustration about a situation which is possible, but difficult, to change.
  I wish I could speak *English more fluently.*
  My friend wishes he could get *a job in the film industry, but it's very hard to get in to.*
- We use *wish* + *would/wouldn't* + **infinitive** to express irritation at another person's behaviour or at an or annoying situation. We use it in the hope that the person or the situation will change.
  I wish you'd listen *to what I'm saying for once.*
  I wish my parents wouldn't treat *me like a child.*
  We all wish the weather would improve.

Note We cannot say ***I wish I would*** *do something.*

If only

We use *if only* to express strong wishes or regrets. It can be used instead of ***I wish*** to add strength to the wish or regret.

- *If only* + **past simple** expresses unhappiness about a situation which it is impossible to change.
  If only I were/was *a teenager again.*
- *If only* + **past perfect** expresses regret for something in the past which is impossible to change.
  If only I hadn't spent *all my savings on that car.*
- *If only* + *could* + **infinitive** expresses frustration about a situation which is possible, but difficult, to change.
  If only I could speak *English more fluently.*
- *If only* + *would/wouldn't* + **infinitive** expresses irritation at another person's behaviour or at an annoying situation. We use it in the hope that the person or the situation will change.
  If only you'd listen *to what I'm saying for once.*
  If only it would stop *raining.*

Practice

1 Choose the correct verb.

1. I really wish everyone in the world *speaks / spoke* the same language.
2. Don't you wish English *didn't / wouldn't* have so many irregular verbs?
3. I wish I *didn't / hadn't* stayed up so late last night.
4. If only they *can / could* forecast the weather more accurately.
5. I wish you *would / could* say what you mean.
6. If only I *don't / didn't* have to go to the dentist today.

2 Complete the sentences with the correct form of the verb in brackets. You may need to add an auxiliary verb.

1 Katie wishes she .... (work) harder when she was at school.
2 I wish I .... (find) the present I bought for my mum's birthday. It must be here somewhere.
3 I wish my sister .... (be) so untidy. Her bedroom is always a mess.
4 If only you .... (tell) me when you were going to arrive. I'd have come to meet you.
5 I wish I .... (not eat) so much chocolate. I'm starting to feel sick.
6 I wish you .... (not keep) interrupting me.
7 I wish people .... (stop) criticising our football team.
8 If only I .... (not turn down) that job offer. I'd be working in Milan now.

3 Complete the email with the correct form of the verb in brackets. There may be more than one correct answer.

Dear Grandad,

Just a quick message to apologise for being so rude at the weekend. I really wish I [1] .... (make up) for some of the things I said. If only I [2] .... (think) about how my words would affect you. To be honest, I wish I [3] .... (be) more patient and considerate like you.

My only excuse is that I'm really not happy at work and realise I've made a mistake. I just wish I [4] .... (listen) to your advice and [5] .... (not apply) for the job in the first place. Anyway, I've now handed in my notice and am looking for a new job.

I'd really appreciate another chat with you. I know you said you wouldn't give me any more advice, but I wish you [6] .... (reconsider) your decision. I promise I'll listen to you this time.

Love,

Mark

UNIT 9 CLEFT SENTENCES

'Cleft sentence' is the name given to sentence structures which are used to emphasise certain information. These two examples compare the structure of normal sentences with cleft sentences. The emphasised information is in bold type.

Normal sentence	Cleft sentence
They bought things online.	*What they did was* ***buy things online.***
Pete paid for our flights.	***It was Pete*** *who paid for our flights.*

Common cleft sentence structures start with ***What, Why, All*** and ***It***.

What, Why

- ***What*** **clause + verb +** ***is/was*** **+ noun phrase**
  What I'd really like is a long cool drink.
  What my brother wanted for his birthday was a new car.
- ***What*** **clause + verb +** ***is/was*** **+ infinitive without** ***to***
  What you should do if you have toothache is arrange a dental appointment.
  What I intended to do was to quit my job at the end of the year.*
  What I really wanted was to sleep.*
  *We use ***to*** **+ infinitive** if the verb in the first part of the sentence is followed by ***to*** **+ infinitive** (e.g. *intend, want, decide*).
  We use the bare infinitive (i.e. without *to*) if the verb in the first part of the sentence is followed by the infinitive without *to* (e.g. *should*).

It

- ***It*** **+** ***is/was*** **+ noun phrase + relative clause**
  It's her sense of humour that I really enjoy.
  It was my sister who made all the decorations for the party.
- ***It*** **+** ***is/was*** **+ adverbial phrase + relative clause**
  It's in this office that we're having our meeting next week.
  It was in 2010 that we first met.
- In ***It*** cleft sentences we can choose which information to emphasise. For example, from the sentence below we can make three cleft sentences.
  Pete had his bike repaired last weekend.
  It was Pete *who had his bike repaired last weekend.* (It was Pete, not Ben.)
  It was last weekend *that Pete had his bike repaired.* (It was last weekend, not yesterday.)
  It was his bike *that Pete had repaired last weekend.* (It was his bike, not his car.)

Practice

1 Rewrite these sentences as cleft sentences starting with the word given. There is sometimes more than one correct answer.

1 I really need a new computer. (*What*)
2 He bought his computer online, not his printer. (*It*)
3 Tim goes to the gym every day to keep fit. (*What*)
4 We're all worried about global warming and climate change. (*What*)
5 I don't want to end up with nowhere to live. (*What*)
6 I particularly enjoyed the music in *La La Land*. (*It*)
7 20th century classical music interests me most. (*What*)
8 I've never understood why some people need hardly any sleep. (*What*)

2 Rewrite these sentences as cleft sentences starting with *It*. Emphasise the information in bold type.

1 The sculptor Anthony Gormley was born **in 1950**.
2 Gormley's most famous work *The Angel of the North* is situated **in Gateshead**.
3 Gormley uses **his own body** as the model for many of his sculptures.
4 Gormley's favourite medium to work in is **cast iron**.
5 Gormley met his wife, Vicken Parsons at **the Slade School of Fine Art**.

3 **Rewrite each sentence three times, emphasising different information each time.**

1 I met Carla in Florence in 2012.
2 I first saw *Les Misérables* in London was I ten years old.

4 **Answer the questions with *No* followed by *What … did/ said was*.**

1 Did he say he was busy? (tired)
2 Did you put that money you earned into your bank? (spend it all)
3 Did your friends say they'd arrive this morning? (tomorrow)
4 Did you borrow that money from your parents? (take out a loan)

UNIT 10 INVERSION

Inversion for emphasis

Inversion refers to a sentence structure in which the normal word order of subject and verb is reversed. The purpose of using this sentence structure is to emphasise a point by making it sound more important or dramatic. It is associated with more formal speaking or writing.

- Here are two examples of inverted word order, followed by the same idea in a sentence with normal word order.

  Not once *during the interview* ***did I feel*** *nervous.*
  – I didn't feel nervous once during the interview.
  Only when *the staff receive better pay* ***will*** *their performance* ***improve****.*
  – The staff's performance will only improve when they receive better pay.

Inversion after words or phrases with a negative meaning

- The negative words or phrases in the examples below are underlined and the inverted subject and verb are in bold.

  Never ***have I been*** *so bored by new a James Bond film.*
  No way ***am I going*** *to say I'm sorry.*
  Under no circumstances ***should you open*** *that email.*
  Not for one moment ***did I dream*** *we'd ever meet again.*
  Not once ***did she call*** *me during her holiday.*
  Not only ***has James lost*** *his job, but he also has to find somewhere new to live.*
  Not since last summer ***have I been swimming*** *in the sea.*

Inversion after words or phrases with a limiting meaning

Little ***did I know*** *what they were plotting, so the party came as a complete surprise!*
Rarely ***have I been*** *so disappointed by a film.*
Not until I checked my diary, ***did I remember*** *we had a meeting this afternoon.*
Only when we arrived and there was nobody there to meet us ***did we realise*** *we were a day early.*

Practice

1 **Rewrite the sentences in inverted form starting with the word or phrase in brackets.**

1 You shouldn't under any circumstances give your personal details to a stranger on the phone. (Under no circumstances)
2 Kate had never felt so excited in her life. (Never)
3 We don't realise how dependent we have become on computers until they let us down. (Not until)
4 There's no way we are going to agree to those conditions – they are completely unfair. (No way)
5 I've rarely witnessed such a moving ceremony. (Rarely)
6 We only noticed the hole in the roof when it rained heavily. (Only)

2 **Correct any mistakes in these sentences. Two sentences are correct.**

1 It's been such a busy day that not until I got home I realised I'd left my phone at college.
2 Not once we didn't have pizza while we were in Italy.
3 Never have they forgotten my birthday.
4 Not only I have to work from Monday to Friday, but I also have to go in on alternate weekends.
5 Not since she left school Laura had so many good friends.
6 Rarely will you taste such wonderful food.

3 **Complete this email with words and phrases from the box.**

little	never	no way	not only	not since	only when

Last weekend, I decided to visit my aunt and uncle who live in an old cottage in a very rural area. [1] .... is their house in the middle of nowhere, but it also has no running water or electricity. [2] .... did I realise they lived in such primitive conditions. My relatives were very welcoming but as soon as I arrived they announced it was time for bed. I couldn't believe it. [3] .... I was a child had I gone to bed as early as 7 o'clock. I didn't object but I said to myself [4] '............ am I going to go to sleep straightaway. I'll read my book until I'm tired.' We said goodnight and I went to my bedroom. [5] .... had I seen such a dark room! I opened my book, but [6] .... I moved nearer to the window could I make out the words on the page.

GRAMMAR REFERENCE AND PRACTICE

UNIT 11 THE PASSIVE

The passive has the same range of forms as the active, but only transitive verbs have passive forms. (A transitive verb is one that can have a direct object.)

We use the passive form when we want to focus attention on **the person or thing affected by** an action rather than **the doer of** the action.

Forming the passive

- The passive is formed with the verb ***be*** + the past participle of the main verb.

Verb form	Passive	Active
present simple	*Cotton **is grown** in Egypt.*	*They grow cotton in Egypt.*
present continuous	*Traffic **is being diverted** because of an accident.*	*They are diverting traffic because of an accident.*
past simple	*The match **was cancelled**.*	*They cancelled the match.*
past continuous	*I **was being followed** by a stranger.*	*A stranger was following me.*
present perfect simple	*Our house **has been damaged** by the high winds.*	*The high winds have damaged our house.*
past perfect simple	*The painting **had** already **been bought**.*	*Someone had already bought the painting.*
will future simple	*My phone **will be activated** tomorrow.*	*They'll activate my phone tomorrow.*
modal verbs	*Everyone **must be informed**.* *We **could be fined**.*	*They must inform everyone.* *They could fine us.*

Note The following continuous passive forms are possible, but sound awkward and so are rarely used: present perfect continuous, past perfect continuous and future continuous e.g. *Candidates **will be being interviewed** all next week.*

- ***get*** + the past participle of the main verb can be used as an informal alternative.
  *My computer **got stolen** from my bag on the bus.*
  *Too much of the food people buy **gets wasted**.*

Passive sentence structure

- The **object** of this active sentence (*newspapers*) is the **subject** of the equivalent passive sentence.
  *Ben was delivering **newspapers**.*
  ***Newspapers** were being delivered by Ben.*
  The **subject** of the active sentence (*Ben*) becomes the **agent** of the passive sentence.

Including the agent or not?

Passive sentences may not include an agent for these reasons.

- The agent is understood or obvious.
  Cotton is grown in Egypt.
  (We could add *by farmers* but this is understood.)
  The burglar was arrested as he left the house.
  (We could add *by the police* but this is obvious.)
- The agent is unknown.
  My house has been broken into.
  (We could add *by someone* or *by an unknown person*, but this would add little to the sentence.)
- The agent is a secret for some reason.
  The President has been accused of lying.
  (The speaker doesn't want to mention the accuser's name.)

Practice

1 Rewrite these sentences using appropriate passive verbs. Only one passive sentence needs to include the agent.

1 They'll hold interviews for the other top jobs next week.
2 You have to see this form to believe it. The applicant has written it in pencil.
3 They have appointed no one to replace Ms Kirkby since they promoted her last year.
4 They asked applicants to send in hand-written letters to accompany their CVs.
5 You must send your application as a PDF.
6 The company will require successful applicants to start work on Monday.
7 Jeffrey Bowman will announce the name of the new CEO at the next board meeting.
8 You couldn't expect someone with experience to work for that salary.

2 Read this newspaper story about a damaged building, making the active verbs passive.

Illegal squatters have finally abandoned a city centre mansion worth £5 million after a week of destruction. They had covered three of the bedroom walls with graffiti and had ripped cupboards apart. They had chopped up most of the furniture and used it as firewood. They had torn up the carpets and smashed the mirrors and windows. Builders have estimated the damage at more than £1 million.

3 **Rewrite these short texts about 'memory', replacing the underlined active verbs with passive verbs. You do not always need to include the agent in your answer.**

1 We use the term 'amnesia' to refer to a partial or complete loss of memory. It is usually a temporary condition which only affects a certain part of a person's experience. Specific medical conditions can cause amnesia.

2 We all know that our real experiences form our memory. But could someone put a false memory into our heads? Could they persuade us that we had experienced something that never actually took place?

3 We use our semantic memory to store our knowledge of the world. Everyone has this knowledge base, and normally we can access it quickly and easily.

4 We can think of our working memory as the ability to remember and use a limited amount of information. However, this information is erratic. If someone distracts you, you can lose the information and you have to start the task again.

UNIT 12 PASSIVE GERUND & INFINITIVE

to infinitive passive and gerund (*-ing* form) passive

- In Unit 6 you learned that certain verbs are followed by *to* + the infinitive and others by the gerund (*-ing* form). For example:

  want *+ to infinitive* — *Paul* ***wants to learn*** *Spanish.*
  risk *+ gerund* — *I can't* ***risk meeting*** *Margot.*

  The same pattern applies in the passive sentences.

  want *+ to infinitive* — *Paul* ***wants to be taught*** *Spanish.*
  risk *+ gerund* — *I can't* ***risk being seen*** *by Margot.*

  Here are some more examples of these patterns in the passive.

- with *to* infinitive

  hope — *He* ***hoped to be awarded*** *first prize for his invention.*
  expect — *Sue wasn't* ***expecting to be promoted*** *this year.*

- with the gerund

  imagine — *Just* ***imagine being attacked*** *by a bear!*
  avoid — *Many celebrities* ***avoid being seen*** *in public.*

to be + past participle

- We can use ***to*** *be* + ***past participle*** after adjectives.

  I'm happy ***to be corrected*** *if I'm wrong.*
  Is it ***possible to be invited*** *to the ceremony?*

be + past participle

- We can use ***be*** + **past participle** after modal verbs.

  Our flight ***might be delayed.***
  What everyone says at the meeting ***must be recorded*** *accurately.*

being + past participle

- We can use ***being*** + **past participle** after verbs or adjectives + prepositions.

  I ***insist on being told*** *the moment they arrive.*
  I was angry ***about being given*** *the sack by my boss.*

- We can use ***being*** + **past participle** as a noun phrase.

  Being admitted *to hospital can be a scary experience.*
  My earliest memory is ***being taken*** *to the zoo by my parents.*

Verbs with two objects

- Some verbs can be followed by two objects: a direct and an indirect object. Examples:

  give, send, pay, write, offer, show, teach, lend, tell

  In the sentence: *Cassius gave Rufus a book, book* is the direct object and *Rufus* is the indirect object.

  Active sentences with two objects can be made passive in two different ways.

Active sentence	Passive sentence 1	Passive sentence 2
Cassius gave Rufus a book.	*Rufus* ***was given*** *a book by Cassius.*	*A book* ***was given to*** *Rufus by Cassius.*
Our manager sent us all the same email.	*We* ***were all sent*** *the same email by our manager.*	*The same email* ***was sent to*** *us all by our manager.*

Notes

- It often sounds more natural to make the indirect object the subject of the passive sentence. (Passive sentence 1)
- If the direct object is made the subject of the passive sentence the word *to* is often put before the indirect object. (Passive sentence 2)
- When deciding the order of objects, it is more common to put the known information as the subject of the sentence and new information as the object.

Practice

1 **Complete these sentences with the passive form of the verb in brackets. One sentence has two possible answers.**

1 I sometimes miss ______ on holiday by my parents. (take)
2 Zoe hopes ______ as a student at Cambridge University next year. (accept)
3 Our flight today is likely ______ because of fog. (cancel)
4 I can't stand ______ waiting. (keep)
5 Children shouldn't ______ by their parents. (tease)
6 Julian would really like ______ how to sing properly. (teach)
7 You can't insist on ______ if you volunteered for the job. (pay)
8 Nobody likes ______ what to do. (tell)

GRAMMAR REFERENCE AND PRACTICE

2 **Rewrite the sentences using passive verbs in two different ways.**

1. My bank sent me a letter pointing out that my account was overdrawn.
2. The police showed the witness photos of six possible suspects.
3. The headteacher told the students their exam results.
4. Our department has sent emails to hundreds of customers during the last week.
5. They awarded Julius a prize for a story he had written.
6. The company paid a bonus to all employees in the busy summer period.
7. My parents gave me the money to buy a new phone.

3 **Correct any mistakes in these sentences. Two are correct.**

1. Jacob insisted on being given the biggest bedroom in the house.
2. To be shown how to restore photos was fascinating.
3. Don't expect being thanked every time you do something for someone else.
4. She was thrilled to be told that she had passed all her exams.
5. When he retired, the doctor was given his colleagues a wonderful present.
6. Nurses and doctors should be give a pay rise next year.
7. The children hated be told old stories by their father.
8. Jane was excited about be asked to take part in the show.

UNIT 13 CAUSATIVES

In causative sentences, the subject of the verb is the person who arranges the action to be done or the person who is affected by the action.

have + object + past participle

- The subject of this structure is not the doer of an action but the person who intentionally causes or arranges the action.

  *I'm **having** my hair **cut** tomorrow.*
  *He **had** his car **repaired** last week.*
  *You should **have** your windows **cleaned**.*
- The same structure also has a non-causative meaning when it is used to refer to actions which are done to someone with a bad result.

  *Simon **had** his wallet **stolen** on the New York Metro.*
  *We **had** our credit card **declined** because we had gone over our limit.*

get + object + past participle

- When this refers to the intentional causing of an action, it is more informal than *have something done*.

  *I must **get** my coat **cleaned**. It's filthy.*
  *She's going to **get** her hair **dyed**.*
  *You really must **get** your eyes **tested**.*

get + *someone* + *to* infinitive

- In this structure *get* is similar in meaning to *ask* or *persuade*. The emphasis here is on the person who does the action that the subject of the sentence arranged.

  *We're **getting** a friend **to do** our shopping for us this week.*
  *I wish I could **get** my brother **to keep** his room tidy.*

have + *someone* + infinitive without *to*

- This has the same meaning as *get someone to do something* but is more formal.

  *I'll **have** my secretary **send** you an application form.*
  *Can you **have** your driver **bring** the car round to the front door, please?*

make + *someone* + infinitive without *to*

- This has the same meaning as *to force* or *require* someone to do something.

  *He **made** his daughter **finish** all her homework before going out to meet her friends.*

let + *someone* + infinitive without *to*

- This has the same meaning as *allow* or *permit* someone to do something but is less formal.

  *The manager **lets** employees **wear** casual clothes on a Friday.*

Practice

1 **Put the words in the correct order to make sentences.**

1. next / alarm / getting / a / we / fitted / are / week / burglar

   ……………………………………………
2. bedroom / have / painted / we / blue / might / our

   ……………………………………………
3. fixed / had / Michael / yet / car / his / has ?

   ……………………………………………
4. phones / let / their / school / classroom / doesn't / students / bring / the / into / the

   ……………………………………………
5. mend / tablet / someone / I'm / on / getting / my / screen / to / the

   ……………………………………………
6. pay / teenager / the / was / window / to / for / broken / the / made

   ……………………………………………

2 **Rewrite these sentence in two ways using *have* and *get*.**

- *have* something done
- *get* someone to do something

1. You'd better go to the optician's. Your eyes need testing.

   ……………………………………………
2. You should call a builder. Your roof needs repairing.

   ……………………………………………
3. Why don't you arrange for the dentist to check your teeth?

   ……………………………………………
4. It's about time I went to see my hairdresser. My hair needs trimming.

   ……………………………………………
5. You'd better ask the supermarket to deliver your shopping.

   ……………………………………………

3 **Give two negative answers to these questions using the words in brackets**

1. Do you cut your own hair? (hairdresser)

   ……………………………………………
2. Did you clean the car yourself? (my son)

   ……………………………………………

3 Did you repair your computer? (a technician)

4 Will you cut down those trees yourself? (a professional tree surgeon)

5 Did you clean that jacket yourself? (a local dry cleaning firm)

UNIT 14 REPORTED SPEECH

Changes to verb tenses

- The tense of the verb in reported speech is usually further in the past than in the actual words which were spoken. Compare these examples of direct speech and reported speech. After the verb *said* we can, but we don't have to, include the word *that*, as in the first example.

Direct speech	Reported speech
*'I'm **feeling** tired.' (Angie)*	*Angie said (that) **she was feeling** tired.*
*'The rain **has stopped**.' (Omar)*	*Omar said the rain **had stopped**.*
*'I **walked** all the way.' (Sarah)*	*Sarah said she **had walked** all the way.*
*'We **will help** if we **can**.' (They)*	*They said they **would help** if **they could**.*

- Past perfect tenses and *would, could* and *should* cannot move further into the past so they do not change.

*'I **hadn't eaten** falafel before.' (Sue)*
*Sue said she **hadn't eaten** falafel before.*
*'I **wouldn't** go sailing again.' (Jeff)*
*Jeff said he **wouldn't** go sailing again.*

Without tense changes

- The tense of the verb in reported speech does not always change, for example if we want to show that what the speaker said is still true now or if the reporting verb is in the present.

*'I **love** strong coffee.' (Jan)*
*Jan said she **loves** strong coffee.*
*'I'm **expecting** a delivery.' (Ed)*
*Ed says he's **expecting** a delivery.*

Pronoun and possessive adjective changes

- We often have to change pronouns and possessive adjectives, especially when the reporter is not the original speaker.

*'I'll email **you**.' (Dan)*
*Dan said **he'd** email **me**.*
*'The book is not **yours**, it's **mine**.' (Ed)*
*Ed said the book was not **mine**, it was **his**.*

Time and place adverbs

- These words change if the time or place is no longer the same.

*'I'll see you **tomorrow**.' (Mia)*
*Mia said she'd see me **the following / next day**.*
*'I've worked **here** for two years.' (Max)*
*Max said he'd worked **there** for two years.*

More time reference changes

(ten minutes) ago	*(ten minutes) before/earlier*
last week/year	*the previous week/year, the week/ year before*
now	*at that time, immediately, then*
this week	*last/that week*
today	*that day, yesterday, on Monday, etc.*
tomorrow	*the next/following day, the day after*
yesterday	*the previous day, the day before*

Reporting verbs

- If we are reporting advice, a suggestion, an apology, etc. we can use different structures.

verb + *to* infinitive: *agree, offer, promise*
'I'll take you to airport.' (Sue)
*Sue **offered to take** me to the airport.*

verb + object + *to* infinitive: *advise, invite, tell, persuade, remind, warn*
'If I were you, I'd drive there.' (Mo)
*Mo **advised me to drive** there.*

verb + *-ing*: *recommend, suggest, deny, admit*
'Let's watch a movie.' (Tom)
*Tom **suggested watching** a movie.*

verb + preposition + noun OR **verb + *-ing***: *apologise for, complain about, insist on*
*'I'm sorry that I **didn't arrive** on time.' (Jack)*
*Jack **apologised for not arriving** on time. / for his late **arrival**.*

Impersonal reporting structures: *It* + passive

- To report speech without saying who the reporter is, we can start sentences with *It* + a passive verb.

***It is said that** the price of petrol will rise sharply this year.*
***It has been reported that** the suspect is in hiding.*

Practice

1 Change the direct speech to reported speech. Use *say* and change all time and place references.

1 'I'll see you tomorrow morning.' (Rob)
2 'I didn't do anything wrong.' (Irina)
3 'We can meet at my office.' (Steve)
4 'I'd never expected to be here today.' (Ahmet)
5 'Megan and I were here yesterday. We waited for you until 7 o'clock.' (Polly)
6 'Pedro's looking forward to starting his new job next week.' (Sacha)
7 'You can come on holiday with us.' (Zoë)
8 'It's been raining here all night.' (Luisa)

2 Rewrite the reported speech in direct speech.

1 They said they were looking for someone with my qualifications.
2 The manager said I had the right experience for the job.
3 He said I wouldn't have to work at weekends.
4 He said they'd provide me with a company car.
5 They said employees were allowed to work from home occasionally.
6 He said I could start the following Monday.

3 Choose the correct option.

1 James denied *to steal / stealing* the money.
2 Mandy insisted *to come / on coming* to every meeting.
3 Pierre's father agreed *to help / on helping* him with his assignment.
4 The doctor warned Alex *not to take / not taking* the pills without water.
5 Eva suggested *to have / having* the party at her place.
6 Can I persuade you *to give / on giving* me a hand?

UNIT 15 RELATIVE CLAUSES

Relative clauses provide extra information about people, things, places and possessions. They are usually linked to the rest of the sentence they are in by relative pronouns.

Relative pronouns

- ***who, whose,*** and ***that*** refer to people.
  *My son, **who** composes big band jazz music, lives in Birmingham.*
  *That's the couple **whose** house we bought.*
  *Are you the person **that** offered to give me a lift?*
- ***whom*** refers to people and is usually used with a preposition.
  *The person **to whom** this letter is addressed no longer lives here.*
- ***which***, ***that*** and ***whose*** can refer to things or ideas.
  *They've got a car **that/which** runs on electricity.*
  *They live in a very old house **whose** roof recently collapsed.*
- ***where*** and ***when*** refer to places and times.
  *The village **where** they live is in the middle of nowhere.*
  *I can't remember the year **when** we moved here.*
- ***why*** refers to reasons.
  *The reason **why** I'm so late is that my flight was cancelled.*

Defining relative clauses

There are two main types of relative clause: defining and non-defining.

- Defining relative clauses provide information which is essential to the meaning of its sentence. The clause defines or identifies the person or thing we are talking about.
  *The couple **who brought me up** were not my real parents.*
  *The car **which was used** in the robbery had been stolen.*
  The relative clauses in these sentences make it clear which couple and which car the speaker is referring to. The relative pronoun in them is the subject of the relative clause.
- When the relative pronoun is the object of the relative clause, it is often left out.
  *The couple <> **you met last week** were not my real parents.* (<> replaces *who(m)* or *that)*
  *The car <> **I bought last weekend** has broken down.* (<> replaces *which* or *that)*
  *2017 was the year <> **I started my new job**.* (<> replaces *when)*
  *That's the reason <> **I'm so excited**.* (<> replaces *why)*

! Note Defining relative clauses which include prepositions can be structured in two ways:

- In formal speech or writing, we would say:
  *The book **about which he was talking** is a world-wide best seller.*
- In informal speech or writing, we would say:
  *The book **he was talking about** is a world-wide best seller.*

Non-defining relative clauses

- Non-defining relative clauses provide extra information which is not essential to the meaning of a sentence. They are separated from the rest of the sentence by commas.
  *My daughter, **who lives in Colchester**, is a teacher.*
  *The hotel, **which has a hundred bedrooms**, is in the city centre.*
- They can be used to introduce a comment on a previous clause.
  *We'd been kept waiting at the airport for six hours, **which I found very frustrating**.*
- *That* cannot be used instead of *who* or *which* in a non-defining relative clause.
- The relative pronoun cannot be left out of a non-defining relative clause.

Practice

1 Finish the sentence beginnings A–D with two endings from the box. Add a relative pronoun where necessary.

has the best weather
said he couldn't come to the meeting
I'd buy if I had enough money
most tourists come here
Mike recommended
Barbara's going on holiday with
we celebrated your birthday
won an award for outstanding design

A That's the house …
1 *That's the house that / which won an award for outstanding design.*
2 ....

B What's the name of that hotel …?
3 ....
4 ....

C Which is the season … ?
5 ....
6 ....

D Is it Pete or Marty …?
7 ....
8 ....

2 Complete the sentences with a relative pronoun if one is necessary. Add a preposition if necessary. Add commas to sentences which include a non-defining relative clause.

1 Farmville .... is a popular online game is usually played through Facebook.
2 Players have a "home" farm and several themed farms .... they can grow a range of crops.
3 The main way .... a player earns money is by harvesting crops or visiting neighbours.
4 People .... I know quite well spend several hours a day playing Farmville.

5 Anyone ________________ has experienced it knows all too well that video game addiction is real.
6 There are some people ________________ lives have been changed forever by their addiction to video games.
7 There are many adults and children ________________ video games are an escape from the pressures of real life.
8 A self-confessed addict ________________ has been hooked on playing computer games for years, admits it causes him problems.

3 Combine sentences in these extracts from film reviews using relative clauses. Reorder the information if necessary.

Libero

A boy is only eleven years old. The boy tries to understand his family. He tries to stop it from breaking apart. At the same time, he has to deal with his mother's absence. He finds this very difficult.

I Am Legend

A military scientist is left completely alone in New York City. A virus has wiped out the residents of the city. The scientist is played by Will Smith.

UNIT 16 PARTICIPLE CLAUSES

Participle clauses involving different grammatical structures can be used to link actions within sentences. These clauses can go before or after the main clause.

Present participle clauses

- We use these to describe actions happening at the same time as the main action or immediately before the main action.

  *I drove to work, **thinking about our forthcoming holiday to Austria.***
  ***Putting down my book,** I turned off the light and went to sleep.*
- We can also use present participle clauses to describe the result of an action.

  *The waiter dropped the tray, **spilling** the drinks everywhere.*

Present participle clauses with conjunctions

*I learnt basic Spanish **while living in Barcelona.***
*They left **without saying a word.***
***On hearing** that I had passed my exam, I went out to celebrate.*

Perfect participle clauses: *having* + past participle

- We use this structure to describe something that happened **before** the main action.

  ***Having failed his driving test six times,** Don bought himself an electric bicycle.*
  *Jeff felt quite ill, **having eaten fours bars of chocolate.***

Past participle clauses

- A past participle clause is used when the meaning is passive.

  ***Taken regularly,** vitamin C can help to prevent colds.*
  ***Built in 1930,** the Empire State Building is one of the most recognisable buildings in the world.*

Participle clauses used instead of relative clauses

- These are called 'reduced relative clauses'.

  *The tree **growing in our garden** is an oak.*
  *Most of the people **involved in the discussion** were teenagers.*

With a full relative clause these sentences would be:

*The tree **which is growing in our garden** is an oak.*
*Most of the people **who were involved in the discussion** were teenagers.*

Participle clauses used instead of subordinate clauses

- Time clauses with *while, when, as, on* can be replaced with a participle clause.

  ***As we walked to work,** we chatted about a film we'd seen.*
  Walking to work, …
- Reason clauses can be replaced with *because* or *as*.

  ***Because I wanted to improve my English,** I enrolled in an online course.*
  Wanting to improve my English, …

Practice

1 Choose the correct participles in these sentences.

1 We came out of the theatre *wondered / wondering* what the play had been about.
2 We'd seen a play *based / having based* on a contemporary novel.
3 *Reading / Having read* the novel, I was interested to see how they would make it into a play.
4 It was the first play *written / having been written* by this young director.
5 I'd read a review of the play in a magazine *specialising / specialised* in modern drama.

2 Replace the participle clauses in these sentences with a non-participle clause.

1 Adventure training centres are designed for people wanting to do outdoor activities.
2 Arriving at the centre, I was surprised to see that there were people of all ages there.
3 Not having been to one of these centres before, I didn't know what to expect.
4 Putting my boots on, I chatted to the person next to me.
5 Having been there three times before, he thought he was an expert at the climbing wall.

3 Complete the participle clauses using a verb from the box. Use the negative form if necessary.

be able to   buy   eat   spend   visit

1 ________________ speak French, I couldn't make myself understood.
2 ________________ snails before, I didn't know if I would like them.
3 The shop was full of tourists ________________ souvenirs to take home.
4 While ________________ the Eiffel Tower, I bumped into an old friend.
5 ________________ all my money by the end of the first week, I couldn't afford to eat out for the rest of the holiday.

Acknowledgements

Anthony Cosgrove would like to thank the editorial team for all their help and for making *Prepare* such an enjoyable project to work on.

The authors and publishers are grateful to the following for reviewing the material during the writing process:

Bridget Bloom, Tom Bradbury, Annie Broadhead, Hilary Day, Mark Fountain, Simon Harwood, John Hayward, Helen Tiliouine, Graham Ward, and Susan White.

The authors and publishers acknowledge the following sources of copyright material and are grateful for the permissions granted. While every effort has been made, it has not always been possible to identify the sources of all the material used, or to trace all copyright holders. If any omissions are brought to our notice, we will be happy to include the appropriate acknowledgements on reprinting and in the next update to the digital edition, as applicable.

Key: U = Unit, LS = Life Skills, R = Review, EA = Extra Activities.

Text
U16: Greta Thunberg for the text about Greta Thunberg. Copyright © Greta Thunberg. Reproduced with kind permission; Rishab Jain for the text about Rishab Jain. Copyright © Rishab Jain. Reproduced with kind permission.

Photography
The following photographs have been sourced from Getty Images.

U1: Jonathan Knowles/Stone; JGI/Jamie Grill; milanvirijevic/E+; Brothers91/E+; Andrii Lutsyk/Ascent Xmedia/DigitalVision; Flashpop/Stone; BFG Images; Bruce Laurance/Photographer's Choice RF; SolStock/E+; Bruce Laurance/Photographer's Choice RF; **U2:** Eternity in an Instant/Stone; Ashley Ezrachie/EyeEm; Richard Sharrocks/Moment; fstop123/E+; Sam Bassett/Stockbyte; Juanmonino/E+; Blue Images/The Image Bank; Ron Krisel/Photodisc; SensorSpot/E+; pixelfit/E+; Julian Elliott Photography/Stone; sturti/E+; **LS1:** Image Source; Sarah Casillas/DigitalVision; PeopleImages/E+; **U3:** SCIEPRO/Science Photo Library; Dorling Kindersley: James Graham; LittleBee80/iStock/Getty Images Plus; BSIP; Science Photo Library; Carol Yepes/Moment; FatCamera/E+; SDI Productions/E+; Henglein and Steets/Cultura; LWA/Stone; sturti/E+; **U4:** SDI Productions/E+; Nattakorn Maneerat/iStock/Getty Images Plus; Flashpop/DigitalVision; Morsa Images/DigitalVision; Terry Vine/DigitalVision; Portra/E+; HASLOO/iStock/Getty Images Plus; kali9/E+; Ariel Skelley/DigitalVision; sturti/E+; **LS2:** Hill Street Studios/DigitalVision; Monty Rakusen/Cultura; Johner Images; **R1**: Robert Daly/OJO Images; **U5**: Justin Sullivan/Getty Images News; Keystone-France/Gamma-Keystone; GraphicaArtis/Hulton Archive; Simon Song/South China Morning Post; Historical/Corbis Historical; Sean Gallup; JUNGE, HEIKO/AFP; HELENE DAUSCHY/AFP; WLADIMIR BULGAR/Science Photo Library; franz12/iStock/Getty Images Plus; monkeybusinessimages/iStock/Getty Images Plus; londoneye/iStock/Getty Images Plus; **U6**: Axelle/Bauer-Griffin/FilmMagic; Pascal Le Segretain/Getty Images Entertainment; NurPhoto; Manfred Schmid/Getty Images Entertainment; Taylor Hill/FilmMagic; Samir Hussein/Getty Images Entertainment; **LS3:** jayk7/Moment; Prostock-Studio/iStock/Getty Images Plus; pondsaksit/iStock/Getty Images Plus; Big Cheese Photo; ozgurdonmaz/E+; **U7**: The AGE/Fairfax Media; Sporting News Archive; THOMAS KIENZLE/AFP; MARTIN BUREAU/AFP; kylewolfe; BEHROUZ MEHRI/AFP; Central Press/Hulton Archive; aluxum/E+; mmphoto/DigitalVision; Chloe Knott - Danehouse/Getty Images Sport; DMEPhotography/iStock/Getty Images Plus; ullstein bild; Prostock-Studio/iStock/Getty Images Plus; **U8:** Prasit photo/Moment; Colin Anderson Productions pty ltd/DigitalVision; Westend61; API/Gamma-Rapho; SW Productions/Stockbyte; sturti/E+; FatCamera/E+; Juan Silva/Photodisc; DreamsNavigator/iStock/Getty Images Plus; **LS4**: sturti/E+; kali9/E+; **R2**: John Phillips/Getty Images Entertainment; **U9**: Maskot; Halfdark; skynesher/E+; seksan Mongkhonkhamsao/Moment; Prostock-Studio/iStock/Getty Images Plus; skynesher/E+; aldomurillo/E+; **U10:** South_agency/E+; urbazon/E+; Erik McGregor/LightRocket; Westend61; kali9/E+; Heide Benser/The Image Bank; Mixmike/E+; RichLegg/E+; Fertnig/iStock/Getty Images Plus; CasarsaGuru/E+; **LS5:** skynesher/E+; **U11:** Rosemary Calvert/Stone; Thanasis/Moment; amoklv/iStock/Getty Images Plus; Jupiterimages/Photodisc; mariusFM77/E+; Alexander Spatari/Moment; Niphon Khiawprommas/iStock/Getty Images Plus; Heather Winters/Photolibrary; **U12:** © Marco Bottigelli/Moment; Dario Cingolani/EyeEm; MB Photography/Moment; Morsa Images/DigitalVision; izusek/E+; Morsa Images/DigitalVision; Ezra Bailey/The Image Bank; Hinterhaus Productions/Stone; Tuul & Bruno Morandi/The Image Bank; fstop123/E+; Sergio Monti/EyeEm; **LS6:** © RAZVAN CIUCA/Moment; Afriadi Hikmal/Moment; andresr/E+; s-cphoto/iStock/Getty Images Plus; Peter Dazeley/The Image Bank; **R3:** Ben A. Pruchnie/Getty Images Entertainment; **U13:** trait2lumiere/E+; recep-bg/E+; filadendron/E+; Aja Koska/E+; Ryan McVay/Photodisc; Motortion/iStock/Getty Images Plus; mixetto/E+; Ghislain & Marie David de Lossy/Cultura; **U14:** Elisaveta Ivanova/E+; twinsterphoto/iStock/Getty Images Plus; svetikd/E+; stock-eye/E+; SDI Productions/E+; **LS7:** Daisy-Daisy/iStock/Getty Images Plus; FluxFactory/E+; LJM Photo; alengo/E+; martin-dm/E+; FatCamera/E+; NoSystem images/E+; **U15:** NiseriN/iStock/Getty Images Plus; Image captured by Joanne Hedger/Moment; Enrique Aguirre Aves/The Image Bank; Barcroft Media; User10095428_393/iStock/Getty Images Plus; Munib Chaudry/Moment; SUMY SADURNI/AFP; Paul Souders/Photodisc; sweetpeatoad/Moment; moodboard/Brand X Pictures; richgreentea/Moment; Savushkin/E+; Klaus Vedfelt/DigitalVision; South_agency/E+; Martin Harvey/The Image Bank; **U16**: Daniel Berehulak/Getty Images News; MARCO DE SWART/AFP; Kevin Winter/Getty Images Entertainment; Anadolu Agency; Ezra Shaw/Getty Images Sport; Saturnino Pérez Garrido/EyeEm; Cavan Images; Halfpoint/iStock/Getty Images Plus; David Ramos/Getty Images Sport; Leigh Vogel/WireImage; **LS8**: monkeybusinessimages/iStock/Getty Images Plus; **R4**: Danita Delimont/Gallo Images; **EAU3**: Obradovic/E+; Rana Faure/Photodisc; Jamie Grill/The Image Bank; JGI/Jamie Grill; Xavier Arnau/E+; Bambu Productions/DigitalVision; **EAU8**: Jose Luis Pelaez Inc/DigitalVision ; Martin Barraud/OJO Images; BSIP/UIG; Morsa Images/DigitalVision; **EAU8:** SDI Productions/E+; **EAU15**: Hightower_NRW/iStock/Getty Images Plus; SolStock/E+; Imazins/ImaZinS.

The following photographs have been sourced from other libraries/sources.

U2: John Michaels/Alamy Stock Photo; **U5**: Lina YING/Alamy Stock Photo; Newscom/Alamy Stock Photo; **U6:** Book cover from THE HUNGER GAMES by Suzanne Collins. Jacket cover © 2008 by Tim O'Brien. Reprinted by permission of Scholastic Inc.; Book cover from Jurassic Park by Michael Crichton. Reprinted by kind permission of Penguin Random House LLC; 'THE DEVIL WEARS PRADA' © 2006. Twentieth Century Fox. All rights reserved. Reprinted with permission;

Ben Molyneux/Alamy Stock Photo; Photo 12/Alamy Stock Photo; **U8**: Michael Barera; © South West News Service; **U13:** agefotostock/Alamy Stock Photo; **U16**: © Greta Thunberg. Reproduced with kind permission; © Rishab Jain. Reproduced with kind permission.

Front cover photography by Carlina Teteris/Moment/Getty Images; krystiannawrocki/E+/Getty Images.

Illustration
emc design ltd.

Audio
Audio production by Leon Chambers.

Typesetting
Typeset by emc design ltd.

The publishers are grateful to the following contributors:
Life Skills sections: Daniel Vincent; Grammar reference and practice: Simon Haines; project management: Emma Ramirez; editing: Alyson Maskell.